APR -- 2005

WITHDRAWN

DATE DUE

2005

WINNETKA-NORTHFIELD
PUBLIC LIBRARY DISTRICT
WINNETKA, IL
446-7220

ACES AT WAR

Books by Eric Hammel

76 Hours: The Invasion of Tarawa (with John E. Lane)
Chosin: Heroic Ordeal of the Korean War
The Root: The Marines in Beirut
Ace!: A Marine Night-Fighter Pilot in World War II
(with R. Bruce Porter)
Duel for the Golan (with Jerry Asher)
Guadalcanal: Starvation Island
Guadalcanal: The Carrier Battles
Guadalcanal: Decision At Sea
Munda Trail: The New Georgia Campaign
The Jolly Rogers (with Tom Blackburn)
Khe Sanh: Siege in the Clouds
First Across the Rhine (with David E. Pergrin)
Lima-6: A Marine Company Commander in Vietnam
(with Richard D. Camp)
Ambush Valley
Fire in the Streets: The Battle for Hue
Aces Against Japan
Aces Against Germany
Six Days in June
Air War Europa: Chronology
Aces Against Japan II
Carrier Clash

ACES AT WAR
The American Aces Speak
Volume IV

Eric Hammel

Pacifica Press

Copyright © 1997 by Eric Hammel

All rights reserved.
No part of this book may be reproduced or transmitted in any form or by any means, electronic or mechanical, including photocopying, recording, or by any information storage and retrieval system, without permission in writing from the publisher.

Requests for permission to make copies of any part of the work should be mailed to: Permissions, Pacifica Press, 1149 Grand Teton Drive, Pacifica, California 94044 ♦ (650)355-6678

Manufactured in the United States of America.

Typography by Words To Go, Inc., Pacifica, California

ISBN 0-935553-24-X

Library of Congress Cataloging-in-Publication Data

Hammel, Eric M.
    Aces at war / Eric Hammel
       p. cm. — (The American aces speak ; v. 4)
    Includes bibliographical references and indexes.
    ISBN 0-935553-24-X
       1. United States—History, Military—20th century—Sources. 2. Air pilots, Military—United States—Biography. 3. United States—Armed Forces—Airmen—Biograpy. 4. Battles—History—20th century—Sources. 5. Military history, Modern—20th century I. Title. II. Series: Hammel, Eric M. American aces speak ; v. 4.
D790.H254 1992 vol. 4
[E840.4]
358.4'00973 s—dc21
[358.4'0092'273]
[B]   97-10571
                                                                                  CIP

For Dad

CONTENTS

Glossary and Guide to Abbreviations   xi

PROLOGUE
    Flight   1
        Norman Fortier
        Civilian Pilot Training Program

PART I: At War Against Japan
    Down in Flames   7
        Vice Squadron Commander Charlie Bond, AVG
        Paoshan, China—May 4, 1942
    Ducks in a Row   14
        2d Lieutenant George Hollowell, USMC
        Guadalcanal—September 14, 1942
    The Safest Thing   23
        1st Lieutenant Larry O'Neill, USAAF
        Marilanan, New Guinea—September 13, 1942
    Command   29
        Lieutenant Commander Tom Blackburn, USN
        Rabaul—February 4, 1944
    Dancing in the Dark   33
        Lieutenant (jg) Connie Hargreaves, USN
        Mariana Islands—June 20, 1944

Busy Day, Sad Day	42
Ensign Jojo McGraw, USN	
Off Samar—October 25, 1944	
Going South	49
1st Lieutenant John Bolyard, USAAF	
Amoy, China—November 3, 1944	
Two of Our Planes Are Missing	52
Major Ed Roddy, USAAF	
Clark Field, Luzon—January 3, 1945	
The Pilot-Making Machine	57
Ensign Don McPherson, USN	
Nittigahara, Japan—March 19, 1945	
Piece of Cake	64
Lieutenant Jim Pearce, USN	
Kyushu Area—March 21, 1945	
Long-Range Escort	69
Major John Loisel, USAAF	
Indochina Coast—March 28, 1945	
VLR	73
Major Jim Tapp, USAAF	
Tokyo—April 7, 1945	
Part II: At War Against Germany	
Mustangs Over Dieppe	89
Flying Officer Holly Hills, RCAF	
Dieppe, France—August 19, 1942	
Slaughter Over Cap Bon	94
Captain Darrell Welch, USAAF	
Cap Bon, Tunisia—April 5, 1943	
Bomber Escort to Paris	104
Major Jack Price, USAAF	
Paris—November 26, 1943	
A Long Wait	111
1st Lieutenant Bob Curtis, USAAF	
Lorenzo Nuovo, Italy—February 19, 1944	
Little Friends	118
Colonel Mort Magoffin, USAAF	
Kaiserlautern, Germany—April 24, 1944	

All for One 122
    2d Lieutenant Dwaine Franklin, USAAF
    Northern Italy—June 9, 1944
Daylight Ranger 126
    Flight Lieutenant Clarence Jasper, RCAF
    Off Rostock, Germany—June 27, 1944
Unbalanced 128
    1st Lieutenant Bob Goebel, USAAF
    Budapest, Hungary—July 2, 1944
Last Mission 133
    Captain Bud Fortier, USAAF
    Lechfeld Airdrome, Germany—July 24, 1944
The Rescue 142
    2d Lieutenant Deacon Priest, USAAF
    Franco–German Frontier—August 18, 1944
Never Smoke in the Cockpit 155
    2d Lieutenant Harley Brown, USAAF
    Saarbrucken, Germany—August 28, 1944
Save the Bombers 158
    1st Lieutenant Frank Gerard, USAAF
    Annaberg, Germany—September 11, 1944
Prey 163
    Captain Jim Carter, USAAF
    Langensbold, Germany—November 18, 1944
Outnumbered 166
    Major Niven Cranfill, USAAF
    Merseberg, Germany—November 27, 1944
Shot Down 171
    Captain Tink Cole, USAAF
    Stendal Airdrome, Germany—February 25, 1945
Night Stalker
    1st Lieutenant Herman Ernst, USAAF
    Rhine River Area—March 2, 1945
Jumped 187
    1st Lieutenant Ivan Hasek, USAAF
    Limburg, Germany—March 16, 1945

Part IV: At War in the Middle East
    Engagement Over Sinai   193
        Rudy Augarten
        El Arish, Egypt—December 22, 1948

Part IV: At War Over Korea
    It Goes With the Territory   201
        Lieutenant Colonel Jerry Brown, USAF
        Tokchon, North Korea—November 30, 1950
    Glider Time   205
        Captain Brooks Liles, USAF
        Korea—March 15, 1952
    The Longest Dogfight   208
        1st Lieutenant Cecil Foster, USAF
        North Korea—September 7, 1952
    Out of Control   213
        Lieutenant Colonel Ed Heller, USAF
        Yalu River Area—January 27, 1953
    Crossing the River   221
        Major Jack Bolt, USMC
        Yalu River Area—July 11, 1953
    Navy Night Ace   229
        Lieutenant Guy Bordelon, USN
        South Korea—June 29–July 16, 1953

Part V: At War Over Vietnam
    The Hanoi POL Strike   239
        Major Jim Kasler, USAF
        Hanoi, North Vietnam—June 29, 1966

Bibliography   251
Index   255

GLOSSARY AND GUIDE TO ABBREVIATIONS

A-20 USAAF Douglas (Havoc) light bomber
A6M IJN Mitsubishi Type 0 (Zero, Zeke, Hap, Hamp) fighter
AA Antiaircraft
AAA Antiaircraft artillery
ack-ack Antiaircraft gunfire
AD USN Douglas (Skyraider) carrier attack bomber
Airacobra USAAF Bell P-39 or P-400 fighter
API Armor-piercing incendiary (bullet)
AT-6 USAAF North American (Texan) advanced trainer
Avenger USN/USMC Grumman TBF or TBM carrier torpedo/level light bomber
AVG American Volunteer Group of the Nationalist Chinese Air Force (Flying Tigers)
B-10 USAAC Martin twin-engine light bomber
B-12 USAAC Martin twin-engine light bomber
B-17 USAAF Boeing (Flying Fortress) four-engine heavy bomber
B-18 USAAC Douglas twin-engine medium bomber
B-24 USAAF Consolidated (Liberator) four-engine heavy bomber
B-25 USAAF North American (Mitchell) twin-engine medium bomber
B-26 USAAF Martin (Marauder) twin-engine medium bomber

B-29 USAAF Boeing (Superfortress) twin-engine very heavy bomber
B-52 USAF Boeing (Stratofortress) jet strategic intercontinental bomber
B5N IJN Nakajima Type 97 (Kate) carrier torpedo/level bomber
B6N IJN Nakajima (Jill) carrier torpedo/level bomber
Baka American slang (meaning "stupid" in Japanese) reference to IJN Yokosuka MXY7 (Ohka) manned suicide attack aircraft
Bearcat USN Grumman F8F carrier interceptor
Betty IJN Mitsubishi Type 1 (G4M) twin-engine medium bomber
Bf-109 German Messerschmitt fighter
Bingo fuel Predetermined amount of jet fuel required to return to base
Bogey Unidentified aircraft
Boston British varant of Douglas A-20 Havoc twin-engine light bomber
Buffalo USN/USMC Brewster F2A carrier fighter
Buster Emergency speed
C-46 USAAF Curtiss (Commando) twin-engine troop carrier/cargo transport
C-47 USAAF Douglas (Skytrain) twin-engine troop carrier/cargo transport
C6N IJN Nakajima (Myrt) carrier reconnaissance plane
CAP Combat air patrol
CO Commanding officer
Corsair USN/USMC F4U carrier fighter
CPT Civilian Pilot Training program
CV Fleet carrier
CVE Escort carrier
D3A IJN Aichi Type 99 (Val) carrier dive-bomber
D4Y IJN Yokosuka Type 2 (Judy) carrier dive-bomber
Dauntless USN/USMC Douglas SBD carrier scout/dive bomber
Dinah IJA Mitsubishi Type 100 (Ki-46) twin-engine command/reconnaissance airplane
Dumbo Air-Sea rescue airplane or helicopter
E base USN elimination training base
E7K IJN Kawanishi Type 90-3 (Alf) twin-float reconnaissance biplane
F-86 USAF North American (Sabre) jet interceptor
F-105 USAF Republic (Thunderchief) jet fighter-bomber
F1M IJN Mitsubishi Type 0 (Pete) reconnaissance float biplane
F2A USN/USMC Brewster (Buffalo) carrier fighter
F4F USN/USMC Grumman (Wildcat) carrier fighter

Aces At War

F4U USN/USMC Vought (Corsair) carrier fighter
F6F USN Grumman (Hellcat) carrier fighter
F8F USN Grumman (Bearcat) carrier interceptor
F9F USN/USMC Grumman (Banshee) carrier jet interceptor
FDO Fighter direction officer
Flak Antiaircraft gunfire (from *Flieger Abwher Kannon*)
FM USN General Motors (Wildcat) carrier fighter variant
Form 5 USAAF pilot flight log
Frank IJA Nakajima (Ki-84) fighter-bomber/interceptor
FW-190 German Focke-Wulf fighter
FW-200 German Focke-Wulf (Kondor) four-engine maritime reconnaissance bomber
G Force of gravity (x 1)
G4M IJN Mitsubishi Type 1 (Betty) twin-engine medium bomber
GCI Ground-control intercept
George IJN Kawanishi N1K2 land-based interceptor
He-111 German Heinkel twin-engine medium bomber
HEI High-explosive incendiary (bullet)
Helen IJA Nakajima Type 100 Ki-49 twin-engine heavy bomber
Hellcat USN Grumman F6F carrier fighter
Helldiver USN Curtiss SB2C carrier scout/dive bomber
IFF Identification Friend or Foe (radio device)
J2M IJN Mitsubishi (Jack) high-altitude interceptor
Jack IJN Mitsubishi J2M high-altitude interceptor
jeep carrier Refers to escort carrier
(jg) junior grade
Jill IJN Yokosuka B6N carrier torpedo/level bomber
JP-4 jet fuel
Ju-52 German Junkers tri-motor transport
Ju-86 German Junkers twin-engine medium bomber
Ju-87 German Junkers (Stuka) dive-bomber
Ju-88 German Junkers twin-engine light bomber/dive-bomber
Judy IJN Yokosuka Type 2 (D4Y) carrier scout/dive bomber
kamikaze Refers to Japanese suicide aircraft
KC-135 USAF Boeing (Stratotanker) tanker/aerial refueler jet
Ki-21 IJA Mitsubishi Type 97 (Sally) twin-engine bomber
Ki-27 IJA Nakajima Type 97 (Nate) fighter
Ki-43 IJA Nakajima Type 1 (Oscar) fighter

Ki-44 IJA Nakajima Type 2 (Tojo) fighter
Ki-45 IJA Nakajima Type 2 (Nick) twin-engine fighter
Ki-46 IJA Mitsubishi Type 100 (Dinah) twin-engine command/reconnaissance aircraft
Ki-48 IJA Kawasaki Type 99 (Lily) twin-engine light bomber
Ki-49 IJA Nakajima Type 100 (Helen) twin-engine heavy bomber
Ki-61 IJA Kawasaki Type 3 (Tony) fighter
Ki-84 IJA Nakajima (Frank) fighter
La-11 Soviet-built Lavochkin fighter
Liberator USAAF Consolidated B-24 four-engine heavy bomber
Lightning USAAF Lockheed P-38 twin-engine fighter
Lily IJA Kawasaki Type 99 (Ki-48) twin-engine light bomber
LSO Landing signal officer
Mach Speed of sound
Me-110 German Messerschmitt twin-engine heavy fighter/night fighter
Me-262 German Messerschmitt twin-jet fighter
MiG-15 Soviet-built jet fighter
Mitchell USAAF North American B-25 twin-engine medium bomber
Mosquito British de Havilland D.H.98 twin-engine two-seat bomber/fighter-bomber/night fighter
Mustang USAAF/USAF North American P-51 fighter; RAF/RCAF North American ground-cooperation fighter
Myrt IJN Nakajima (C6N) carrier reconnaissance plane
N1K2 IJN Kawanishi (George) land-based interceptor
Nick IJA Nakajima Type 2 (Ki-45) twin-engine fighter
OS2U USN Vought (Kingfisher) observation-scout floatplane
Oscar IJA Nakajima Type 1 (Ki-43) fighter
P-35 USAAC Seversky fighter
P-36 USAAC Curtiss (Hawk) fighter
P-38 USAAF Lockheed (Lightning) twin-engine fighter
P-39 USAAF Bell (Airacobra) fighter/fighter-bomber
P-40 USAAF Curtiss (Warhawk) fighter
P-43 USAAC Republic Lancer fighter
P-47 USAAF Republic (Thunderbolt) fighter
P-51/F-51 USAAF/USAF North American (Mustang) fighter/fighter-bomber
P-61 USAAF Northrop (Black Widow) twin-engine night fighter
P-70 USAAF Douglas (Havoc) night fighter variant

P-80/F-80 USAAF/USAF Lockheed (Shooting Star) jet fighter-bomber
P-400 USAAF Bell (Airacobra) export variant fighter/fighter-bomber
PBY USN Consolidated (Catalina) twin-engine patrol bomber/rescue aircraft
Pete IJN Mitsubishi Type 0 (F1M) reconnaissance float biplane
Point Option Refers to spot at which USN carriers are expected to be when strike or scout aircraft return from a long-range mission
POW Prisoner of war
PSP Pierced steel planking
PT-17 USAAF Boeing or Stearman primary trainer biplane
RAF Royal Air Force
RCAF Royal Canadian Air Force
ROTC Reserve Officers' Training Corps
RPM Revolutions per minute
R&R Rest and recuperation
Sabre USAF North American (F-86) jet interceptor
SAM Surface-to-air antiaircraft missile
SB2C USN Curtiss (Helldiver) carrier scout/dive-bomber
SBD USN Douglas (Dauntless) carrier scout/dive-bomber
Seabee Refers to USN construction battalions (CB)
Shooting Star USAAF/USAF Lockheed P-80/F-80 jet fighter-bomber
Spitfire British-built Supermarine fighter
Stuka German Junkers Ju-87 dive-bomber
T-6 USAF North American (Texan) air control aircraft (variant of AT-6)
TBF USN/USMC Grumman (Avenger) torpedo/level bomber
TBM Same as TBF, but manufactured under license by General Motors
Thunderbolt USAAF Republic P-47 fighter
Thunderchief USAF Republic F-105 jet fighter-bomber
Tojo IJA Nakajima Type 2 (Ki-44) fighter
Tomahawk An export variant of the Curtiss P-40 fighter
Tony IJA Kawasaki Type 3 (Ki-61) fighter
Tu-2 Soviet-built Tupelov light bomber
USAAC United States Army Air Corps
USAAF United States Army Air Forces
USMC United States Marine Corps
USN United States Navy
USS United States Ship
V-1 German flying bomb

Val IJN Aichi Type 99 (D3A) carrier dive-bomber
VBF USN fighter-bomber squadron
VF USN fighter squadron
VLR Very long range
VMF USMC fighter squadron
VMO USMC observation squadron
VMSB USMC scout-bomber squadron
VS USN scouting squadron
Wildcat USN/USMC Grumman F4F or General Motors FM carrier fighter
Yak-18 Soviet-built Yakovlev twin-engine trainer
YP-38 USAAF Lockheed (Lightning) in-service test fighter
Zeke IJN Mitsubishi Type 0 (A6M) carrier fighter
Zero IJN Mitsubishi Type 0 (A6M) carrier fighter

Prologue

FLIGHT

NORMAN FORTIER
Civilian Pilot Training Program
Nashua, New Hampshire—1941

The idea that I might someday fly an airplane never entered my mind until my second year at St. Anselm College. I had never built a model airplane or even read an aviation magazine; I wasn't interested in the occasional barnstormers who came to the local airport. I had never yearned to "slip the surly bonds of earth," as Pilot Officer McGee put it in his memorable poem "High Flight." It never occurred to me.

After World War II started in Europe, President Roosevelt recognized the probability that the United States would sooner or later became involved. Perhaps disturbed by the reports of German air power, and especially the assessment of that air power by Charles Lindbergh, he pushed through Congress the Civilian Pilot Training (CPT) program to provide a source of trained pilots for future military applications.

The CPT was offered to colleges and universities—with government funding—throughout the United States. St. Anselm College accepted the program—maybe it helped pay the bills in otherwise lean times—but soon ran into a problem: getting students to sign up for it.

During my freshman year, Father Houde tried to recruit me into the program, but I declined because I was only seventeen; the minimum entry age was eighteen. Father Houde was the proctor at St. Anselm—the university official appointed from the academic staff to see that undergraduates observed the regulations. He was about 6'4" tall, with a stern demeanor and unsmiling face. In his black garments, he was an intimidating figure. In my sophomore year, without the age excuse, I agreed to sign up, but my heart wasn't in it. I just wanted Father Houde off my back.

The ground school and flight training both took place at Pete Goldsmith's Flight School at the Nashua Municipal Airport. "Goose" Gosselin was our ground school instructor. We learned about air navigation, meteorology, the theory of flight, aircraft engines, and Civil Air regulations. Just as we were beginning to wonder if we'd ever get into an airplane, ground school ended and flight training began.

George Harmon was my instructor. He wasn't much older than I, probably in his early twenties. We walked out to a two-seater Piper Cub and he showed me what to look for in a pre-flight inspection.

The engine-start procedure was simple: turn the magneto switches on, yell "Contact," somebody spins the propeller, and the engine coughs into life. The Piper Cub had a tail skid, not a tail wheel, so taxiing wasn't exactly the simple procedure it became a few years later.

I was a bit apprehensive as we headed for the take-off position—I had never been higher off the ground than in an ill-fated skiing episode. Before takeoff, we checked the magnetos, George released the brakes, and we lurched forward. It was a bumpy ride at first, but it gradually became smoother as we gathered speed. Then we lifted easily off the ground. We were no longer a part of the earth below—we were in our own detached world.

I cannot describe my feelings the moment that Piper Cub lifted off the ground. I had "slipped the bonds of earth;" I knew what McGee meant. The course of my life had been changed.

At the end of the forty-hour flight program, in early summer of 1941, I had my private pilot license and I was hooked. The CPT included a secondary phase—forty hours of advanced flying training in a Waco UPF-7 biplane. I needed no urging from Father Houde to sign up.

The Waco UPF-7 was an open-cockpit biplane that looked like a holdover from the Great War. My instructor was Al Hirsch, a ham-fisted pilot from Pelham, the town of my birth. He was heavy-set, just under six feet tall, and he looked and spoke like an old New England farmer. But he knew how to fly that Waco, and he knew how to teach flying.

He sat in the back cockpit and spoke to me through the gosport, a simple tube connected to the headphones in my cloth helmet. He called it the profanity strainer. I don't recall that I had any way to answer him. This was a one-way conversation. If I knew what he was saying, I simply nodded my head.

Al is high on my list of unforgettable people. And the Waco UPF-7 is high on my list of favorite airplanes. Unlike the Piper Cub, it was rugged enough to withstand the aerobatics that were part of the flight-training program. It was a great airplane for loops, slow rolls, snap rolls, Immelmanns, lazy eights, Cuban eights, hammerhead stalls, and even an outside spin which, once experienced, I was never tempted to try again. The Waco was almost identical to the Stearman PT-17 that I would fly as an aviation cadet, and that gave me a considerable edge.

The secondary phase of the CPT ended just before Pearl Harbor. The final flight was in a Stinson 105, Pete Goldsmith's pride and joy, on a solo three-leg cross-country.

The flight included landing at two different airports, filing the flight plan for each leg, and making weather checks and all the required radio calls—sort of a graduation flight.

The weather was generally fair, and the flight was uneventful—until I approached the Nashua airport. The wind had become strong and gusty, and there was a direct cross-wind on the runway. I was in radio contact with Pete and Al, who told me to land into the wind, at right angles to the runway, and to be aware of the gusty conditions.

This meant landing directly toward the main hangar, and across the shortest part of the airfield. Al told me later that Pete was really worried that I would smash up his pride and joy, and he kept reassuring Pete that I could handle it with no problem. He probably had his fingers crossed.

Unaware that this was a big problem, I landed the plane with little difficulty. Goldsmith was so relieved, he almost hugged me when I got out. Al just stood there with a big grin on his face.

On December 7, the Japanese bombed Pearl Harbor. I had more than eighty hours of flying time and a private pilot's license. In January, I left St. Anselm College and enlisted as a Flying Cadet in the Army Air Corps.

PART I

At War Against Japan

DOWN IN FLAMES*

Vice Squadron Leader CHARLIE BOND, AVG
1st Fighter Squadron, American Volunteer Group
Paoshan, China—May 4, 1942

Charles Rankin Bond, Jr., was born in Dallas, Texas, on April 22, 1915. He joined his high school ROTC unit in 1929, served for five years in the Texas National Guard, entered the U.S. Army Air Corps Flying Cadet program in 1938, and emerged from flight training in February 1939 as a second lieutenant assigned to fly B-17 heavy bombers from Langley Field, Virginia.

Lieutenant Charlie Bond resigned his Air Corps commission in September 1941 and shipped out to China on September 24 as a member of the first American Volunteer Group draft. After reaching China, Wingman Bond was assigned to the 1st AVG Fighter Squadron. In his very first encounter with Japanese airplanes—on December 20, 1941—Bond was

---

* Bond, Charles R., Jr. and Terry H. Anderson. *A Flying Tiger's Diary.* College Station, Texas: Texas A&M University Press, 1984. Quoted verbatim with permission of the publisher.

credited with probably shooting down an Imperial Army Ki-21 twin-engine bomber near Kunming, China.

On January 29, 1942, Flight Leader Charlie Bond shot down two Imperial Army Ki-27 fighters, and probably downed a third, near Rangoon, Burma. He scored probables on February 6 and 21, then achieved ace status on February 25, when he downed three more Ki-27s. He next downed a Ki-27 over Rangoon on February 26, 1942.

From Charlie Bond's Diary:
May 4, 1942
[Squadron Commander] Bob Neale's plane was hit by some return fire from the Jap reconnaissance ship, and Mickey Mickelson showed up sick this morning. Bob decided he and Mickey would go to Kunming and pick up a replacement for Mickey and another P-40.

Later we heard some noises overhead and stepped out of the alert shack to find two Japanese reconnaissance ships high overhead. Bartling and I took off in hopes of catching them. By the time we got to eighteen thousand feet they were gone.

On the way back to the field I heard Bob Neale on the radio. He was returning from Kunming and near Paoshan. A few minutes later both Bob and Mickey showed up over the field: Mickey was feeling better.

Bob Little and I were cleaning our pistols when Neale yelled for us to man our ships. We dashed out to the planes, and by the time I had started my engine I looked up and saw the Jap bomber formation high above heading toward our field. Looked like about twenty-five bombers at eighteen thousand feet. Neale started shooting his pistol in the air to get everyone's attention; then he ran for the ditch. My engine had warmed up, and I sat there in the cockpit with my hand on the throttle. I paused a second. Hell, I can make it! I shoved the throttle open and headed straight across the field. I had not gotten into my parachute or put my helmet on. I didn't even have my seat belt on, and my canopy was open. My only thought was to get airborne and beyond the edge of the field before the bombs hit. My speed built up unusually slowly, and suddenly my tail literally jumped off the ground. Damn, I had not even put up my flaps, which was pre-takeoff procedure. I had quite a lot of field yet, so I put them up. I leaped forward and just did manage to clear the rock barricade at the far end of the field. I turned to the left and got into my flying gear as I started a maximum climb. I could see the bomber formation clearly now. They skipped the field and were bombing the city.

I wasn't climbing nearly as fast as I expected. Something was wrong I had full throttle and RPM. Oh, hell! I forgot to raise my landing gear in all the haste and excitement. I got it up and then started gaining on the bomber formation. They were now in a wide sweeping turn to head back south after dropping their bombs. I cut across and pulled up in a steeper climb. In the meantime I stole a quick look at the city below. The bombing was almost perfect—right in the middle of the city.

I looked around for possible enemy fighter escort and saw none, but I did pick up a second wave of about the same number of bombers. I had a better chance against them, since they were trailing the first wave. I positioned myself to concentrate on them. They were at eighteen thousand feet and in a single vee formation. I got about a thousand feet above and off to the right. I made a diving left turn and pulled up into the right rear quarter of the outside flank of the formation. I closed in on the outside bomber and squeezed the trigger. My bursts completely enveloped the fuselage, but I saw no smoke or fire. The two adjacent bombers immediately started streaming a bluish white smoke to attract me to them as "wounded" aircraft. We had been briefed about this trick, but this was the first time I had seen it. I wasn't about to take that bait. The bomber on the extreme flank end pulled away a bit, and this made it even more obvious.

I continued my rear right quarter attacks. On my third attack I saw his right engine disintegrate and ignite into a flaming torch. He went down and through the overcast. I turned on the bomber at the tail of the vee, but suddenly my guns quit firing. I had become too engrossed and had been firing long bursts, by far too long. Recharging the guns produced no results. Hell, I was out of ammunition!

I pulled away sharply and made a diving 180 turn to head back. Now, where am I? I had chased some fifty enemy bombers down across northern Burma and had only gotten one. I was downright disappointed in myself and in my gunnery. I had them all to myself and there was no enemy fighter escort.

There was nothing to do but return to Paoshan. I spotted the Burma

Road bridge over the Salween River and felt better about my position. I knew where I was, had sufficient fuel, so I relaxed and changed my course slightly to head directly to the field. I began evaluating the flight, filled with remorse that I didn't get more Japs. The field appeared, and I tried to pick up our ground station on the radio. Several calls brought no reply, and I was now in a steep dive towards the field. I leveled out and did a slow roll as I crossed over the alert area. I tried the radio again with no results and decided that they were probably in the ditches. I thought I'd make a wide turn around the city to examine the bomb damage while spreading out my traffic pattern. What a sight. Before, the city had been spilling over with evacuees, and now they were jammed all over the place. The Japanese bombs had caught them without any warning. Fires engulfed the city. Many buildings and houses were blown to bits.

After one last look I concentrated on my landing approach. I slowed down and moved the lever for the flaps and landing gear forward. Suddenly I heard several loud explosions. The noise stunned me. I immediately concluded that my landing gear hydraulic system had blown up. I had been having trouble with it operating correctly the last several days but couldn't find anything wrong with it. I decided to try to recycle the gear lever. When I reached down, I cried out in pain. I had stuck my left hand into a raging fire!

I swung my head around and looked to my rear. There they were. Three Jap Zeros right on my tail and firing like mad! The explosions were their rounds of ammunition hitting my armor plate behind my seat. The bullets had gone through my fuselage tank, which still had a few gallons of fuel in it, before impacting the armor plate. The fuselage tank had exploded, and the fire was whipping into my lower rear cockpit and then up around my legs.

What a stupe I had been. I had become so engrossed with the bombing scene below that I had made the fatal mistake that a fighter pilot should never get caught doing: I didn't suspect enemy fighters in the area.

The Japs had laid this attack on a little differently. They knew our situation from the two reconnaissances flights that preceded the bombers. They decided to forego the fighters as bomber escorts and hold them off and away from the field with the hope of catching all of us when we returned—low on ammunition and gas.

For a split second I considered giving up, but something wouldn't let me. I leaned forward as far as my seat belt would permit, closed my eyes because the fire had begun to engulf me, and reached over with my right hand to grasp the canopy crank and rolled it fully back. I unhooked my seat belt with my left hand and put both hands on the stick to make the ship climb abruptly and roll over one-half turn to the right. I took my hands off the control column and reached for the right side of the cockpit to get out of the seat.

The airstream grabbed me as the upper part of my body protruded outside the cockpit. It dragged me out. I had forgotten my earphone connection to the radio plug, but the force of the wind tore it loose. I knew I was out of the airplane and opened my eyes. One second the blue sky and the next the ground. I was tumbling. I looked down to find the metal ring to pull my parachute and jerked it wildly. I felt a tugging and then a violent jerk. I was in the parachute straps, floating.

Suddenly I became terrified. Those dirty bastards will strafe me like they did Henry Gilbert at Rangoon. Automatically I started praying—out loud. I prayed devoutly to God with my eyes closed, and then opened them to look for the Zeros. Fortunately, they had pulled away and were heading south.

Looking down, I saw the ground rushing up at me. I would hit backward if I didn't do something, so I tried to kick around in my harness, and I did get about halfway around when I hit. I fell across some large clods of earth in a rice paddy. The parachute gradually floated to the ground beside me. I sat up and realized that I still had the rip cord ring tightly grasped in my right hand.

I landed in a Chinese cemetery, about a mile and a half from the field. I quickly came to my senses and punched the release on my parachute harness. The straps fell away, and I ran to the closest burial mound and used it as a barrier against possible strafing by a Jap fighter. I squatted there watching the remaining Japs make passes on the field.

I felt a burning sensation on my neck and shoulders and suddenly realized that my scarf and flying suit were on fire. I hurried to a small stream flowing through the cemetery and laid down on my back and wallowed in the water. My head ached. I reached up to rub it and felt something wet and drew my hand away to look at it. It was blood. Christ! I looked down at my hands. They were badly burned, and the skin had been torn loose in several places. Blisters were forming. My face and neck and upper shoulders were scorched; my eyebrows were gone. Pain was setting in.

There were many Chinese in the cemetery crouching behind the burial mounds. I motioned for one of them to come over to me. He reacted warily but did start walking towards me. He had one hand behind his back. I went through the gestures of picking up a telephone and calling while uttering the usual Chinese greetings, "Wau. Wao. Whoo. Wa." I did not have my flying jacket, on the back of which was sewn the Chinese flag and directives written in Chinese to help us. Nevertheless, he seemed to get the message, smiled lightly, and then brought his hand from behind his back, revealing a large rock. He was ready to give me the works, thinking I was the enemy. He motioned for me to follow him and led me off to a cluster of huts. We entered one, and a group of Chinese peasants looked at me without any emotion. Fortunately, there was a telephone.

It's amazing what one can do in an emergency with sign language. I got them to understand that I needed an American doctor. A Chinese man got on the phone and got the word back to our AVG hostel. Eventually Doc Richards appeared in the doorway.

The agony of my burns had me on the verge of passing out. I wanted to die to get out of the pain. I would lie down, get up, walk around, lie down, get up, hold my hand in the air to reduce the circulation and throbbing pain, cry out aloud, and pray.

Doc took off my clothes and examined me. My helmet had too long rips in it. Apparently the armor plate in the P-40, which tapers off at the top to resemble the narrowing shoulders and head of a man, had barely kept all but a couple of bullets from hitting me. Otherwise I would've been killed. Two bullets barely missed the armor plate and ripped past my head close enough to cut my scalp and bring blood. My eyelashes and eyebrows were gone. My face was blistered on the left side. Around the hairline of my neck was an open wound of burnt flesh where the helmet plug to my aircraft radio had dug into my flesh when I forgot to unhook it upon bailing out. My shoulder blades were heavily blistered, and one blister ran down the middle of my back about six inches. My right thumb was blistered, and my left hand looked terrible, third-degree burns.

Doc gave me a shot in the arm and a couple of capsules of something, and I sat down for a minute to let the stuff set in. Then he started pulling the skin off the blisters. He looked at the USAAC ring on my left hand and said that it had to come off. I just peered back as the dope began to grab me. Nevertheless, when he pulled off the ring and the burned flesh on my finger, I nearly hit the ceiling. Then he started pouring peroxide on the open, raw places. That put me on the verge of convulsions, but fortunately the dope began to take hold. He smeared gentian violet all over the upper part of my body and very heavily over the burned portions. I became a gooey mess.

Doc asked me if I could walk, and I could. My socks were wet, since I had lost my boots. A Chinese gave me a pair of sneakers, and we walked out toward the jeeps. My flying suit had been tied at my waist to keep it off my burns on the upper part of my body. On the way through the rice paddies to the jeeps, Bob Neale came up and told Doc Richards that Benny Foshee was in a bad way from bomb shrapnel. A Chinese doctor had wanted to amputate one of Benny's legs, but he would not have it and kept yelling for Doc Richards. I urged Doc to go on and take care of Benny.

We met Bob Little at a main junction in the city, and we tried to joke about the whole deal. By now the dope had taken over and I couldn't feel a thing. Bob Neale, Bob Little, a Chinese interpreter, and I drove through the city towards the hostel, an eight-mile trip. Neale and Little had to fire their pistols into the air to get space for us to drive by the panic-stricken natives on the main road.

I shall never forget the horrible sights as we made our way through the bombed-out city. We drove past what had been shacks, homes, buildings, and factories, and now they were either leveled or still burning. There were bodies lying everywhere, in and under charred debris. Some were completely dismembered, and others were burned so badly the teeth were showing from fleshless faces. I saw one body with no leg, arms, or head, and another with the skull half gone. Once Bob Little had to get out of the jeep to move a timber from our path. When he heaved it aside, a human head rolled across the road. The air was filled with the smell of burning flesh. Once you smell that odor you never forget it. One very pitiful sight was a wailing Chinese mother on her knees in the middle of the road with her dead child in her arms and her dead husband at her side. Had I not been under the influence of the dope I would have upchucked right there. Many times I thought Neale and Little would vomit. None of us said a word during the trip.

When we arrived at the hostel, we learned that Benny Foshee had died before Doc Richards could get to him, apparently from loss of blood. Doc Richards was busy sewing up the buttocks of an airman. A bomb splinter had ripped him open. The hostel had taken two bombs, and the place was a mess.

Everyone told me they had watched from the ground as I was shot down. Doc Richards and Bob Neale had fired their pistols at me to warn me that the Zeros were on my tail. They also said the Japs had been firing at me while I was over Paoshan. Joe Peeden, a mechanic, said my plane hit and bounced for a hundred yards and then burst into a ball of fire.

They all congratulated me on being alive, and I went to the hostel. My number-one boy shook the debris off my bunk, and Doc gave me some sleeping pills. I thanked God I was still alive, lay down on my blistered back, and fell asleep.

The twin-engine bomber (probably a Ki-21) Bond downed on May 4 was his last aerial victory. He mustered out of the AVG when it ceased operations on July 4, 1942, but flew several more missions while Army Air Forces fighter pilots staged into China to take over where the AVG had left off. Following a brief home leave, Bond reentered the Army Air Forces with the rank of major and was assigned as an instructor to the School of Applied Tactics. Bond served a tour with the American mission in the USSR, returned home in 1944, and remained in the service after the war. He retired from the Air Force in 1968 with the rank of major general.

DUCKS IN A ROW

2d Lieutenant GEORGE HOLLOWELL, USMC
VMF-224
GUADALCANAL—September 14, 1942

George Lindley Hollowell was born in Kansas City, Kansas, on December 6, 1920. After graduating from high school in 1938, he attended

Kansas State College, in Manhattan, Kansas. One day during Hollowell's junior year, Navy and Marine recruiters showed up on campus to show a movie titled Your Navy Wings of Gold, *and that did it for young Hollowell; he was hooked on the notion of becoming a naval aviator! According to the rules at the time, a young man who wanted to enlist in the V-5 Naval Aviation Cadet Training Program had to be at least twenty years old and, if only twenty, had to obtain parental consent. George Hollowell was twenty, and he did obtain the required consent. When he reported to the Navy Elimination Air Base at Fairfax Airport in Kansas City, he turned in the consent forms and was given a physical and mental examination, which he passed. Then he was given ten hours of dual instruction, including check rides and a fifteen-minute solo flight. He passed the "E"-base course and was accepted for duty on May 3, 1941.*

Hollowell's next stop was Jacksonville, Florida, where he reported in as a seaman 2d class awaiting appointment as an Aviation Cadet. During June and July 1941, he and many other prospective cadets washed airplanes, pulled wheel chocks, and cranked the engines for those who already were cadets. His appointment came through at the end of July 1941 and he was sent to Corpus Christi, Texas, for training with the base's first training class. Hollowell graduated from Corpus Christi on February 9, 1942, as a Marine second lieutenant.

I proceeded on June 1, 1942, to the North Island Naval Air Station in San Diego, but I stopped in Kansas City en route to visit my parents and future wife. On arrival at the 2d Marine Aircraft Wing headquarters, I joined a group of second lieutenants and was told not to send any laundry out. This proved to be good advice, for in a few days we were sent to the Marine Corps Air Station at Ewa, Hawaii, on the island of Oahu. There, a large group of second lieutenants was gathered together in a room and introduced to Captains Robert Galer and John Smith, who tossed a baseball bat into the air and went "hand over hand" to the end of the bat in order to determine who would get first choice. The lieutenants didn't realize it, but we were about to be picked for our future combat squadrons. John L. Smith was the commanding officer of Marine Fighter Squadron 223 (VMF-223) and Robert E. Galer was the commanding officer of VMF-224. I was picked by Bob Galer.

My first flight in VMF-224 was my first flight in a Grumman F4F

Wildcat fighter. It was July 20, 1942. We trained in familiarization, tactics, formation gunnery, field carrier landing practice, and the use of oxygen.

The trip to the South Pacific was not a pleasure cruise. VMF-224 flew from Ewa, named for the sugar plantation it was carved from, to Ford Island, the Navy landing field right in the middle of Pearl Harbor. Here our Wildcats were loaded aboard the aircraft transport USS *Kitty Hawk* along with twenty flight officers, one ground officer, and forty-two enlisted men. This was on August 14, 1942, the same day we qualified for carrier landings aboard the USS *Hornet*. Also aboard the *Kitty Hawk* was Marine Scout-Bomber Squadron 231 (VMSB-231), which was equipped with Douglas SBD Dauntless dive-bombers.

Before conversion by the Navy, the *Kitty Hawk* had been a banana boat working in the Gulf of Mexico. She still had railroad tracks in the boat deck, so the fruit could be left in the rail cars to reduce handling between picking and unloading. She pitched and rolled at the whim of the ocean. Almost every night we had rain, which did much to dampen the spirits of those who were sleeping on the main deck in canvas cots, even though the pitching and rolling caused the cots to slide on the rain-slick deck.

The monotony of the trip was broken on August 15, 1942, when Captains Bob Galer, John Dobbin, and Kirk Armistead accepted commissions as majors. On August 20, those of us who had never crossed the Equator became "shellbacks" and were initiated into the "Ancient Order of the Deep." At 2400 hours, we lost an entire day as we crossed the 180th meridian.

We arrived at Vila Harbor, Efate, New Hebrides Islands, at 0900 on August 28, 1942. We tied up "dead in the water" to the auxiliary aircraft carrier USS *Long Island,* and our F4Fs and the VMSB-231 SBD dive-bombers were hoisted from the *Kitty Hawk* to the flight deck of the *Long Island,* which was equipped with a black-powder catapult that could get the aircraft into the air most of the time. After being hoisted aboard, we were catapulted into the air while the ship remained dead in the water. We only lost one aircraft when the catapult shot fizzled. The Wildcat fell off the end of the flight deck into the water and sank. The pilot of this aircraft, 2d Lieutenant Matt Kennedy, was not injured in this accident, but he was killed in 1943, in another accident.

After being launched, we flew to the nearby airfield (code named Roses), which was commanded by Lieutenant Colonel Joe Bauer, the commanding officer of VMF-212. At Roses, we mounted belly tanks on our aircraft and tested them. The next day, August 29, we flew to Espiritu Santo, also in the New Hebrides, and landed at the airfield code named Buttons. This was the home of Marine Observation Squadron 251 (VMO-251), which was commanded by Lieutenant Colonel John Hart. VMF-224 and VMSB-231 remained overnight at Buttons and took off at 0700 on August 30 for the flight to join up with VMF-223 and VMSB-232 on Guadalcanal in Solomon Islands, which was code named Cactus.

I had a total of forty-seven hours in the F4F on the day I landed on Guadalcanal. This included carrier qualification aboard the USS *Hornet* on August 14, 1942, and the flight to Guadalcanal from Efate. The next day, August 31, I was one of seventeen VMF-224 pilots Major Galer led off Henderson Field on our first combat patrol.

VMF-212 and VMO-251 were the senior fighter outfits in the South Pacific Area at this time. Both squadrons were to play an important role in the Cactus air war, as was anyone who flew off Guadalcanal between August 1942 and early 1943, but it was a considerable loss of face on their parts that VMF-223 and VMF-224 beat them to Guadalcanal. They sent planes and pilots of division size (four aircraft) to integrate with those of us already there, to fill holes caused by sickness and pilots missing in action. Their pilots would stay ten days to two weeks before being rotated.

At our new base, we faced malaria, dysentery, insects, rain, and poor—and very little—food. Almost every night included several hours spent in a wet slit trench while Henderson Field was bombarded from the air or from the sea by Imperial Navy warships. There was plenty of flying for everyone in the Cactus Air Force, as we called the assortment of fighter and dive-bomber units that arrived at Guadalcanal over the course of time.

On September 2, I shot down an Imperial Navy G4M Betty twin-engine medium bomber, and I got a second Betty on September 13. Both of these airplanes were taking part in the almost daily noontime raids the Japanese launched from their base at Rabaul, nearly 600 miles to the northwest of Guadalcanal. This enemy raid consisted of approximately twenty-five Bettys and an undetermined number of Zero fighters. There were three of us Cactus Air Force pilots against them, but we forced the Bettys to jettison their bombs some distance from Henderson Field, which was a victory for us! These were not unusual odds at the time, as the Japanese always outnumbered our airborne forces by about ten to one.

By then, VMF-223, VMF-224, and P-400 fighters from the Army's 67th Fighter Squadron were operating from a grass airstrip known as Fighter-1. Fighter-1 was an ordinary unimproved field—literally a field—and we tried to keep it that way. There were no bulldozers, no matting, and as little taxiing as possible. We tried to keep the grass growing on the field to avoid mud holes and ruts. We had moved to this field from the main one, Henderson, because we were having so much trouble with takeoffs, landings, and taxiing there. Parking was also a problem because of SBDs and their bomb loads. Also, transport aircraft were bringing in fuel and supplies, and Seabees from a naval construction battalion were always working on the field due to the almost continual bombing. The Seabees, by the way, were some of the real heroes during the August–November 1942 stage of the war. They would be out on the runway, making repairs, almost before the bombing runs had finished. They cleared the damaged Marston Matting (pierced steel planking), filled the holes, compacted the fill, and refitted the matting. They had to work fast, because no one knew when the field would be needed for another alert or an emergency landing by aircraft damaged in contact with the enemy. We moved the fighters to the grass field on September 9 and continued to use it for as long as we were there.

The VMF-223, VMF-224, and VF-5 ground crews did an almost superhuman job during September and October 1942. They had F4Fs from their own squadrons as well as VMF-212 and VMO-251 all depending on them to refuel aircraft, clean guns, and service oxygen equipment, and they also had to dodge the frequent air raids. Finding time for even one meal a day was hard. Here I need to acknowledge my plane captain, Sergeant Raymond Sorenson. He was a redhead, with a redhead's coloring and about a million freckles—a real Norman Rockwell picture. His smiling face and salute as I taxied away for each takeoff were the last thing I took note of, and his smiling face and thumb's-up signal would be the first thing I encountered on each landing. Raymond Sorenson had an unquenchable desire to serve and take care of his aircraft and me. Without my plane being serviced and ready, I would not have been an ace and not even telling this story.

Often we didn't know who was in control of the field as we approached it following a scramble. Skirmishes near the airfield between the enemy ground forces and our own during the night and early morning hours were not uncommon.

◆

On September 14, I joined three other pilots from VMF-224 in an early-morning scramble caused by two Zero-type float fighters. We climbed too high to make contact with these enemy aircraft, but both of the float fighters were shot down by Wildcat pilots from the Navy's veteran Fighting Squadron 5 (VF-5), which had flown from the USS *Saratoga* until she was damaged by a torpedo. VF-5 had arrived at Cactus on September 11.

It must be pointed out that at the time of our arrival at Guadalcanal, radar and combat air control were both in their infancy. To be specific, our "early warning" was the product of some of the real heroes of the early war, the coastwatchers, usually Australians based on Japanese-held islands with very primitive radios and one or two islanders to assist them. As enemy aircraft flew overhead on the way from Rabaul to Guadalcanal, the coastwatchers would actually count by type and radio this information to Cactus Control with an altitude estimate of high, low, or medium. This is what we used to alert our aircraft. Sometimes the enemy would not show for various reasons, such as low fuel, a change in weather, a change in flight direction after being spotted, or just whim, but we had to scramble anyway.

A second alert took place at noon on September 14. It was spurred by an undetermined number of Imperial Navy Mitsubishi G4M Betty medium bombers and Mitsubishi A6M Zero fighters. A number of VMF-223 and VF-5 Wildcats, and four of us from VMF-224, took off and climbed to altitude, about 26,000 feet. There, at around 1300 hours, Bob Galer and John Dobbin each shot down a Zero, the VMF-223 pilots got two Bettys, and the VF-5 pilots also got two Bettys.

On good-weather days it was typical to scramble three or more times in response to calls from the coastwatchers. At times, the number of aircraft available for a scramble was limited because of the need to refuel, rearm, or repair fighters that had taken part in an earlier scramble. But usually within an hour or so of each scramble, a section of two aircraft or a division of four aircraft would become ready and take off to join the fray. In general, the available pilots would be in a ready tent, just a few feet from the aircraft, and would run to the planes when the alert was sounded. Each pilot had an assigned airplane, so the procedure was simple. Also, the in-service aircraft were used so often that the heat on the island did not let the engines cool enough for starting to be a problem.

We were in the ready tent when the third alert came at about 1930. It was just twilight when we took off, but the field was not yet under attack.

I got in my aircraft with the assistance of my plane captain, who helped with the parachute and shoulder straps. After spotting the leader roll by on takeoff, I waved to my plane captain to start the engine, and then I started my take-off run. As soon as I was off the ground, I adjusted the throttle with my left hand and tightened it in that position so it wouldn't creep. Next, flying with my left hand, I reached down with my right hand to crank up the landing gear, which took thirteen full turns from down to fully retracted. During this period of time, I was adjusting my oxygen mask and looking for the enemy. As soon as the landing gear was up, it was necessary to readjust the throttle, after which I started to pump the wobble pump with my left hand while flying with the right.

Climbing to altitude in my F4F was almost always an adventure. To begin with, my aircraft was different from most of the others, which is why other pilots seldom took it in a scramble. I had a hand wobble pump, while the others had electric wobble pumps that were activated by a simple toggle switch. Mine had a rod with a pistol grip sticking out of the instrument panel that had to be hand pumped for flights above 10,000 feet, because our fuel tanks weren't pressurized. The throttle and wobble pump were not so critical and I could work them with my left hand, but the exertion using the hand wobble drained my oxygen and my energy level. Fortunately, despite food and parts shortages, my plane and I remained reasonably healthy throughout the Guadalcanal Campaign.

I was normally Major Galer's wingman, but on this last scramble late on September 14, it was a matter of what pilots and aircraft were available, so I became Major Dobbin's wingman. Typically, whoever could get off joined those already airborne, and in this case I joined Dobbin on his right wing. Three other VMF-224 pilots also took part in this scramble.

After joining up as best we could, we headed for a high altitude intercept because that was where we were told the main attack would come in. When the word came from Cactus that float aircraft were coming in low over the field, Major Dobbin signaled for me to stay on his wing. We left the other three planes at 25,000 feet, at what we called a high CAP (combat air patrol), just in case there were more enemy aircraft at altitude.

The two of us started descending without seeing the enemy, but Major Dobbin finally spotted them from about 2,000 feet. They turned out to be Imperial Navy F1M Pete reconnaissance float biplanes, which were often used as strafers and even as interceptors. Often, they dropped light bombs while they were strafing. I had a hard time picking them up, but I did see them as I passed below about 1,500 feet.

Cactus Control had told us that there were about thirty enemy aircraft, but I didn't try to count them. I was trying to stay in formation with my flight leader while we were in the high-speed dive, and I only had a chance to look for the enemy when we were close to the ground and Dobbin gave me the signal to break off. It was nearly dark by then and they were coming across Henderson Field from southeast to northwest at nearly treetop level in two strings of about equal numbers.

When we picked them up, the Petes were below us, over Fighter-1. To add to the excitement, we had to fly through our own antiaircraft fire, which was bursting around the Petes.

John Dobbin just naturally took the left string, because he was on that side, which left the right string to me. We came in above them and cut in somewhere in the middle of each string. I fired my first shots about 1,000 yards from the nearest Pete in front of me. I filled my gunsight with the first plane, opened fire, then just "walked" my bullets down the line of airplanes. The enemy pilots were helping me in this effort by being too low to dive, and the fire put out by the rear-seat gunners firing at me provided a good aiming point. They also helped by mostly staying in trail formation.

Major Dobbin and I had to break off after only one pass, because the enemy aircraft were heading away from the island and there wouldn't have been enough time for another pass. I was able to see what damage we had inflicted when I looked back over my shoulder as I pulled up from the attack. I saw four of the enemy aircraft still in the air but on fire. The remaining enemy planes disappeared in the darkness and did not return. They were last seen streaking away from the island. It is believed that they came from the seaplane anchorage at Gizo Island, about 210 nautical miles from Guadalcanal.

It was very dark as we recovered from our engagement and prepared to land. All of our planes from this scramble landed safely. Major Dobbin and I were each given credit for shooting down three of the Petes. This made each of us an ace, Dobbin with six victories (including a Zero downed during the afternoon scramble) and me with five.

When I rotated out of Guadalcanal with the other VMF-224 survivors, I was still twenty-one years old. I had flown with three future Medal of Honor winners (John Smith, Bob Galer, and Joe Bauer), was an ace myself, and had participated in one of the breakthrough battles of World War II. After all this, I felt very good and also competent with my Wings of Gold. I had survived the air battles, the sickness, and the poor food, and I was on my way home to marry the girl who, after fifty-three years, is still my guardian angel.

Following his September 14, 1942, rise to acedom, 2d Lieutenant George Hollowell downed a Betty over Henderson Field on September 27 and another Betty and a Zero over Guadalcanal on October 11.

Following home leave and service in the United States, he served as a senior F4U Corsair pilot with VMF-111 in the Central Pacific and flew sixty ground-attack missions against bypassed Japanese bases in the Marshall Islands. He remained in the Marine Corps after World War II and served in Korea and Vietnam. After twenty-eight years on active duty, Colonel George Hollowell retired on July 1, 1968.

THE SAFEST THING

1st Lieutenant LARRY O'NEILL, USAAF
342d Fighter Squadron, 348th Fighter Group
Marilinan, New Guinea—September 13, 1943

Lawrence Frederick O'Neill was born on February 28, 1921, in St. Louis, where he lived while attending elementary school and high school.

St. Louis has a long association with aviation, and I suppose that background motivated me toward aviation and flying. Beyond that, my love for adventure drew me toward enlisting in the Army Air Corps. In September 1940, it was apparent that the United States would enter the war, and I wanted to have a part in it. I was nineteen, just one year out of high school. I had completed a Civil Aeronautics Administration ground school course for a private pilot's license, but I couldn't afford flight lessons. The next best thing was enlisting in the Army Air Corps, which sent me to the Aviation Mechanics School at Chanute Field in Rantoul, Illinois. My first duty station after graduating from Chanute was Maxwell Field, Alabama, an advanced flight training school where cadets flew North American AT-6 Texan trainers. As often as possible, I begged a ride with instructors and thus got a good feel for flying.

Later, while on detached duty at Greenville, Mississippi, I learned that the Air Corps had instituted a "college equivalency" examination for entrance into the Aviation Cadet program. Until that time, a minimum of two years of college was required to apply, but by passing the scheduled exam, this requirement could be satisfied. A friend and I studied for three months to take the exam in the fall of 1941.

In early January 1942 I received word that I had passed the equivalency exam and I was given orders to Pre-flight training at Kelly Field in San Antonio, Texas. I like to think that I passed on my merits, but the bombing of Pearl Harbor while I was waiting to hear the results may have had something to do with my acceptance into the program.

I completed Pre-flight training at Kelly and was assigned to Class 42-I. I went on to Primary at Chickasha, Oklahoma; Basic at Waco, Texas; and Advanced at Lake Charles, Louisiana. Our class graduated on

October 9, 1942, and I was ordered to Windsor Locks, Connecticut, to check out in a brand new fighter, the Republic P-47 Thunderbolt. In November, some of us with P-47 time were ordered to the newly formed 342d Fighter Squadron of the 348th Fighter Group, which had been activated on September 30 at Westover Field, Massachusetts, under Major Neel Kearby.

The group headquarters and the other two squadrons trained at Providence, Rhode Island, but the 342d Fighter Squadron went to Bedford, Massachusetts, where we were the sole occupants of the brand new base. We lived in wooden barracks with potbellied stoves, in the middle of the coldest winter in years. The temperature went as low as minus-25 degrees, and the toilet huts were outside.

One memorable event during our time at Bedford was an acrobatic training flight I had at high altitude. I had inadvertently set my oxygen to Emergency, so I passed out from lack of oxygen and woke up headed straight down to the sea. The controls were immovable, but full trim-tab action and many Hail Marys, plus all my strength on the stick, brought the plane out in a zoom. I leveled off at about 3,000 feet, so you can imagine how close I must have come to the water. I was out of sight of land and I could tell that all was not right with the plane or the pilot. I made my way back to Bedford, and when we examined the plane, we found that all the control surfaces were damaged, and the wheel wells and air intakes were bulged out. I had been in what became known as compressibility. As one of the first groups to get P-47s, we had heard of problems, such as a P-47 in a dive having its tail come off. This was one problem we never worried about after my dive, since the plane had held together pretty well.

In April 1943, we loaded up for overseas deployment. We all had about 200 hours in the P-47 when we sailed and were a good, confident fighting unit.

We were sure we were going to England. We left New York in a convoy, but we could see that we were headed south, rather than east toward Europe. It was soon announced that Australia was our destination. The convoy went through the Panama Canal and on to Brisbane, Australia. After being trained in one of New England's coldest winters, and having all of our cold-weather flying gear with us, it was quite a surprise to be headed to a tropical area.

We arrived in Brisbane in June 1943, and our new P-47Ds arrived by freighter from San Francisco. They were assembled at a field called Eagle Farms. Believe it or not, they did not have belly or wing tanks at that time, so all hands went to work improvising belly tanks. The P-47 was so big compared to other fighters at that time that the Aussies thought they were some kind of bomber, and they kept looking for bomb bay doors.

Why was a P-47 unit, with airplanes that had very limited range, being sent to the Southwest Pacific? It was something of a puzzle. Looking back on it, apparently the Fifth Air Force commander, Major General George Kenney, and the Southwest Pacific Area commander, General Douglas MacArthur, had had success in their demands for more air support, and we were the first fighter unit that became available. However, I imagine Kenney was unhappy that he got short-range P-47s instead of long-range P-38s, because he needed long-range support if he needed anything. As a result, our group commander, Colonel Neel Kearby, had a selling job to do.

We flew to New Guinea in July 1943 and were based near Port Moresby. Initially, we went for weeks without seeing the enemy as we flew routine cover missions for transports and bombers. Later on, it felt like months were passing with little or no action.

I think the weather and living conditions were the greatest problems we faced. With no real navigation equipment, the threat of the buildup of vast tropical thunderheads was a constant concern to all of us. Many combat squadrons lost planes and pilots to violent weather—I would guess as often or more often than to enemy action. And the living conditions—a steady ration of dehydrated foods, malaria-infected mosquitoes, mud, and humidity—proved to be the undoing of some of the men, including pilots.

Later, when Colonel Charles Lindbergh toured the fighter bases in the Southwest Pacific, he showed us how to greatly extend the range of our fighters. He visited most of the V Fighter Command squadrons to demonstrate methods for setting the throttle manifold pressure and propeller pitch to get hours more time from the fuel available.

Colonel Kearby really wanted to prove to General Kenney that our P-47s could go out and fight, so he initiated small flights to undertake fighter sweeps over Japanese air bases. The group's first victories came on August 16, 1943, when pilots from the 340th and 341st Fighter squadrons shot down several Ki-43 Oscar fighters around Marilinan, New Guinea. Next, on September 4, Colonel Kearby shot down a Betty bomber and an Oscar over Hopoi.

My turn at the plate came on September 13, 1943. At the time, I was a regular element leader, and I was a flight leader on this specific mission. At about 1030 hours, our formation of two four-plane flights was flying top cover for several transports that were supplying the newly captured strip at Nadzab. The fighter controller vectored us to a large flight of bogeys at 20,000 feet that appeared to be heading back toward Japanese territory. We were probably at 15,000 or 16,000 feet, so we had to climb.

Following the vector, we soon found a flight of Imperial Navy twin-engine Betty bombers near Marilinan. They were pretty well spread out, so I assumed they were returning to base, possibly Wewak. The Bettys were slightly higher than we were and headed away from us, so we had to give chase as well as climb. Records of the time say there were an estimated fifty fighters and twenty bombers in the formation, but I have no recollection of numbers like that. In fact, I did not see any fighters, but I was sure they were in the area. As a result, I wanted to attack the bombers as soon as we could.

Our final approach was toward the bombers' 3 o'clock position, and that meant a tough full-deflection shot. Since we had lost some speed in the climb to their altitude, I pushed over in a quick dive as we approached the enemy flight, to try to pick up speed and come up toward the underside of the bomber formation. I attacked the first group of bombers I could reach. They were going from my left to my right, so my pushover and pullup were toward the right rear of the closest bomber.

As I pushed over and came to within about 200 yards of the plane I was attacking, my canopy instantly became totally covered with oil. I couldn't see a thing and I didn't know how bad the oil leak was. Since I had already started my firing pass, the safest thing for me to do was start shooting and then get out of the area. I fired a burst of a few seconds with the six .50-caliber machine guns. (In order to save weight, we carried only six of the eight guns the P-47s could have carried.) I started shooting mainly on instinct and to complete what I had started. But I was in a very fearful state, having no idea why the plane was suddenly covered with oil, or if the oil flow would continue, or if the engine was about to stop or start burning, or what!

I made a sharp evasive turn and dove toward Mother Earth. I was in a slight panic; I didn't know what was happening around me. Imagine driving along and having a dark blanket thrown over your car! I felt very vulnerable as I was, in effect, flying on instruments. I feverishly reviewed all the instruments while in my dive away from the fight, to see any sign of a drop in oil pressure, or a rise in temperature, or a loss of power. Everything seemed to be okay, and the engine didn't miss a beat. As far as I could tell, I had not been hit.

As I got out of the area, I opened the small vent in the windshield so I could see ahead at least a little bit. That little vent saved my life; it helped me get oriented toward the ground. Previously, it had served as a diversion, for watching chewing-tobacco juice get sucked out into the airstream.

Not knowing how much oil I had lost was a real concern, but I could see that the oil had apparently not gotten any darker, which is to say, thicker, on the glass. I calmed down and leveled out on a course for Nadzab. When I had the base in sight, within about thirty minutes, I was a happy and relieved man! By this time, Nadzab was an operational advance base. Army aviation engineers had repaired damage and built taxiways and ramp areas.

My contact with the tower was brief—I had an emergency and they cleared me to land on the operational runway.

As I approached the strip, I had the canopy open and could see over the side. However, as I turned onto the final leg into the runway, I could no longer see it, and that was the thing that had me most concerned. Fortunately, there must have been little or no crosswind, because I hit the runway just fine and could taxi in the usual way.

The rest of my flight also landed at Nadzab soon afterward, and to my happy surprise, 2d Lieutenant John Nagle said that I had shot down a Betty bomber! When the others had seen the black cloud of oil come from my plane as I was making my gunnery pass, they all thought I had been hit. And when they lost me in my mad dive, they thought I was gone.

I must say that I was able to make a landing at Nadzab because of the great work done by Army engineers in completing repairs and additions to the landing strips in the period from September 5 to 13, when the mission took place. Our squadron had been part of the fighter cover for the paratroop landing at Nadzab on September 5, 1943.

My victory was the first by anyone in the 342d Fighter Squadron. Coincidentally, Captain William Banks, also of the 342d, shot down an Oscar fifty miles northwest of Marilinan at exactly the same time.

A check of my plane showed that the servicing crew had failed to use safety wire on the oil-tank cap, and the cap had worked its way off. When I pushed over, oil shot out into the windstream and covered the canopy.

I used up a large amount of luck on this mission—getting a victory, not getting attacked myself, and effecting a safe landing.

First Lieutenant Larry O'Neill next tangled with the Japanese on December 26, 1943, and he achieved ace status that day when he shot down four more Bettys near Umboi Island. He rotated home to the United States in October 1944 and was separated from active duty with the rank of captain in October 1945.

O'Neill entered the engineering school at Washington University in St. Louis in late 1945, and in 1946 he transferred to the Missouri School of Mines at Rolla. By going straight through the summers of 1946 and 1947, and carrying heavy credit-hour loads, he was able to graduate in June 1948. In February 1948, he took a competitive oral and written exam for the Navy Civil Engineer Corps, and won an appointment as a lieutenant junior grade. In 1965, Commander Larry O'Neill, Army Air Corps fighter ace, retired from the Navy.

COMMAND*

Lieutenant Commander TOM BLACKBURN, USN
VF-17
Rabaul - February 4, 1944

John Thomas Blackburn, the son and brother of professional Navy officers, graduated from Annapolis in 1933, grudgingly served his obligatory two years in the surface fleet, and at the first opportunity, volunteered for flight training. He was a fighter pilot all the way—by choice and by temperament.

When war broke out, Lieutenant Blackburn was teaching tactics to novice fighter pilots at the Navy's new fighter-training center at Opa-Locka, Florida. He asked to be returned to a carrier squadron and was refused, but eventually wangled orders to form and command Carrier Escort Fighter Squadron (VGF) 29, which he led during the first day of the invasion of North Africa (during which he was forced to ditch after a radio failure left him far from the fleet without fuel). On returning to the United States, Lieutenant Commander Blackburn was ordered to form and command VF-17, the Navy's first Vought F4U Corsair squadron, for duty aboard the new fleet carrier USS Bunker Hill. *The Corsair needed to be tamed for carrier duty, and Blackburn and his crew of youngsters did that, but the Hellcat was coming on strong and it was decided to put VF-17 ashore in the Solomons to avoid the hassle of keeping the Corsairs maintained from a supply line otherwise dedicated to Grumman F6F Hellcats.*

VF-17's first tour was in mid and late 1944, out of one of Munda's satellite fields. In covering the Torokina landings and associated operations, Tommy Blackburn destroyed four Japanese aircraft, including three fighters. Even more important, his command hit the victory columns in a big way. After a break in Australia, VF-17 was reassigned to one of the new Bougainville fighter strips to cover Rabaul-bound bombers. Thereafter, VF-17 racked up kills with chilling regularity, and the innovative Blackburn oversaw the development of quite brilliant new fighter tactics. By January 31, his own score stood at seven, all fighters but one.

---

* Blackburn, Tom, with Eric Hammel. *The Jolly Rogers: The Story of Tom Blackburn and Navy Fighting Squadron VF-17*. Pacifica, California: Pacifica Press: 1997.

VF-17 and Tommy Blackburn were riding high with nearly 150 aerial victories at the expense of just nine of its number lost.

I led off twenty of our Corsairs on February 4. Once again, our charges were B-24s, this time bound for Tobera Field. I had a newly arrived lieutenant on my wing, a solid-seeming senior pilot I wanted to check out before moving him up to lead a section, or even a division.

Only twenty Zeros and ten Tonys appeared to challenge us. On the approach, however, Ensign Percy Divenny, who had joined us in Espiritu but already had two kills under his belt, made a really dumb mistake. Instead of opening the valve that released CO_2 into the Corsair's wing-purging system, he opened the adjacent valve, which actuated his emergency landing-gear system. Once down by this means, there was no way to get the wheels back up while in flight. We were by then too close to the target to allow Perce to abort, so, as soon as I saw the reason why he was dropping back, I radioed to tell him to tuck in beneath the heavy bombers. If Perce had understood and done exactly what he had been told—and stayed put—he would have it made; the Zekes would never be able to get at him.

We were virtually retiring from the bomb-drop point when, to my utter horror, I saw Divenny's Corsair slowly dropping behind the B-24s. We could never figure out what happened; Perce was a cool hand, so the only theory that held water was that his Corsair suffered some sort of engine power loss. In any case, by this time, the Zeros were nipping at our flanks, looking for an opening so they could get at the Liberators or bounce exposed fighters. Our job was to protect the B-24s, and we all had our hands full doing that, so I made the brutal decision to withhold cover for Divenny. Naturally, the Zeros—at least eight of them—pounced on Perce. As they started in, Lieutenant (jg) Earl May broke from his position in the bomber cover and led his wingman, Ensign Wilbert "Beads" Popp, to the rescue. The two got to Divenny's lagging fighter, and they did get their talons into one of the Zekes. Earl got credit for an assist and Beads got full credit for the kill. However, the rest of the Zeros bore down on them, and May and Popp had to dive to safety. A Zeke came down on Perce's tail and hammered him into a fatal dive.

As the retiring bombers were clearing the coast, six Zekes hit the formation from 500 feet above the low-cover flight. Attacking from the rear, these Zekes put in a series of aggressive high-side runs. The rear division, under Lieutenant (jg) Paul Cordray, turned back to take on the Zekes, and the Zekes broke contact. However, when Paul turned again to rejoin the bombers, two Zekes slipped in and set up a firing pass at the rear element, Lieutenant (jg) Hal Jackson followed by Lieutenant (jg) Don Malone. Jackson was well behind Cordray and his wingman, and Malone was lagging even farther behind Jackson.

Cordray gave a frantic "Close up" zooming signal, and Jackson promptly moved in. Malone, who had a long history of lagging in formation, did not respond to the unmistakable series of short dives and zooms, nor even to "Don! Don! Close up! Close up," which Paul frantically broadcast by radio. When the Zekes pulled up at the conclusion of their single firing run, Malone's Corsair was burning and falling away. Attracted by Cordray's vain warning, several of us saw Don's chute blossom. We hoped he would get down safely, but we had to leave. No one ever saw Don again.

As soon as we landed, I confronted Earl May at the ready room and let him have my fury. I had been literally sick to my stomach when I saw Divenny going down, but I had made the painful decision to carry out our responsibility to defend the bombers. I had determined that we could not do that and cover Divenny, too. It was, in my mind, a tough fact of life that Perce had been lost because he had been unable to stay under the heavy bombers. The only thing that kept me from grounding Earl was the lucky fact that no enemy fighters had attacked through the hole his departure had left in our formation.

"Get this straight, Earl. Nobody has ever questioned your courage. You don't have to prove yourself like some show-off schoolboy. You had no goddamn business breaking out of your cover position with Beads to take on all those Japs. For what? Sure, you and Beads flamed one, but you damn sure didn't help Divenny. You were lucky as hell you and Beads didn't get it, too. You *know* that if the enemy hadn't muffed their chance they'd have had three easy kills instead of just the one. Worse than that, you exposed the rest of us and the bombers. Our job is to get those klunkers in and out in one piece. I'm *proud* that we haven't lost one yet. They *depend* on us. This is a team operation. There's no place for some wild-ass who shoves off to be the heroic White Knight riding to the rescue. I will not tolerate this kind of shit. Is that clear?"

Earl was angry with me—his body language said as much—but he was wrong and I was right, and he knew it. I got a sheepish, "I understand, Skipper."

"If you weren't such a good man who's always done a top job before, I'd throw your ass out. As it is, you're no longer a division leader. You'll fly wing, where I can keep my eye on you."

I was so obviously angry for the rest of the day that no one got within ten feet of me if he could help it.

My overall reaction and anger over the two losses might seem unreasonable, but both were firmly grounded in my life-long perception of how duty must come before my personal feelings for my subordinates, strong as they were. All hands—even late arrivals like Perce Divenny—knew that our responsibility was to guard the bombers *at all costs*.

In part, however, the display of anger was a mask for my profound grief. The two unnecessary losses were almost more than I could bear. I privately judged myself at least a little culpable in both cases.

With respect to Perce's fatal lapse, I had allowed the wing-purging and emergency landing-gear CO_2 bottles to remain side by side even though I easily could have gotten Vought or even our own mechanics to relocate one safely away from the other. The potential for error was *so* obvious! Amazingly, Divenny's gaffe had been the first of its sort in hundreds of combat sorties.

Malone's loss was a little different, and I bore more direct responsibility. All hands knew that Don had a marked propensity to lag. Maybe I should have ridden him harder, or moved him forward from the definitively vulnerable tail-end slot. We knew that the Imperial pilots, like us, were quick to spot and nail a laggard.

Worst of all was my conviction that I had seen both situations developing. I had certainly seen Divenny fall behind, and I am sure I had seen Malone do so earlier in the mission. In Divenny's case, I *could* have taken the chance and gone back or have sent help, but I deliberately chose not to. In Malone's, Cordray could have gone to help, but Paul knew—and accepted—my thinking, so he did not dangerously expose his division and put others at risk, as May had done.

These were two more painful examples of the loneliness of command. I found, after a long search through my soul, that I would not have acted differently in either case. But I had contributed to Malone's death by being too lenient; I should have grounded him when his inability to correct a long-apparent problem. It was a bomb that had ticked away—that I had heard ticking—until it blew up in Don's face.

Two days later, over Rabaul, Tommy Blackburn raised his score to eleven confirmed victories and five probables. And shortly thereafter, Rabaul caved. In the end, VF-17 returned home and was decommissioned. In its day, it was the Navy's top-scoring squadron, with 154½ confirmed victories.

The end of the war found Commander Tommy Blackburn whipping a new carrier air group into shape for duty in the Pacific. He remained in the Navy—in aviation, of course—until 1962, when he retired as a captain. He passed away in 1994.

DANCING IN THE DARK

Lieutenant (jg) CONNIE HARGREAVES, USN
VF-2 (USS *Hornet*)
Mariana Islands—June 20, 1944

Everett Carleton Hargreaves was born in Wadena, Saskatchewan, on May 10, 1921, and lived there for his first year, until his father, a minister, took over a congregation in Grand Haven, Michigan. Later, the family moved to Eagle River, Wisconsin. While still quite young, Carl, as he was called by his family, accompanied his father several times in an old World War I Jenny flown by a local barnstormer, and this fixed him on the road to a flying career. Hargreaves completed high school in Edgerton, Wisconsin, in 1939 and went on to Westminster College in New Wilmington, Pennsylvania, where he signed up for the primary Civilian Pilots Training course in his sophomore year. He then transferred to Knox College in Galesburg, Illinois, simply because Westminster College was unable to offer the secondary CPT course.

Once through the secondary CPT course, Hargreaves made a beeline for the nearest Army Air Corps recruiting office, but his efforts to enlist were stymied by the fact that having been born in the Canadian boondocks, he had never been issued a birth certificate and had been naturalized simply as "minor son" on his father's naturalization papers. After gathering the requisite paperwork to prove that he both had been born and was a United States citizen, Hargreaves was still turned down by the Army Air Corps, which did not believe the written statements he had collected. So he signed up for the Naval Aviation Cadet program, which welcomed him with open arms because the Navy's air arm had been so depleted during recent Pacific War battles.

Cadet Connie (for "Wisconsin") Hargreaves began his Elimination training at Glenview Naval Air Station, Illinois, and then moved on to flight training at Corpus Christi Naval Air Station, Texas, from which he graduated as an ensign on March 17, 1943. He attended fighter operational school at Opa-Locka Naval Air Station, Florida, and underwent carrier qualifications back at Glenview. Ensign Hargreaves then received orders to VF-2, which was forming at Atlantic City Naval Air Station under Lieutenant Commander Bill Dean, who had been one of his advanced fighter instructors at the Kingsville Naval Air Station, Texas. In short order, VF-2 began training for combat in the first production batch of new Grumman F6F Hellcat fighters. On October 4, 1943, after undergoing gunnery training at Quonset Point Naval Air Station, Rhode Island, and carrier qualifications at Norfolk, Virginia, VF-2 was ordered to Pearl Harbor for eventual assignment to a fleet carrier.

We arrived at Pearl Harbor in mid-October 1943 and were assigned to the Barbers Point Naval Air Station as part of the Hawaiian air defense. We were soon taking part in a live practice for the Marines going ashore on Maui while we operated from the new USS *Lexington* for several days. As a result of this exercise, Commander Butch O'Hare requested that VF-2 replace VF-6 in his Air Group 6 aboard the USS *Enterprise*. This was because VF-6 had sustained more than fifty percent losses in its last operation. Thus, our initiation into combat was at Makin and Tarawa atolls in the Gilbert Islands, and on a short raid on Kwajalein Atoll in the Marshall Islands. Then we headed back to Pearl.

Bill Dean received orders in early January 1944 to have seven volunteer pilots available on a temporary basis to report to the escort carrier

USS *Kalinin Bay,* which was loaded with new Hellcats to be used as replacement planes, along with us "experienced" pilots. We headed for Majuro Atoll, where I received orders to catapult off the *Kalinin Bay* and land aboard the USS *Bunker Hill* to join VF-18 for the raids on Truk in the Caroline Islands, Saipan and Guam in the Mariana Islands, and Eniwetok Atoll in the Marshalls. We received the Presidential Unit Citation for this round of operations. Upon the *Bunker Hill's* return to Pearl, I was detached from VF-18 to rejoin VF-2, which, with the rest of Air Group 2, had just been assigned to the new USS *Hornet* (CV-12) upon her arrival from the States. We were to be her first combat air group. We boarded officially on March 7, 1944, for the new *Hornet's* first tour of combat duty.

We headed for the Caroline Islands, with Palau and Woleai for targets. We were resupplied at Majuro and then went on to attack Hollandia, New Guinea, and the nearby Wakde Islands. This was followed by attacks against Truk and Ponape in the Carolines and against Wakde once again. After this, we went to Kwajalein for resupply, then sailed to support the invasion of the Marianas. On June 11, 1944, we opened strikes on Saipan and Guam, where we lost three planes at 14,000 feet to very accurate antiaircraft fire. Only one pilot was able to bail out. He landed just to the west of Guam and had to lasso the periscope of the rescue sub so he could be towed far enough out of the range of shore guns for the sub to surface safely and take him aboard. Our next targets were Chichi Jima and Haha Jima in the Bonin Islands, and Iwo Jima in the nearby Volcano Islands. The purpose of these strikes was to head off any Japanese planes coming down from Japan to hit our Marines landing on Saipan. But our task group commander, Rear Admiral Jocko Clark, had received word that the Japanese fleet had left its home ports and was heading for an engagement to protect Saipan, so we returned to the Marianas to rejoin the rest of Task Force 58.

On June 18, 1944, many of us took assignments to search 380 miles out from the carriers with a 50-mile cross leg. This was an unusually long search for fighters. We had to trust that the *Hornet* would be able to continue on its anticipated course and that we would be able to notice any change in the force or direction of wave caps to enable us to plot more accurately our navigation back to the fleet. Most of the search flights wound up being five hours or more in length, with a maximum fuel supply for just six hours. This meant we required a most accurate navigation, for we might still have to wait for the carrier to respot aircraft on the flight deck before bringing us aboard. It was our best effort, but none of us was able to report a sighting of the Japanese fleet.

June 19 started out on the same program as the previous day, but before long our combat air patrol was vectored out to intercept incoming bogeys, which turned out to be Japanese carrier planes trying to strike our fleet. These planes were to fly on to Guam, refuel, and then make the long flight back to their carriers. However, most of those planes never got to complete their mission. The day was later tagged as the Marianas Turkey Shoot. Our squadron was credited with seventy-six kills and several probables on June 19, but some of us never got to even see a Japanese plane during the entire day, as we were assigned to fly escort for our dive-bombers and torpedo planes going in to drop their bombs on the airfield on Guam. However, as a result of the bombing, the few Japanese who made it to Guam piled up in their attempts to land between bomb craters on their runway.

By dawn of June 20, we knew that two-thirds of the first-line Imperial Navy carrier pilots and planes had been downed, and that their fleet had to be somewhere close, but our searches continued to be futile. That is, they were futile until about 1600, when a contact was made and the Japanese fleet was reported to be only about 200 miles west of us.

I was one of a dozen pilots relaxing in Ready Room 1 when the word came in, but it didn't take us long to bring our plotting boards up to date. We were all ready to go when the Task Force 58 commander, Vice Admiral Pete Mitscher, decided to launch a strike. Air Group 2 contributed twelve fighters to escort twelve dive bombers and nine torpedo planes. Even the fighters were loaded with 500-pound bombs, for maximum striking power, since this was the first time a Japanese carrier fleet had come out since October 26, 1942. We could always jettison the bombs in the event we ran into enemy planes.

After we joined planes from all the other carriers, one of our Hellcats had to return to the *Hornet* because of engine problems. The rest of us flew with the strike force to the reported sighting position, but no Japanese fleet was there.

We were at the point of having to turn around and increase ground speed some if we were to have a chance at landing aboard our carriers before darkness set in, but our air group commander gave the word to continue west in hopes of finding the enemy. We passed the 300-mile mark on our plotting boards before we sighted the Japanese fleet just as the sun was setting. Air groups from the other carriers had separated in an effort to lengthen our search line, and they stumbled onto a second Japanese task group, which launched a few fighters to combat the attack. But our force had no aerial opposition—just antiaircraft shells bursting all around us, though it got to be very heavy as we approached the push-over point.

As I remember it, Bill Dean took his division in first, flying low in order to protect the bombers as they came out of their dives, when they were most vulnerable to attack by enemy fighters. My division stayed high to protect the bombers until they had all made their dives. Then we finally got in position to commence our own dives. I think that dive was about the longest I ever made, if not in altitude, then certainly in the time I spent watching my own tracers and trying to distinguish them from all the AA that was coming up at me. It seemed like the point of release for that bomb I had been loaded with would never arrive, even though I had the guns going in short bursts all the way down.

The sun had been setting at the approach altitude, but after our dives of some 10,000 feet, the sun had disappeared and it was almost totally dark, which made rendezvous difficult until we got far enough away and out of range of the Japanese guns so we could turn running lights on to help us find each other among the many clouds that restricted visibility. There was no air traffic controller with radar out there in the deep, dark, cloudy ocean to warn us of near misses—just sharp eyes looking for another set of running lights to join up on. We joined up regardless of what the tail markings indicated, as long as it was another fighter. There was no moon to help light the way, and there were no lights from cities reflecting off the clouds to help us navigate, as there had been back in the States. We simply faced sheer darkness for flying on instruments in and around the clouds. It was a precarious and very scary flight back to our carriers.

About halfway back, we began to hear calls of "Going down, out of gas." The dive-bombers, with the lowest fuel supply, were first to ditch. Then the torpedo bombers, which had a few more gallons of gas than the dive-bombers, started going down. And then I began to think of the instructions we had been given when standing night-fighter duty in combat areas: "If launched before midnight, bail out when you get low on fuel, for the admiral won't take a chance of putting the carriers into the wind long enough to land you aboard and give the Japanese Bettys or submarines their chance at the fleet." And, "If launched after midnight, try to conserve gas so we can bring you aboard as soon after sun-up as we can after respotting the deck for landings." But as we flew along toward home in that pitch darkness, I began to think, Certainly they won't stick to those instructions with so many planes in the air—not only from our *Hornet*, but from all the other carriers in the task group.

Very few of our carrier pilots had ever made a night landing on a carrier, even back in the States, where the ships probably had the deck lights on and the landing signal officer spotlighted. Out there, the carriers would most likely not even show the dim blue deck lights that could be seen only from airplanes approaching from just the right position in the groove. There would only be a black light showing on the "skeleton suit" the LSO would probably have to haul out so we could at least see any instructions he might have to signal to assist us in the final groove after we had made three-plus legs of a normal landing pattern. And that pattern would have to be made with the only visual guide being the fluorescent wake from the carrier.

It's strange, the thoughts that go through your mind, besides those associated with trying to mentally prepare for a landing. As we flew on and on in that pitch darkness, I began to question my navigation, for it seemed like we should have found our own carriers a long time ago. But checking my watch indicated that we still had more than half an hour to go before we should be sighting the wakes of our task group—if we had been lucky and plotted our navigation correctly to the Point Option of the moving carriers. All the plotting had to be done in the dull glow of a red-lens flashlight, which was used to help preserve night vision. As I thought about possible navigation errors, I leaned my fuel mixture a little more, as long as the cylinder-head temperatures didn't change beyond acceptable limits.

When we finally spotted the wakes of our fleet below, the letdown was granted first to the few remaining torpedo and dive bombers, for them to get aboard as soon as possible. But in their haste to land on a deck rather than in the dark, black water as so many of their mates had been forced to do, many of the bomber pilots, who lacked experience landing in total darkness with only a dimly lit LSO to guide them, just couldn't seem to handle their planes properly after getting the Cut. Many of them crashed on deck, and this caused quite a delay in landing the next plane. With so many crashes happening, Admiral Mitscher gave the word to "Turn the light on." This helped reduce the number of crashes, although when it was my turn to land, the plane ahead of me crashed, so the *Hornet* LSO was forced to give me a Waveoff.

I still had a little more gas than others reporting in, so I climbed back out of the landing pattern and circled until I could no longer see any more airplane running lights circling the carrier for landing. Finally the deck cleared, and I got a chance to land without another waveoff. I let down and made a standard pattern with wheels and flaps down, got the speed down to the usual 72 knots, "hung on the prop" on the cross leg, and picked up the LSO as I turned in for final. I got a Roger all the way in to the Cut and landed without incident on the number-four wire. Then I taxied out of the gear with a blast on the throttle to clear the deck in case any more planes needed to come in. After I folded the wings, the taxi director parked me mid-deck, about 50 feet forward of the number-5 barrier, the last one that was usable after all the crashes.

As I climbed out of the cockpit, my plane captain dropped everything and ran to starboard, away from me. For good reason, too! He happened to have glanced back in time to see another Hellcat come barreling up the deck, missing all the landing wires and heading straight for us. I had been reaching back into the cockpit to get my plotting board, and for the next few seconds my heart was in my mouth, for I didn't really have any place to go in a hurry. Because the wings were folded, the usual exit was to the rear of the wing and down to the deck, but that would have put me closer to the approaching plane, and that I didn't need.

Fortunately, the number-5 barrier itself slowed the Hellcat somewhat and jerked it to a course crossing to port. It missed my plane by inches but struck another plane, which forced it farther to the left until it slid over the side of the deck and landed on top of the forward port quad-40mm antiaircraft gun mount. The pilot turned out to be our newly promoted air group commander, Jack Arnold, who had previously been skipper of the dive-bomber squadron and thus had hardly any air time in the Hellcat, and very few carrier landings in it, even in daylight. I guess I was saved by a fortunate roll of the ship coupled with the number-five barrier jerking Commander Arnold's Hellcat to port.

The Big Boy crane was on the way over to steady the plane in its precarious perch until the commander could be assisted out of the cockpit. Then the crane gave the Hellcat a gentle nudge to topple it on over the side so the gun crew could commence repairs to get the quad-40 back in usable condition. Unfortunately, no one thought of retrieving the cameras from the plane before it was toppled over the side, and the commander's photographic efforts during the strike went for nought. I know that Commander Arnold was shaken up, but he couldn't have been any more frightened than I was when watching his plane, with its still-whirling propeller, coming straight for me while I had no place to go. But we survived and stumbled on down to our fighter ready room, where the air group flight surgeon had the ingredients for "sick call" ready for us to relax on while we tried to learn more about the rest of our buddies who had been on the flight.

Only six of us were in the ready room, and as time dragged on with no other landings being made, we realized that five of our VF-2 planes were out there somewhere. On the other hand, we had several pilots from other carriers sitting in the ready room with us, so we had hope that our missing buddies were similarly on some of the other carriers. It was a glum, somber ship, but as we unwound, word came in that two of our Hellcat pilots were on the *Yorktown* and one was on another carrier. Much later, word came in that the fourth had been picked up by a destroyer. And finally we heard that the last one had been plucked out of the water by a cruiser. It was probably after midnight before we could really relax, knowing our gang was all safe, although five planes had been lost and we would need replacements.

On June 24, 1944, aircraft from Rear Admiral Jocko Clark's Task Group 58.1, including many from the Hornet's *Air Group 2, once again struck*

Iwo Jima. Of more than 140 Imperial Navy fighters and bombers dispatched from the island in three separate waves to challenge the attackers, 116 were claimed by F6F pilots. Lieutenant (jg) Connie Hargreaves, who had not even seen a Japanese airplane during eight months in the combat zone, shot down four of the Zero fighters (and probably shot down another) directly off Iwo Jima during a single morning strike mission. And during an afternoon scramble to challenge land-based fighters and bombers dispatched to attack Task Group 58.1, Hargreaves shot down another Zero to become an ace in a day.

Adding to his score, Connie Hargreaves shot down three more Zeros, and probably shot down another, on July 3, during yet another Task Group 58.1 foray against Iwo Jima. And, finally, on September 21, 1944, as Air Group 2's fabulously successful combat tour was in its last days, Lieutenant (jg) Hargreaves brought his final personal victory tally to 8.5 when he shared in the downing of a Yokosuka D4Y Judy dive-bomber at sea in the Philippines.

More than a half-century after his World War II combat, Hargreaves still feels he owes his ascent to acedom to two of the men he followed into battle in 1944: "Our task group was supposed to be heading for Eniwetok, as the other task group was doing 'by the book,' but Rear Admiral Jocko Clark took the responsibility for detouring to within 250 miles of Iwo Jima to launch a pre-dawn fighter sweep. That was June 24, 1944, and between the sweep and subsequent scrambles to meet the Japanese retaliatory attempts, our task group set an all-time Navy record for number of enemy planes destroyed in the air by a single task group in a single day. It was also Jocko who jumped the gun on the July 3 fighter sweep, when the other task group assigned to the mission stayed back for the scheduled Fourth of July fireworks display. Fifteen of us came back from that sweep with thirty-three Japanese aircraft destroyed, plus a few probables. As a result, on July 4, we covered our carrier bombers without finding any opposition, except for a horrible amount of anti-aircraft fire.

"Commander Bill Dean could have been a very high-scoring pilot, had he taken all the flights when opposition was anticipated. But he always tried to keep the scores for all his pilots as even as possible, not catering to a favored few, as some of the other fighter squadron skippers did. Often, Bill took assignments for the combat air patrol or bomber *escort instead of leading all the fighter sweeps. That gave us all an opportunity to get into action. Thus, Fighting-2 had twenty-eight aces in our one tour of duty, a Navy record that still stands."*

Following VF-2's return to the United States and home leave, Lieutenant (jg) Hargreaves was assigned to VF-27, with which he served aboard the light carrier USS Independence *during the final two months of the Pacific War. After returning to the United States, Connie Hargreaves made full lieutenant and civilian on the same day, just before Christmas 1945. He remained in the Navy Reserve until 1958, when half the Reserve squadrons based at the Glenview Naval Air Station were decommissioned due to budget cutbacks.*

BUSY DAY, SAD DAY

Ensign JOJO McGRAW, USN
VC-10 (USS *Gambier Bay*)
Off Samar—October 25, 1944

Joseph Dennis McGraw was born in Cleveland, Ohio, on November 17, 1923, and raised in Dewitt, New York, near Syracuse. He graduated from high school in June 1942 and entered the U.S. Navy flight program in October of that year, at the age of eighteen. Cadet McGraw attended Pre-flight training at Chapel Hill, North Carolina, and went on to flight training at Hutchinson, Kansas, and Corpus Christi, Texas, where he earned his wings and commission on July 24, 1943.

Ensign McGraw completed operational fighter school, where he flew old Brewster F2A Buffalo fighters, and was assigned to VC-10, with which he trained for carrier duty in the General Motors FM-2 Wildcat fighter. First combat for VC-10 and Ensign Jojo McGraw came in the Marianas, where on June 18, 1944, McGraw shot down a Betty medium bomber off Guam. On the morning of October 24, 1944, while covering the Leyte invasion force, Ensign McGraw shot down two Ki-48 Lily twin-engine light bombers.

In October 1944, I was still assigned to VC-10 aboard the USS *Gambier Bay* (CVE-73). We were part of a support escort carrier group and were supporting General Douglas MacArthur's landing on Leyte. There were three groups of "jeep" carriers in our Task Group 77.4, and all were assigned to cover the landing force and provide support for the U.S. Army ground forces ashore. Six of the jeeps were in our group, which was designated Taffy 3; six more were in Taffy 2, to the south of us; and another six were in Taffy 1, which was to the south of Taffy 2. We could put up a pretty good cloud of airplanes, about 450 in all, depending on how many were down for repairs or in maintenance.

On the morning of October 25, the *Gambier Bay* had just launched a combat air patrol of eight planes to cover our task group, several of our TBMs were out on antisubmarine patrol, and the first strike group was supporting MacArthur's troops ashore. I was not assigned to any of the early missions, so I was in the wardroom, about to have breakfast.

At about 0645, Taffy 3, which was composed of three U.S. Seventh Fleet destroyers, four destroyer-escorts, and the six Task Unit 77.4.3 escort carriers, was standing off Samar south of the San Bernadino Strait when we were suddenly attacked at long range by four Imperial Navy battleships, eight cruisers, and thirteen destroyers that had traversed the San Bernadino Strait during the night, a difficult feat.

When the first airplanes from Taffy 3 spotted them, the Japanese warships were close enough to start shooting, and they attacked us immediately upon sighting us. The *Gambier Bay* went to battle stations and all the pilots remaining aboard ran to the ready room. In the ready room, the squadron intelligence officer was shouting, "Man your planes! Man your planes!"

I grabbed my helmet, plotting board, and parachute harness, but I didn't take time to gather all my other gear. I headed on the run to the flight deck, and as I got there, I could that see most of Wildcat engines were already started up and the planes were manned by other pilots. I sprinted to the last plane in the row on the aft end of the ship, which happened to be my own plane, B-6. It was tied down, and no one was in it yet, so I climbed aboard. I no sooner climbed into the cockpit than my good friend and sometime wingman, Ensign Leo Zeola, climbed up the other side. When he saw me in the cockpit, he really looked discouraged. He said, "Good luck," and then, when he saw some huge colored shell splashes landing alongside the ship, he added, "So long," and got down and went back into the ready room. I did not see him again for many weeks.

I got the airplane started up, but as it was spotted on the portside aft corner of the flight deck, I was going to be the last fighter that would take off. I had to wait for all the other planes to take off, so I sat there counting shell splashes and getting in some real quality prayer time. When my turn to take off finally came, I had to dodge a big shell hole on the port forward corner of the flight deck—just as the skipper, Captain Walter Vieweg, was throwing the ship into an evasive turn. The carrier deck slanted quite a bit in the opposite direction of the sharp turn, and the captain had it at a pretty good angle by the time I was getting off. Given the left torque of the fighter's engine, it made for a real interesting takeoff.

As soon as I got off, I joined up with the skipper of our squadron, Lieutenant Commander Edward Huxtable, who was flying the command TBM. He had rendezvoused his small bomber force and the rest of the fighters that had gotten off before me, and we headed out to attack the Japanese battle fleet.

There was cloud cover at about 2,500 feet, so we couldn't start our attack from very high up and still see our targets. As a result, we came in at the base of the clouds. As we approached, the skipper said, "Fighters in to strafe," and we went in to strafe the ships in order to draw the antiaircraft fire to us, and to diminish it with our own fire. As we did, the TBMs attacked with bombs or torpedoes, whatever they happened to have.

After the initial strafing-bombing-torpedo attack, we spent two and a half hours harassing the Japanese fleet. I used up my ammunition strafing battleships, cruisers, and destroyers. It was something I had never dreamed I'd be doing, but there I was, along with everybody else. Long after we had run out of bombs, torpedoes, and bullets, many of us, including Commander Huxtable in his TBM, continued to make dummy runs at the warships, so airplanes that were coming into the fight with ordnance could deliver it while the antiaircraft fire was more dispersed. We had a cloud of airplanes over the Japanese force, so the antiaircraft fire was pretty well distributed, but it was fairly heavy nonetheless, especially against aircraft low on the water.

In due course, we all started getting low on fuel. Some of the fighters went to Leyte, to the beach at Tacloban, where Army engineers were

Aces At War

putting in an airfield for Army bombers and P-38 fighters. The muddy runway was already pretty crowded with airplanes when I got there. I felt that if I landed at Tacloban, they wouldn't have much fuel and ammunition, and so I would be out of the fight. I chose to try to find another carrier rather than land on the airfield.

I flew south until I found Taffy 2, which was steaming hard to the south of Taffy 3. These jeep carriers had not come under fire yet, but they were running to the south and east while taking aircraft aboard. Several of the carriers were launching aircraft, so I got into the traffic pattern over the *Manila Bay,* behind a huge SB2C Helldiver that must have been left behind from a strike force sent down from the fast carrier task force, which was well out of range to the north of us. I don't know what happened to the Helldiver, but it sure did take up a lot of room on that jeep carrier deck.

As soon as I landed, I asked to be allowed to fly with the *Manila Bay's* squadron, VC-80. It was getting ready to strike the Japanese fleet, which by then was really being pounded and was about to break off its attack.

Commander William Fowler led this large strike. As we got back to where the Japanese warships were, about 30 miles, he ordered the fighters in to strafe first. As we went in, he dived right behind us. The TBMs were being used as glide bombers, not straight-down dive-bombers.

I first strafed a pretty good-sized ship, which I thought was a battleship. As I was pulling out over the line of destroyers on the outboard edge of the battle group, I looked back over my shoulder, and it seemed to me that the battleship had taken quite a heavy hit from Commander Fowler's bombs.

As I was pulling away on the water, jinking as much as possible to stay away from the thick antiaircraft fire, I heard a loud bang. It was as loud as any AA fire I had ever heard. It *had* to be loud for me to hear it over that roaring radial engine, right there at my feet. So I did a reflexive fast break to the left and looked over my shoulder. I saw a giant phosphorous shell that had been fired at me by the battleship. It was sending out rolling balls of fire and trails of smoke. It looked like an octopus, and it scared the heck out of me, but it didn't do any damage.

As we regrouped on the other side of the enemy task force,

Commander Fowler asked if anyone had any bombs left. There still were some aboard a few of the TBMs, so we climbed up a few thousand feet and turned around. Once again, he said, "Fighters in to strafe," and down we went again. This time I strafed right up a line composed of a battleship, a big cruiser, and a destroyer. I don't remember us losing many airplanes. There were quite a few of us in the air, so the AA was dispersed, but we did lose two TBMs on the water. I saw them going in.

We reformed again to the south of the battle group and climbed back up high. I was then flying cover on the left side of the reforming TBMs, and I could see what I took to be several enemy fighters flying high above us, looking us over. But they didn't attack, and were too high for me to reach. When the TBMs had reformed, we went back to the *Manila Bay.*

After rearming and refueling aboard the *Manila Bay,* VC-80 utilized me again, this time as a member of their combat air patrol. It was my third flight of the day. I was the section leader in a division of four FM-2s. We were a good fifteen or twenty miles out from the task force and at our orbit point when we received a vector from the Taffy 2 fighter director. He vectored us out to find what he called "a small incoming bogey." And since it was a small bogey, he only sent four of us out to look it over.

The fighter director had us on a real good track, but when we got there, we found some eighteen Imperial Navy Aichi D3A Val dive-bombers and twelve Zeke fighters coming out of the line of clouds. It wasn't what *I* would have called a "small bogey."

The four of us were vectored into such a beautiful position by the fighter director that all we had to do was make a diving left turn to execute a high-side run on the lead Vals. Each of us picked one of the two front Vals in the two front sections. The division leader—Lieutenant Jack Morrissey—and his wingman took the front two, and my wingman and I took the second two. The Vals were flying in vees of three planes each, but the first Wildcat section took the lead airplane and his inboard wingman, and I and my wingman did the same with the second vee—I took the leader and my wingman took the inboard Val on the section leader's wing. We all fired at about the same time, and we took all four of them at once—flamed them all. It must have been a real surprise to them, because all of sudden we were right there, and *bang,* four of their Vals went down in flames.

I'm sure the lead airplanes of the first two sections were flown by the lead pilots, and that the greener guys were in the back of the formation. We surprised them so bad that they broke up and let their bombs go. Some of them just broke formation and wobbled around, but others stayed in a tight formation.

As soon as we started our firing pass on the Vals, the Zeros in the high cover started diving on us. But they were late enough to give us time to get our shots off, and we were able to pull up really steeply, right into them, so they wouldn't end up on our tails. I pulled up so steeply that I lost my wingman, but I avoided the Zeros as they went by.

The leader of the Zeros was pretty good. He hit Lieutenant Morrissey as Morrissey was climbing. The Zero pilot shot out the Wildcat's engine from head-on, and that put Morrissey in the water.

I went up as the Zeros came down, and thus avoided their fire. I rolled around left out of my climb. As I did, I saw that the lead Zero and his wingman were just pulling up from downing our division leader. As it happened, I was in a great position above and to the right of the wingman, so I lined up and shot him in his engine and wing root with a long enough burst to cause him to flame and explode. That either surprised the Zero leader or made him really mad, because, to try to get on me, he did the tightest turn that I have ever seen any airplane make. But I pulled up into a tight left turn into him, so he missed; he put his shots right behind me. My tight turn must have surprised him, because I got around quickly enough again to get into a head-on run with him, and I got off the first shots, putting a fast burst into his engine before he could get his 20mm cannon going. I think that kind of made him mad, too, because he quickly pulled up hard into me in what I thought was an attempt to ram me. Of course, I also pulled up hard to avoid him, but it was a close thing!

As I looked over my shoulder in another tight turn, I saw that he was smoking heavily. He had turned by then, and was already diving for the clouds. I continued turning to get on him, but as I did, I saw three more Zeros turning into me to cut me off from their smoking leader. I took a long-range shot at the nearest Zero as I turned again and dove for the water, but I didn't damage him very heavily; I only sieved his tail.

I got away and enjoyed the satisfaction of looking back and seeing the Zeros also turning back to where they had come from. As I was diving for the water, I saw a few of the Vals that were still in the area, but they were fast retreating. I tried to catch two of them before they got to the clouds, but I couldn't overtake them from my position before they got into the clouds.

All of a sudden there weren't any airplanes around, so I dived down close to the water on a track back to where we had started our first dive, to where I thought the others might be. Fortunately, I found my wingman and Lieutenant Morrissey's wingman circling our downed division leader. Morrissey was okay and had gotten into his one-man life raft. The others were circling to keep an eye on him. I climbed in a tight circle above the other Wildcats until the *Manila Bay's* radar intercept officer got a position fix on us. Then I called the other two and we went on back to the ship. Morrissey was picked up later.

By the time we got back to the ship, the sun was going down and it was beginning to get dark. I had put in around eleven hours of flying that day. It had been a hectic day for the whole fleet, of course. I had scored two victories, the Zero leader's wingman and the Val. I got a confirmed on the Val and the Zero leader's wingman, but only a damage credit on the Zero that I sieved in the tail, and a probable on the Zero leader.

The Zero leader was certainly an old combat hand, and he was a really good shot: taking out our division leader while he was diving and the division leader was climbing right up into him required excellent marksmanship. He really knew how to handle that Zero. I expect that when he saw our Wildcats, he thought he had finally gotten some easy prey; we weren't Hellcats or Corsairs, so he probably thought he had some easy game there. But he must have been really surprised by the FM-2s we were flying. Apparently he didn't know how much improved they were over the Grumman F4F Wildcats our Navy pilots had flown early in the war. I know he was surprised by the tight turns and my ability to get back around as fast as I did, into a head-on run, so he got kind of rattled and made some mistakes. I don't know what happened to him, but with his engine shot up and smoking, I don't think he made it back to his base.

That ended my day. We were scheduled for strikes the next morning to continue our support of MacArthur's troops ashore, and to chase the remnants of the Japanese fleet that were retreating from the central Philippines. But that was another day.

Aces At War

When I landed aboard the *Manila Bay* for the last time that evening, I received the bad news that my own carrier, the *Gambier Bay,* had gone down right in the middle of the Japanese fleet. I was worried about the rest of my squadron and my shipmates who had gone down with the ship. I wondered where the rest of VC-10 was scattered. Next day, I was issued temporary orders to VC-80 and was to fly with them for another week or so, before the recall went out for the survivors of the *Gambier Bay* to do their best to get back to certain pick-up points from which we would be transported to the rear to be given aid and help. When the time came, I left my airplane with VC-80 and went back into the recovery area to look for my squadron.

October 25, 1944, was a sad day for me. Even though we had won that great battle, my ship had gone down and I had lost so many shipmates.

Ensign Jojo McGraw, ace, veteran, and survivor at twenty years of age, was awarded a Navy Cross in recognition of his single-minded devotion to duty throughout October 25, 1944. When he completed his survivor's leave, he was promoted and assigned as a combat tactics instructor, and was awaiting reassignment to the fleet when the war ended. McGraw remained in the service, flew eighty combat missions in Korea in carrier-based jets, and retired in 1967 with the rank of captain.

GOING SOUTH

1st Lieutenant JOHN BOLYARD, USAAF
74th Fighter Squadron, 23d Fighter Group
Amoy, China—November 3, 1944

John Wesley Bolyard was born on July 2, 1921, and raised in Kingwood, West Virginia. He attended college for two years and enlisted in the Army Air Forces as an aviation cadet. Lieutenant Bolyard graduated from flight school at Spence Field, Georgia, with Class 43-G on July 28, 1943, and was shortly shipped to Karachi, India, for advanced combat training. He arrived in China in December 1943 and was assigned to the 74th Fighter Squadron, which was then based at Kweilin and later moved to Kanchow in southeastern China.

Major John "Pappy" Herbst, the commanding officer of the 74th Fighter Squadron, briefed me on the day's mission. I was to proceed to Amoy on the China coast and check out the airfield. My wingman was Captain Reece, who had just joined our squadron. We were flying the recently acquired P-51B-2. There was no specific target; we were just to go take a look and inflict the most damage on anything that could be of value to the Japanese. Almost all of our flying involved ground support—bombing bridges, compounds, river traffic, road traffic, and the like.

For me the Japanese Army and Navy air forces were almost invisible. The only time we saw them was when they came for their usual nightly bombings of our airfield. We were bombed almost every night, but we sustained very little damage. On this flight, I did not anticipate encountering any Japanese aircraft.

The weather was excellent and the flight to the coast was uneventful. We hit the coast northeast of Amoy, increased power, dropped the noses of our airplanes, and planned to hit the airfield at low altitude with lots of airspeed.

The city of Amoy and its harbor were off to our right. The airfield was located on a peninsula jutting into the harbor. We were lined up perfectly with the single runway. Reece and I kept our heads on a swivel so as to clear each other's tail.

Great balls of fire! Dead ahead at about one mile, two Zeros were taking off in formation, going straight away from us. I told Reece to take the one on the right and he nodded "Okay." This was the stuff fighter pilots dream about. We were closing fast. The Zeros retracted their gear and continued to climb almost straight away in close formation.

I was always amazed at how steep an angle of climb the Zero pilots could maintain when they put their mind to it. We dropped to the deck on the runway so the Zeros were always above us. At the right time, I pulled up on his tail and at about 200 feet I gave him a long burst. In rapid succession, the Zero lurched violently, fairly large pieces flew off of the fuselage, smoke and flames appeared, and it pitched nose-down out of my sight. None of its pieces struck my plane.

I glanced to my right and was surprised to find that I was joined in loose formation with the other Zero. He was slightly above me and climbing rapidly. His right gear was partially extended, but otherwise he appeared in good shape. The Japanese pilot did not look to his left; he appeared to be looking straight ahead and upward. I had just cut power to keep from popping out in front of him when he started a roll. Instinctively, I went to full power, dropped the nose, and executed a shallow diving turn to the left.

I got some airspeed back by the time I had completed the 180-degree turn and again pulled up the nose. As if by magic, there he was—dead ahead, at point-blank range, and climbing flat out. His gear was still slightly extended. He was real close, and I gave him a long burst. Some pieces flew off his airplane; I saw the canopy or parts of it fly off. Smoke and flames followed, and it abruptly pitched nose-down out of my sight.

I got my nose down and rolled to the left for a look-see. I was surprised to see a parachute open and immediately hit the water. I did not see the pilot exit the aircraft. I came around at about 100 feet and saw the pilot looking up at me.

Since I was just off the end of a Japanese runway, low on airspeed, and no altitude, I hit the deck and hauled for the boondocks. I had not felt or heard any hits from ground fire. All gauges were okay, so I ran full power on the deck and headed for the mountains. I hit the button and called Reece. He was over by the mountains, waiting for me. Enroute to the mountains, I got back some altitude, kept all the speed I could, and kept close attention to my tail.

Bang! I felt a hit on my 51. Yank and bank. Nothing in sight. It was probably a lucky shot by ground fire. *Bang!* Another hit. Yank and bank. And then it dawned on me. My .50-calibers were so hot from the two long bursts that they occasionally cooked off a single round. It did get my attention! I picked up Reece and headed home.

In our China bull sessions, we always figured there were two classes of Japanese fighter pilots that we might run into on the China coast: those going down the coast to the Pacific War—junior birdmen—and the experienced professionals going back to Japan. Given the choice, we preferred to take on the kind heading south. I had apparently encountered a southbound formation.

Years later, the Freedom of Information Act opened a bunch of World War II files, and shortly thereafter I began receiving mail from Japan about the Amoy mission. It seems that Imperial Navy Warrant Officer Takeo Tanimizu was still curious as to what had happened to him over Amoy. He did not write to me—a third party was always involved. Tanimizu had thirty-two victories at the time I shot him down, and he was still puzzled as to how I had done the deed. I did not reply. Keep him guessing. My daughter, a U.S. Navy commander, researched the incident and reported that Tanimizu had written a book on his wartime experiences. It reveals that he was so seriously injured in our encounter that he was unable to fly combat again.

Upon landing I was greeted by "Pappy" Herbst, who told me about my mission. He knew all about it. Sometime earlier, the Navy had deposited a coastal observer on a small island adjacent to the Amoy harbor entrance. He had observed the dogfight from the front-row seats as it happened almost over his head. His radio message to a submarine was relayed to Pappy even before we got home. Now that's the easy way to have two confirmed.

It took Lieutenant John Bolyard nearly a year of combat flying in China to break the ice, but then his score rose quickly. On December 8, 1944, Bolyard downed a Ki-61 and a Ki-44 near Nanking's Tai Chao Chan Airdrome, and he achieved ace status on December 27, when he downed a Ki-44, and damaged another, over Canton's Tienho Airdrome.

In addition to his war service in China, Bolyard served on occupation duty from 1946 to 1949. He retired from the Air Force in 1964.

TWO OF OUR PLANES ARE MISSING

Major ED RODDY, USAAF
58th Fighter Group
Clark Field, Luzon—January 3, 1945

Edward Francis Roddy was born in Cleveland, Ohio, on June 29, 1919. He had taken only a few college night courses in preparation for enlisting in the Army Air Corps when the Flying Cadet program was broadened by means of a three-day equivalency test. Having passed the test, Cadet Roddy was called to active duty in April 1941 and earned his wings and commission on December 12, 1941.

Aces At War

Second Lieutenant Roddy first flew P-36s, P-38s, and P-47s with the 56th Fighter Group, then served in two other P-47 units before being assigned to the 348th Fighter Group's 342d Fighter Squadron and going overseas with it in April 1943.

Captain Ed Roddy's first aerial victories were an Imperial Army Ki-61 Tony fighter and an Imperial Navy Zero fighter that he shot down near Wewak, New Guinea, on November 5, 1943. Roddy shot down a pair of Zeros over Arawe, New Britain, on December 16, 1943, and the next day he achieved ace status when he shot down a Ki-46 twin-engine reconnaissance plane, also over Arawe. On December 26, Captain Roddy downed a pair of G4M Betty twin-engine bombers near Umboi Island, and he brought his final victory tally to eight on February 4, 1944, when he shot down a Ki-49 Helen twin-engine bomber near Boram Airdrome, New Guinea.

By late 1944, Major Ed Roddy was the 58th Fighter Group operations officer.

Like all V Fighter Command units in late 1944, the 58th Fighter Group waited its turn to leapfrog into a quickly established forward airfield. After flying out of Noemfoor Island, near the end of New Guinea, since August, we learned that our next base was to be on the island of Mindoro, immediately south of Luzon. On November 8, 1944, we were alerted for our move into the Philippines. The ground echelon loaded up and moved in convoy for Leyte on November 14 and arrived there on November 18, during a concerted attack by the Japanese. The main body of the ground echelon arriveds on Leyte on November 29 and camped near Dulag. The air echelon, of which I was part, remained at Noemfoor with the P-47s, the pilots, and a few maintenance personnel. The rear ground echelon loaded up on another LST and sailed from Leyte on the December 18 or 19, and arrived off the coast of Mindoro on December 22. While en route, the convoy in which the rear ground echelon's LST was a part experienced one hundred attacks, but it managed to arrive without major damage.

After unloading on December 22, the ground echelon immediately began preparations for the arrival of the air echelon, which started arriving on the twenty-third. Not all of the ground equipment or armaments were in place when the unit was told to prepare to attack a Japanese convoy heading for Mindoro on December 26. The group lost five pilots and thirteen P-47s while attacking a heavy cruiser, a light cruiser, and six destroyers—with only their .50-caliber machine guns.

Meanwhile, I had flown the first leg of the journey to Mindoro, from Noemfoor Island to Morotai in the Halamahera Islands, but they had to lift me out of the cockpit and haul me off to the hospital with "Fever, Undiagnosed Origin." A few days later, when I recovered, the flight surgeon released me to return to my unit. While searching around for any kind of transport to Mindoro, I found that the local service squadron had a P-38 that had been repaired and needed someone to fly it up to Mindoro; they were happy to have me join a flight of A-20s that was also going up to the Philippines.

As soon as I arrived at Mindoro, I turned the P-38 over to the local service squadron, and bummed a ride over to the 58th Group—or what was left of it. Pilots who had been listed as missing in action from the December 26 battle were still coming into camp, and it would be weeks before we were able to determine exactly what the unit's losses were from that night battle. I was briefed on our aircraft and aircrew status and told to get ready to support the scheduled Army landing at Lingayen Gulf, Luzon. I heard many of the experiences of the ground echelon and the aircrews, and I noted that many of the complaints were centered on "Bedcheck Charlie," the nightly nuisance plane the Japanese kept sending over Mindoro to disrupt our sleep.

I called Colonel Roy Brischetto, at V Fighter Command Operations, and asked him to authorize a two-ship flight to Clark Field, Luzon, early the next morning—January 3, 1945—to see if we could catch the Japanese before they could refuel and get back to their sanctuary on Formosa. Ray okayed the plan and, out of a handful of eager volunteers, I picked 1st Lieutenant Crystal Andress, of the 310th Fighter Squadron, to fly with me. Our group CO, Colonel Gwen Atkinson, heard about the mission and turned thumbs down—unless I could get it increased to four aircraft, so he could participate.

V Fighter Command agreed to the increase, so in the wee hours the next morning Andress and I headed for the 310th Squadron dispersal area while the Colonel Atkinson and his wingman, 2d Lieutenant Ray Kindred, headed for the 311th Fighter Squadron area. It was still dark when we arrived at the aircraft, and a Red Alert was sounded before our crew chiefs could finish their inspections. We told them that we would complete the inspections and bring the P-47s back if they didn't check out.

Shortly, still under Red Alert conditions, Andress and I took off, negotiated some friendly ack-ack, and started our climb toward Clark Field. We saw one Japanese aircraft some 5,000 to 6,000 feet above us, heading in the same direction, and figured we could catch him. It was not to be. We were ordered to stay in the local area to provide air defense until P-38s scheduled for the duty could get airborne. Finally, some twenty minutes later—it seemed like hours—we were released to continue our mission.

As we arrived over Clark Field at about 0915 hours, we circled around at 18,000 to 20,000 feet. When we reached the west side of Clark, I caught a glint of sunshine reflecting off the wings of a row of aircraft parked wingtip-to-wingtip on a grass satellite field. I alerted Andress and we dropped our external tanks, turned on our gun switches, and headed for the line of aircraft at full throttle. The ack-ack started right away—puffs nearby—and then they started in with small arms and tracers. As we roared down the line of parked aircraft, all eight guns in each P-47 blazing away, men were jumping off the wings and trucks were moving around. The ack-ack was so intense that we stayed right on the deck, and I got a good look at many apparently serviceable aircraft dispersed under camouflage netting. When we finally got out of range of the ack-ack, we climbed up to the east of the field, where, looking back, we could see that we had set eight or ten aircraft on fire. It was 0922 hours.

It was about this time that Colonel Atkinson and Lieutenant Kindred arrived in the area and asked where we were. As they were closing on Clark Field after being further delayed over Mindoro, they had heard Andress and me talking jubilantly about catching the Japanese on the ground. I referred the colonel to the rising columns of smoke from burning planes at Clark Field, to which Atkinson replied that he and his wingman would also make a strafing pass.

I was climbing back through 10,000 feet, scanning the skies to make sure that we would not be jumped from above, when Atkinson called out, "Roddy, I'm on fire!" I asked him which way he was heading. I planned to drop down on his wing until we resolved the emergency. A few seconds later, Andress radioed, "Look at him burn." I looked down at the satellite strip. There was a fireball off the end of the strip, and another column of smoke was rising off the other end. I called Atkinson. No answer. I called Kindred. No answer. Giving the ack-ack at Clark Field a wide berth, I proceeded with Andress back to Mindoro and reported Atkinson killed in action and Kindred missing.

Months later, we found that the P-47 that Andress and I had seen as it cartwheeled in a fireball off the end of the runway was Kindred's. But when Colonel Atkinson heard Andress say, "Look at him burn"—meaning Kindred's P-47—it was enough to make him get out of his own damaged and burning airplane. Fortunately, Atkinson was able to evade the Japanese, and he was returned to friendly forces several weeks later.

Back at Mindoro, Andress did a slow roll over the strip before landing. My plane had damage to the main wing spar and stabilizer, and it had to be towed over to the service squadron area.

In all, we were credited with destroying eleven aircraft during our strafing attack, plus a Ki-49 Helen twin-engine bomber shot down by Colonel Atkinson. However, a photo-reconnaissance plane that flew over Clark Field shortly after the attack took photos that revealed seventeen planes destroyed on the ground. Moreover, the aircraft destroyed were believed to be a new Imperial Navy fighter type codenamed George.

We drank up Atkinson's booze, divided up his khaki clothes (mildewed clothing was something we didn't want to send back to the next-of-kin), and got on with the war. When U.S. Army Forces took over Clark Field, we sent a team to examine the wreckage off the end of the runway. It was indeed Kindred's P-47, and we were able to pick up parts of his remains and give him a military funeral. By then, Colonel Atkinson had been reassigned to V Fighter Command and I had assumed command of the 58th Fighter Group.

On the morning of August 9, 1945, while leading a sixteen-ship formation of Okinawa-based 58th Fighter Group P-47s on a sweep over eastern Kyushu at 8,000 feet, Lieutenant Colonel Ed Roddy observed a tangerine-colored explosion to his 11 o'clock. After swinging toward the fireball, he watched the dark cloud underneath rise and rise, higher than all the other clouds in the sky. Later, Roddy learned that he had witnessed the detonation of the atomic bomb over the city of Nagasaki.

THE PILOT-MAKING MACHINE

Ensign DON McPHERSON, USN
VF-83 (USS *Essex*)
Nittigahara, Japan—March 19, 1945

Donald Melvin McPherson was born on May 22, 1922, and raised in Adams, Nebraska. When the Navy V-5 program waived its two-year college requirement, McPherson enlisted on January 5, 1943, and was appointed as an Aviation Cadet on February 4. He earned his commission and wings at Corpus Christi, Texas on August 12, 1944.

On August 13, 1944, the day after graduation from flight school, I boarded a train to Daytona Beach, Florida, for advanced training in combat tactics. When I reported to the naval air base there on August 18, I was assigned to Flight 81, a combat replacement unit that would be flying the Grumman F6F Hellcat fighter. Much of the time during my three months at Daytona was spent learning far more about fighter tactics, dive-bombing, and gunnery than we had learned in flight school, and we gained a great deal of experience while learning the proper approaches and methods in our field carrier landings. At the end of our course at Daytona, five of us from Flight 81 were chosen as a replacement team and ordered to proceed together to the naval air station at Glenview, Illinois, for carrier qualifications, which would validate us for overseas carrier duty. We reported to Glenview on November 8, 1944, and entered the carrier qualification unit.

At Glenview, the pilots qualified for carrier landings aboard two converted luxury liners that cruised Lake Michigan. One of the ships, the USS *Wolverine,* was an old paddlewheel job that could only make a top speed of about 9 knots. In order for them to land planes, the wind over the bows had to be blowing at least 25 miles an hour. At first, we were taken by boat to the *Wolverine* to observe carrier landings. The skipper of that vessel was a fireball! He was continually on the bullhorn, yelling at the pilots as they landed. One pilot was having trouble making decent landings and, after the third rough one, the skipper ran down to the flight deck, climbed up onto the wing of the airplane, and pounded the pilot on the shoulder with his fists while reading him the riot act. Right about then, I was hoping I would get the chance to qualify aboard the other vessel! The next day I was assigned an F6F-3 Hellcat to fly and, wouldn't you know, I drew the *Wolverine!* We circled the ship for over an hour, waiting for the wind velocity to increase enough so we could make our landings, but it didn't get strong enough, so finally we were ordered back to the base. On November 14, I was assigned to the other aircraft carrier, the USS *Sable,* for qualification, and I was successful in completing my eight landings. Wow, did that flight deck look small! It wasn't nearly as long as the one on the aircraft carrier that would eventually be my home during my overseas combat tour.

After I completed my training at Glenview, my wife and I proceeded home to Adams, Nebraska, for a fifteen-day leave. After that, I had orders to proceed to the San Diego Naval Air Station for further assignment. On reporting to San Diego on December 8, my team was informed that we would not leave for overseas duty until December 18, so Thelma and I had some time to do some sightseeing in the area and make one trip to Mexico. On the eighteenth, we were put aboard a seaplane tender bound for Pearl Harbor. On December 24, the ship rounded Diamondhead and approached Pearl Harbor. As the color of the water changed from a dark blackish color to a very attractive blue, we were told that the change was caused by the coral bottom. However, as we approached the Pearl Harbor channel, the scene changed dramatically once again. The channel had been cleared of all the ships that had been sunk there on December 7, 1941, but the debris outside the channel was unbelievable; twisted, rusty slabs of metal had been dredged up on both banks. It looked like a huge junkyard!

We stayed in a barracks on Ford Island on Christmas Eve. As I looked across the harbor, I could see the battleship USS *Arizona,* whose superstructure was sticking out of the water where she had been sunk at her moorings. The next day—Christmas Day—we were transported to the Barber's Point Naval Air Station on the southwest shore of Oahu. There we were assigned to Fighting Squadron 100 to undergo refresher training until about February 18, 1945. Much of our flight time at Barber's Point was spent in tactical training to embed in our minds the best ways to react to situations that might arise when we engaged the enemy. We

Aces At War

also spent time improving our gunnery skills by shooting at stationary targets on the ground or a nylon sleeve towed by another airplane. I drew the duty of towing the sleeve on a few occasions, and that was a unique experience. You hoped all the shooters were on target and didn't get carried away with how much lead they gave the towed sleeve! We also qualified for the Pacific Defense Ribbon by flying combat air patrols over the area, which was still considered the war zone. We also continued to sharpen our skills by making field-carrier landings in preparation for landings aboard real aircraft carriers.

On January 6, 1945, I made my first landings aboard a full-sized aircraft carrier. She was an *Essex*-class ship that had stopped off in Hawaii while on her way to the war zone and was briefly assigned to help us sharpen our skills. Her flight deck still seemed pretty small, but it was nowhere near as tiny as the little ones back on Lake Michigan! I made another eight arrested landings over the next few days and was a bit surprised that it went so well. The much larger deck seemed to improve a person's confidence some.

My team's time with VF-100 was a confidence builder that helped us polish the skills we had been taught along the way. At the end of our training, we were feeling much more confident that we had enough repetitions of common tactics that we would naturally do the right things in times of stress. We also had flown together enough to sort of know one another's reactions, so we were a pretty well-honed team. As things turned out, though, the teamwork would not be of help to me, because I soon found out that I would no longer be a part of that team.

February 17, 1945, was my last flight day with the combat replacement team. Air Group 83, whose pilots had all trained together in the United States and on Maui, lost a pilot in carrier landing training. VF-83 wired the command post at Barber's Point to request a replacement pilot. I guess I was closer to finishing my training than anyone else, for I was ordered to report to Air Group 83 on Maui the next day. They put me aboard a twin-engine personnel transport, and we landed at Air Group 83's base at 1500. I immediately learned that the group had completed its training and was to board a troop transport the next morning for shipment to the combat zone. What a feeling I had then! It would have helped greatly if I had had a little time to get acquainted with some of the pilots and fly with them a few times. However, a couple of the guys who took pity on me loaded me into a jeep and said they would show me the island, but about all they were really interested in was showing me the bars at the various officers clubs. I could have cared less about those, but in between stops I did see some of the countryside, which was more interesting to me.

The next day, February 19, we all were put aboard a British troop transport for the ocean voyage to the advance base at Ulithi Atoll in the western Caroline Islands. As we approached the more active combat zone, the tension began to mount and our unknown future was something we now had to learn to cope with. Task Force 58, the Fast Carrier Task Force, was at anchor in Ulithi Lagoon when we arrived. There were ships as far as I could see!

On March 10, Air Group 83 went aboard our new home, the USS *Essex,* the first of the new class of fast carriers that bore her name. She had been commissioned in December 1942 and had spent most of the next two and a half years in combat. At the time, she was the flagship of Rear Admiral Frederick Sherman, the commander of Task Group 58.3. We were soon to find out what a fighting man's admiral Sherman was. He often moved about the ship without any rank insignia on his shirt, so the sailors would not spend time saluting him instead of taking care of their duties. Captain R. L. Bowman was the skipper of the *Essex,* Commander H. T. Utter was our air group commander, and Commander James J. (Jack) Southerland was the commander of my squadron, VF-83.

We didn't have long to get acclimated to the carrier before we were in combat. On our second evening aboard, as we watched a movie on the flight deck, Japanese bombers based on Kyushu in southern Japan made a *kamikaze* run on the fleet as it lay at anchor in Ulithi Lagoon. One of the bombers clipped the *Essex's* radar mast and crashed into the island, and another seriously damaged the fleet carrier USS *Hancock* when it crashed right into her. This sure made us wonder what we had gotten ourselves in for.

On March 13, 1945, I once again climbed into the cockpit of an F6F Hellcat and flew a combat air patrol mission over the atoll. In the forty-eight hours we were at Ulithi, I learned what it would have been like to be island based. The heat and humidity were worse than I had expected.

Aces At War

We even found it difficult to sleep under those conditions. I guess that helped me to appreciate my aircraft carrier home for the next few months. The ship was always clean and comfortable. On the other hand, we were always concerned about finding her when returning from a mission, especially when the weather was bad. Another hardship of going to sea in a carrier was the ability of the fleet mail service to catch up with us. I had once gotten four letters from my wife in one day while at Barber's Point, but it was plain to see that letters from Thelma and my family would not be delivered regularly while I was at sea. Boy, were the letters ever welcome, though, whenever they caught up with us.

It was a little traumatic for me to be taken from the combat team at Barber's Point and sent to an air group that I didn't know and had never flown with. Even when the Fast Carrier Task Force went to sea on March 15 for another round of combat, I was still an unassigned extra pilot. As such, I was not scheduled for the initial strikes against targets in Japan, which began on March 18, 1945, to help clear the way for the invasion of Okinawa, which was to begin on April 1. I did get to fly several combat air patrols over the fleet, but the enemy had not yet located the Fast Carrier Task Force, so it was just routine duty.

Between leaving Ulithi on March 15 and the end of the first day of strikes against targets on the Japanese islands of Kyushu and Shikoku on March 18, the VF-83 Hellcat division known as Wonder-5 had a problem. As the division was taking off from the deck in the dark one early morning, the second pilot in the division lost control of his plane on the wet slippery deck and went over the side into the ocean. An accident like this was often fatal, because the plane could be sucked under the ship and into the propellers. Fortunately, this pilot was picked up by a destroyer and returned to the ship. Two days later, on March 18, he was scheduled for the pre-dawn strike launch, and the same thing happened to him again. And for the second time he was retrieved uninjured. However, this pilot was ruled to be unfit for combat and grounded until he could be returned to Hawaii. His misfortune turned into a break for me, because I was assigned to Wonder-5 in his place, as the division leader's wingman.

Wonder-5 was composed of Lieutenant Carlos Soffe, the division leader; Lieutenant (jg) Lyttleton Ward, the section leader; Ensign Melton

Truax, Ward's wingman; and myself, Lieutenant Soffe's wingman. Lieutenant Soffe was sort of a quiet man, but he made me feel at home very quickly. Three of us were to make ace status by shooting down five or more enemy airplanes, but division leader Soffe was never credited with two or three of the aerial victories he claimed, because his gun cameras didn't work well enough at the time to provide the necessary proof.

My first combat mission was on March 19, 1945, my first full day as a member of Wonder-5. It was a clear day that started with a pre-dawn launch for a 300-mile flight to hit Nittigahara Airdrome at just daybreak, about 0650. The Fast Carrier Task Force was southeast of the target.

There were twenty Hellcats and twenty F4U Corsairs in on the Nittigahara strike, which was one of many strikes sent out against Japanese airfields that day. Most of us were carrying six 5-inch high-velocity aerial rockets. As I recall, Wonder-5 was the fourth or fifth division in the attack formation. We had all had lots of training in strafing ground targets and shooting at towed sleeves, but none of us had ever fired live rockets.

Our planes attacked in sections of two planes each. We approached the airfield from the south at about 14,000 feet and made our first run from southwest of the field. Our recovery from the first target run was to be to the east, toward the ocean. Airborne aircraft were our first priority, but there were none, so we proceeded with our second priority, which was parked aircraft. We would dive in at the normal attitude for dive bombing, about 70 degrees.

The "peel-off" was the normal wingover roll that gives the section leader some interval over the wingman. Each of us picked a target. As we rolled into our first rocket run, I could see people running from their barracks to man the antiaircraft guns. Because we had flown so far to reach the target, we were carrying auxiliary fuel tanks. Though we had been instructed several days earlier to switch from the belly tank to a wing tank before making a dive-bombing run, the stress and excitement of my first engagement with the enemy caused me to forget to switch tanks.

There was a number of smaller planes parked in rows, but a big Betty bomber on the parking strip caught my eye. It was in a position for me to line up on, so I went for it. The rockets were fired by pressing a button on the top of the control stick with the thumb. We used the gunsight to aim the rockets, and the proper procedure was to fire the rockets from a higher altitude, and then the guns would be fired from lower down. Most of the way down, tracers from their antiaircraft guns were passing by me from left to right (north to south). They showed up as a bright pink streak and were quite easy to see.

I fired my rockets from between 3,000 and 2,500 feet and then immediately strafed the Betty with my six .50-caliber wing guns. I stayed in my dive until I saw the bomber blow up. By then I was low enough that I needed to pull out of the dive quickly. As a result of that maneuver, the engine failed to get enough aviation gas and quit!

I worked the manual fuel pump and managed to get the engine going again, but by that time I had lost enough speed that the antiaircraft tracer bullets were crossing in front of me. All of a sudden, I felt an impact and knew that my Hellcat had been hit by at least one antiaircraft bullet. The cockpit filled with smoke from the engine stall, so I rolled the hatch back to get fresh air. But I had enough speed left that the air suction pulled my helmet, goggles, and radio earphones off my head. They went flying off into space! This left me without radio communication, but by that time I was over the ocean and out of harm's way.

As I came out over the ocean, I was below 1,000 feet, but I kept the nose of the Hellcat down slightly to hold my speed, and I leveled out at 500 feet, beyond the range of the antiaircraft guns. I then regained some altitude to join up on Lieutenant Soffe's right wing. As I did, I signaled that I had been hit, so he pulled up as close as possible underneath me to inspect my airplane. He finally gave me a thumbs-up to indicate that he didn't think the damage was serious.

As we flew back toward the *Essex,* I felt that the airplane wasn't responding as well as it should have to the controls. By experimenting with trim-tab adjustments to the tail surfaces, I was able to handle it well enough. However, I had to make a few more adjustments when it was time to slow the plane down for the landing approach. The Hellcat was a very flyable aircraft and would land reasonably well under most circumstances. What I feared most during the long flight back were consequences of the rough handling I had given the engine when I had had to restart it after it became starved for fuel. But in spite of my concern, the engine ran fine all the way back to task force, and I landed safely back aboard the *Essex*. Upon inspection of the damage to the airplane, we found that a 20mm cannon shell had penetrated the fuselage about a foot behind my back and severed one of the cables that controlled the tail surface.

From March 14 to June 1945, a period of seventy-nine days spent in the combat area, Air Group 83 flew 6,560 sorties from the deck of the *Essex,* totaling more than 24,000 hours in the air. Our group alone was credited with destroying 220 Japanese planes in the air and 72 on the ground, and we had 121 planes probably destroyed. And planes from our air group also sank or damaged eleven Imperial Navy warships and forty-seven other vessels. Our biggest day in aerial combat was April 6, 1945, when Air Group 83 fighters shot down sixty-nine planes as the Japanese brought forth their first major *kamikaze* effort to counteract the invasion of Okinawa. Our losses that day were one airplane and one pilot. VF-83 alone accounted for thirty-eight of those aerial victories.

Ensign Don McPherson, who participated in many of the ground-attack strikes that typified carrier fighter duty at that stage of the war, worked his way to ace status by shooting down two Aichi D3A Val dive-bombers near Kikai Shima, off Okinawa, on April 6, 1945 and three Kawanishi E7K float reconnaissance biplanes (flying as kamikazes) on May 5, 1945.

Don McPherson left the service at the end of the war and returned home to Adams, Nebraska, to work as a rural letter carrier and, much later, to take up farming.

PIECE OF CAKE

Lieutenant JIM PEARCE, USN
VF-17 (USS *Hornet*)
Kyushu Area—March 21, 1945

James Lano Pearce was born in Milwaukee on December 29, 1919, and raised in Detroit, where his father was an executive for Ford and, later, General Motors. As a result of his father's association with G.M., Pearce won a coveted spot at the prestigious General Motors Technical Institute, which he attended until he dropped out to attempt to enlist in the

Army Air Corps in 1941. By then, there was no doubt of Pearce's aptitude for flying; he had amassed approximately one hundred flight hours in small planes after taking up sport flying in 1938. Nevertheless, the Army rejected him because its doctors believed he was color blind, an error that soon brought him into the Navy's Aviation Cadet program.

Pearce was ordered to report for elimination flight training at Fairfax Field, in Kansas City, on July 1, 1941, and from there he proceeded to the new Corpus Christi Naval Air Station. He passed through Pre-flight training, but was waylaid for three months by a ruptured appendix. Ensign Pearce finally received his gold Navy wings in July 1942 and was assigned to fly Vought OS2U scout planes with VS-52 in Bora Bora. When the squadron returned to the United States in July 1943, five of its experienced pilots, including Lieutenant (jg) Jim Pearce, were reassigned to VF-18, which was training in the new Grumman F6F Hellcat fighter at the Alameda Naval Air Station in California. VF-18 was to have had months to train, but the shortcomings of the new Vought F4U Corsair as a carrier fighter resulted in the half-trained, Hellcat-equipped VF-18's swapping places with Corsair-equipped VF-17 aboard the USS Bunker Hill *as part of Air Group 17. The result was that Jim Pearce and his VS-52 buddies were on their way back to the Pacific within four months of returning to the States from Bora Bora.*

Long before many of its pilots felt they were ready, VF-18 experienced first combat on November 11, 1943, with a raid against the Japanese fortress at Rabaul. Miraculously, Jim Pearce survived a head-on duel with a Zero, for which he was awarded a probable credit. On Christmas Day, 1943, he took part in downing a Betty medium bomber at sea, for which he was given a one-fourth credit.

After VF-18 returned to the United States in 1944, Lieutenant Jim Pearce requested assignment to a combat unit, even though his two Pacific tours qualified him for duty in the United States. He was reassigned, along with many former VF-18 pilots, to VF-17, which was being reformed as a carrier-based Hellcat unit following its ground-based South Pacific tour in Corsairs. Operating from the USS Hornet, *Pearce's next combat took place over Tokyo on February 16, 1945, in the first carrier-based attacks against the Japanese home islands. After taking part in strikes against Iwo Jima, VF-17 returned to Japanese waters, and on March 18, Lieutenant Jim Pearce received a half-credit for his part in downing a Nakajima C6N Myrt reconnaissance plane. The next day, he shot down an Imperial Army Nakajima Ki-84 Frank interceptor and shared in the downing of a second Frank.*

On March 21, 1945, my division was posted to fly the second combat air patrol of the day over Task Group 58.1. We loafed around the ready room from about 0800. Some of us were reading, but my wingman, Lieutenant (jg) George Johnson, and I played cribbage. Since we were scheduled for takeoff at 1100, I went to the ready room pantry at about 1030 and made myself a Spam sandwich. Our combat air patrols were usually three or four hours long and typically consisted of boredom, hunger, and thirst while circling over the fleet with nothing to do, eat, or drink.

Four divisions of Hellcats, two from VF-17 and two from VBF-17, took off from the *Hornet* on schedule at 1055, and we climbed to relieve the early morning CAPs. One division from each squadron was sent up high while Lieutenant (jg) Hal Mitchell's VBF-17 division and my VF-17 division were held at 12,000 feet. We droned around over the fleet for more than three hours, in what looked to be a typical boring flight to nowhere.

Suddenly, at about 1350, almost three hours into the CAP, our fighter director came on the air with a definite tone of alarm in his voice: "Large bogey at seventy miles, approaching from three-three-one degrees. Angels thirteen to fifteen. Red Five [my division!] and Red Twenty-eight [Hal Mitchell's division] vector three-three-one. Angels eighteen. Gate."

As we took off at Buster speed—full throttle—and climbing on our vector, the *Hornet* immediately scrambled four other Hellcat divisions—two from VF-17 and two from VBF-17—to stand by over the task force in case they were needed. During the climb, we charged our guns and fired short test bursts to be sure they were ready for action.

At about 1405, we picked them up—a large formation of Bettys flying in a vee-of-vees formation at about 14,000 feet, plus a cover of Zeros that were quite high above the bombers. They were all on a course 180 degrees from ours. It turned out to be a force of approximately eighteen Betty bombers with little manned rocket-propelled Baka suicide bombs slung under their bellies—the first we had ever seen.

When I announced the tallyho to the ship, the fighter director came back excitedly and ordered us to attack the bombers and ignore the fighters. The fighter escorts were high above and didn't seem to be paying much attention to the bombers. This looked like a fighter pilot's dream.

At this point, we dropped our belly tanks. I had Mitchell split his division wide to the left of mine as we approached with about a 3,000-foot altitude advantage. When we were all in position to execute a 180-degree course change, I swung a 180-degree turn to the left at the same time Mitch came around in a right turn over the top of the bombers. We ended up in a perfect position to commence high-side firing passes, well ahead of and a couple thousand feet above the Bettys. Each of our divisions was spread into sections to be ready to counter enemy fighter attacks, should any of the Zekes come down to get us.

From this point, we peeled off to make our high-side attacks against the bombers. My division took the right side of the bomber formation, and Mitch's took the left side.

The first target I went after was the formation leader. It was like making a run on a gunnery sleeve. I caught him on fire between the right engine nacelle and the fuselage, and then followed him down for a few seconds to get a better look at the little Baka bomb he was carrying beneath and outside his bomb bay. Almost immediately, the Betty's right wing blew off, so I cycled up into position to make my second run.

The Bettys didn't break their formation; they just kept on going. On my second run, I got sucked in a little flat and saw the tail gunner's muzzle flashes, so I had to waste a little time knocking out the 20mm stinger before I could concentrate on the vulnerable nacelle-wing-fuselage juncture and set the bomber on fire.

I had learned back in my VF-18 days that the only reliable way to shoot down an enemy aircraft was to get so close before firing that it was hit him with bullets or run into him. I made this a practice here, as I had in all my air-to-air combat, and it worked. I set the second Betty on fire.

About this time, as Bettys were flaming all over the sky, what was left of the formation started a right turn, as if to go home. But by the time we were halfway around, there wasn't a single enemy bomber flying that was not burning, and the sea was littered with flaming wreckage.

In a period of approximately fifteen minutes, we had knocked them all down. During all that time, only one Zeke came down out of the escort to shoot up one of our fighters that was attacking one of the Bettys.

Lieutenant (jg) Carl Stone, one of the VBF-17 guys, shot the Zeke down and then went on to get a couple more bombers. All in all, we got all eighteen of them, plus the Zeke. I never even saw an enemy fighter!

A post-war check of Japanese records confirmed that none of the Bettys and only a few of the Zekes returned from this mission. And none of the Baka bombs was launched.

It turned out that the Zekes were pretty well taken care of by some fighters that came in from the *Belleau Wood* and a couple of the other ships. After the fighter directors saw they had a big attack on their hands, they had fighters coming from all the different task groups. I guess that's why we didn't see very many fighters down among us as we were busy picking off the bombers. But it was an exciting fifteen minutes. It was something we didn't get to do very often—to just sit there and whack away at them as they plowed on in toward the task force.

I got two of the Bettys; Lieutenant (jg) George Johnson, my wingman, got three; Lieutenant (jg) Jack Crawford, my section leader, got one; Lieutenant (jg) Murray Winfield, Crawford's wingman, got four and shared a fifth with a Marine Corsair pilot; Lieutenant (jg) Hal Mitchell, the other division leader, got five; and Lieutenant (jg) Carl Stone grabbed two Bettys and shot down the Zeke. So our flight alone got the eighteen Bettys and one Zero fighter.

It was exciting while it was happening, but looking back on it, it seems like a piece of cake. However, in the melee, somehow or other, Mitchell's wingman was lost. No one saw him shot down, but I believe he was the victim of a gunner aboard one of the bombers. It's also sad to note that, about two weeks later, Hal Mitchell was killed in action when his airplane was hit by antiaircraft fire. He bailed out, but when they found his chute, it was open and there was nobody in it.

The Baka bombs were manned suicide bombs that were hung from the bomb bays with their wings out to the engine nacelles of the Betty bombers. Until the time of this melee, the fighter pilots had never been briefed as to their existence. In fact, when we were debriefed right after this mission, our intelligence officers treated us like we were hallucinating when we tried to tell them about the "flying bombs" the Bettys were carrying. But we found in a few days that the intelligence officers *had* heard about such a bomb as this, and they even had some little pictures of them. But they had never told us anything about them; only *they* were supposed to know about them. It was fascinating to me that the Japanese had this thing. It had a cockpit, a canopy that looked like a P-51 canopy, a big load of TNT in the nose, and a rocket engine in the back end to give it some range. It was an advanced kind of thing for a nation that didn't mind putting people in weapons and smashing them into things.

I had one more victory, another Frank that I shot down over Kagoshima Bay on May 14. Our combat tour was cut short when the *Hornet* got mashed up in a storm in July 1945. The ship came home to get her bow put back on properly so she could operate once again, but while she was back, the war ended.

After the war, Jim Pearce served as a test pilot at the Naval Aviation Test Center at Patuxent River, Maryland. He then worked briefly as a test pilot for Grumman and for fifteen years as an engineering test pilot with North American Aviation. In 1960, he was selected to work on the Apollo moon-landing program and wound up as director of testing and operations for seven years. He next worked on the moon lander at Grumman for two years. After retiring from industry, Pearce set up a firm to manufacture water pollution prevention devices—a retirement hobby that has grown into a multi-million dollar corporation.

LONG-RANGE ESCORT

Major JOHN LOISEL, USAAF
475th Fighter Group
Indochina Coast—March 28, 1945

John Loisel was born on May 21, 1920, in Couer d'Alene, Idaho, and raised in Norfolk, Nebraska. After attending the University of Nebraska for two years, Loisel entered the Army Air Corps as a flying cadet on March 8, 1941, and graduated from flight school at Mather Field, California, with Class 41-H on October 31, 1941. He was aboard a transport ship on its way to the Philippines when the Pacific War broke out.

Second Lieutenant Loisel went into combat for the first time in

August 1942, flying a P-39 with the 8th Fighter Group's 36th Fighter Squadron. When the 475th Fighter Group was formed at Amberley Field, Australia, in July 1943, 1st Lieutenant Loisel underwent transition training in P-38s. As a flight leader with the new 432d Fighter Squadron, Loisel scored his first aerial victories of the war, a pair of Ki-61 Tony interceptors he downed near Dagua, New Guinea, on August 21, 1943. His next victory credit was for a Zero he shot down near Finschafen, New Guinea, on September 22, 1943, and he achieved ace status when he downed two Zeros over Oro Bay, New Guinea, on October 15, 1943. Thereafter, Captain Loisel shot down one Zero on December 13, damaged another on December 16, shot down a third on December 21, got a fourth on January 23, 1944; and downed a Ki-43 Oscar and a Zero on April 3, 1944.

In March 1945, the 475th Fighter Group was flying P-38s off the newly operational runway at Clark Field. By then, there was little or no aerial opposition in the Philippines. The fighting had become a mop-up operation, with the air units providing support for Army ground forces. The majority of our missions involved bombing, napalming, and strafing ground targets. Less frequently, our group escorted Far East Air Forces B-24s or B-25s striking distant targets on Formosa, or across the South China Sea to Hainan Island, Honk Kong, and French Indochina. These escort missions, at the extreme range of the P-38s, offered the possibility of encountering enemy fighters and were eagerly sought. As the group operations officer, I could select the missions I wished to fly, so on March 28 I put myself on the schedule to escort B-25s against a Japanese naval convoy in the South China Sea, just off the French Indochina coast. As it turned out, this was my last aerial combat with the Japanese.

Each of the three squadrons of the 475th provided two flights—eight aircraft—for this mission. I was leading the 433d Fighter Squadron's Red Flight, which was to fly close cover on the B-25s. Flights of the 432d and 431st provided the high-cover escort force.

As with all long-range missions of the time, we took off from Clark Field with 410 gallons of fuel in our internal tanks and two 315-gallon drop tanks, a total of 1,040 gallons per fighter. Using optimal cruise-control techniques introduced to us earlier in the war by Charles

Lindbergh, we could achieve a combat radius of more than 800 miles. Many factors go into that range estimation. Going out, the aircraft would be heavily loaded with ammunition for the four .50-caliber machine guns and the 20mm cannon, and the external fuel tanks. Without the drag of the drop tanks and with ammunition expended, the P-38 was much lighter and flew much better. Fuel consumption was minimized when we could fly most of the mission at minimum altitude with lower power and RPMs, and using the leanest mixture-control settings. Speed when not engaged with enemy aircraft was not a factor. Consequently, going out on a mission like this one, we usually flew down on the deck or just above the ocean at 160 to 170 miles per hour, indicated air speed. Coming back with a much lighter "clean bird," the same power setting and techniques added an additional 30 to 40 miles per hour to the indicated air speed.

Our flight path for this mission took us directly westward over the ocean for some 825 miles. Some two to three hours after takeoff, we made rendezvous with the B-25 formation to take up our escort duties. Outbound, we flew a spread formation just above the B-25s, which were only a few hundred feet off the water. To achieve the fuel economy we needed, we had to fly low, reduce our propeller revolutions, throttle back, and lean-out the mixture control. At these long-range cruise settings, our airspeed was low and we could cover the B-25s with a minimum of weaving or fuel-consuming throttle jockeying.

Following several aborts, our escort force consisted of some twenty P-38s. As the combined B-25 and P-38 force approached the Indochina coast, the enemy convoy was sighted and called in to the B-25s by one of the top-cover P-38 flights. The convoy was about 15 miles off the Indochina coast, traveling northward.

The B-25s turned toward the enemy ships to make their bombing and strafing attack. Meanwhile, we picked up speed and climbed to several thousand feet above the lead B-25 formation. Just as flak started coming up from the convoy, which consisted of four or five merchant ships and several escorting warships, I spotted a dozen enemy aircraft in a loose, strung-out gaggle milling around above the convoy at about 7,000 or 8,000 feet. The enemy fighters were just circling, in no particular formation beyond elements of two airplanes.

I dropped my external fuel tanks and rammed throttle and pitch full forward. As my speed increased, I pulled up and bored right into them. Their attention must have been on the B-25s below, because as we closed in on their rear quarter, they took no evasive action. The covering flights from the 431st and 432d Fighter squadrons initiated attacks against the Japanese fighters from above at the same time I initiated my attack.

As I passed through 6,500 feet, I started firing at a pair of Japanese fighters—they were Ki-84 Franks—that I was rapidly overtaking from directly astern. I fired a single burst at the wingman, who immediately broke left. I was out of range when I opened fire, and probably did no damage. The leader, if that's what he really was, continued straight ahead. The two fighters had been close together, so it took only a slight adjustment or minimal turn to switch targets from the wingman to the leader.

I closed to within a few hundred feet and began firing from dead astern. We always used the "All" position for the gun selector, which fired all four .50-caliber machine guns and the 20mm cannon. I observed hits on the fuselage and right wing. The Frank burst into flames from the wing root, executed a left turn, and headed down steeply, flaming badly. It crashed into the ocean just off the enemy convoy.

My speed carried me on past the scattering Japanese fighters. As I started a slow turn back over the convoy and the B-25s, the rest of my flight stretched out in a long string behind me. Above us, the 432d and 431st P-38s were heavily engaged with other Japanese fighters. The air was crackling with excited calls.

I was concentrating on the B-25s, in order to cover their attack and withdrawal, when Red-4—the fourth man in my immediate flight, 2d Lieutenant Wesley Hulett—called out that he had been hit. As I circled to go to his aid, I saw another P-38 flame an enemy fighter that was shooting at Red-4. Then another enemy fighter took its place on the tail of the distressed P-38. I forced this one to break off its attack with a short burst from just out of range. I would have shot him down if he hadn't taken evasive action. This brief diversion caused me to lose sight of Lieutenant Hulett's P-38, so I circled around to look for him after he radioed that both his engines had been shot out, but I couldn't locate him. I told him to head due east and that I'd call the rescue PBY.

After radioing the PBY, I went down to the deck and circled the area, but I sighted nothing. I then climbed back toward the fight, which had drifted westward from Tre Island and the now-burning Japanese ships. I made several more passes at Japanese fighters that were being chased down by the other P-38s, and I saw a 432d pilot shoot down an enemy fighter.

In a short while, as we were getting low on fuel, we were forced to start back home. I made a final pass over the area in which Lieutenant Hulett had gone down and again radioed the PBY to give it the location.

Our fuel was critical. Once again, we throttled back, spread out, and flew several hundred feet above the waves at our most economical cruise settings. As the hours on the return flight passed, each cockpit grew smaller and tighter, helmet and parachute straps were loosened, and pilots squirmed and massaged cramped muscles and posteriors. Finally, three and a half hours later, the Luzon coast was sighted.

One pilot who ran out of fuel bailed out when we reached the coastline. He was never heard from again. The rest of us made it back safely and landed with minimum fuel remaining. I logged eight hours and 45 minutes on that mission. The final score was ten enemy aircraft destroyed for two of our planes and pilots.

John Loisel was promoted to lieutenant colonel in May 1945 and assumed command of the 475th Fighter Group in July. After World War II, he completed work for his degree and then went back on active duty as a career professional. He commanded a jet fighter-bomber group near the end of the Korean War and held a succession of staff and flying jobs until he retired from the Air Force with the rank of colonel in 1970. At the time of his retirement, Colonel John Loisel had flown 323 combat missions and had accumulated 5,400 military flying hours.

VLR

Major JIM TAPP, USAAF
78th Fighter Squadron, 15th Fighter Group
Tokyo—April 7, 1945

James Buckley Tapp was born on December 6, 1920, in Eveleth, Minnesota, where he attended high school and the local community college.

♦

In the fall of 1940, I enrolled in the Civilian Pilot Training program while attending my second year at Eveleth Junior College. Before the school year was out, I had completed the CPT Private and Secondary courses, both of which were sponsored by the Civil Aeronautics Administration. Inside the front page of the Secondary Course Student Pilot Rating Book it says; "The success of the Civilian Pilot Training Program will depend on two factors: (1) The safety record established and (2) the acceptance by the military services of the products of our controlled training. The military standards require proficiency in each maneuver in the course. The quality of training you give your students will largely determine future participation in the program. See that they meet the standard and insure civil aviation's contribution to National Defense."

In the Private Course, I flew Piper J-3 Cubs for 36 hours and 30 minutes, and in the Secondary Course I flew the Waco UPF-7 biplane for 42 hours and 30 minutes. It was in this course, which was mostly acrobatic, that I really decided that I wanted to become a fighter pilot. I also became aware that you could go through the Army Air Corps Flying Cadet training program and after graduation resign your commission and join the RAF or RCAF and fight the Germans. This seemed to be an exciting goal in the spring of 1941, and it was what I decided to do. I took the Flying Cadet physical exam while still in the CPT Secondary Course and found that in order to be accepted I had to have a couple of ice hockey-caused problems fixed. I needed to get my nose straightened out and a tooth capped. After finishing the CPT course, I had these repairs done. When I retook the exam, I passed. I was sworn in as an Flying Cadet on November 7, 1941, and went off to Kelly Field, Texas. One month later the Japanese changed my plans to fly Spitfires in England.

As I progressed through flying school, I was lucky enough to end up in the single-engine Advanced course at Lake Charles, Louisiana. Fortunately, the Air Corps was basing most of its posting decisions in those days on the alphabet, and not your size. Being six foot two, I was always afraid that I would be sidetracked from my goal of becoming a fighter pilot. One evening, about three weeks before graduation, we were called back from our one and only scheduled overnight cross-country flight. After we assembled in the ready room, we were read a message from the War Department. The message asked for volunteers for immediate combat in fighters. Those who volunteered were to be graduated early and assigned directly to a fighter unit without leave. This latter bit was a deterrent to many, but fourteen of us volunteered. We were indeed graduated early, on June 26, 1942, and sent to the 311th Fighter Squadron, 58th Fighter Group, at Dale Mabry Field in Tallahassee, Florida. We were joined there by other volunteers from other schools. Those of us from Lake Charles went directly to Tallahassee with a one-day layover in New Orleans. We started flying P-39D-1s on July 3, and we flew almost continuously through July 26. My Form 5 shows that I missed four days of flying during that period.

On July 28, we were put aboard a special train headed for San Francisco. The train, which was made up of three non-air-conditioned Pullmans, slowly made its way across the southern United States to Los Angeles and then up to San Francisco. After about a week's wait, we left Fort Mason by ship. We had been issued gear in San Francisco for cold and hot weather, so we didn't know where we were headed. After we got out to sea, we were told that we were going at least as far as Hawaii. On arrival in Pearl Harbor, we found that we were going to stay there for awhile. The ten or so squadrons comprising the VII Fighter Command had been decimated by the time we arrived. They were the ones that provided the pilots for immediate combat with the Fifth Air Force in the Southwest Pacific and our units in the South Pacific. We were their replacements. Several of us ended up in the 78th Fighter Squadron, and we flew P-40s practically every day for the next couple of months.

On October 30, new orders were received by twenty-five of us. We were to be sent to Australia on an emergency basis. It looked like things were back on track again. Six of us from the squadron packed up and went to Wheeler Field to await transportation. After about a week, we were recalled to the squadron. The 78th had been selected to replace the 73d Fighter Squadron, which was assigned to Marine Air Group 22 on Midway. The Marine fighter squadron, VMF-221, and their Brewster Buffalos had been wiped out in the Battle of Midway in June. We set a record for long-range over-water flight when we flew from Hawaii to

Midway with the use of special large belly tanks. I was disappointed by the recall from the trip to Australia, but it hadn't been too many months since the Battle of Midway, so it didn't seem too bad. The Japanese might come back, but of course they didn't.

After being relieved by a Marine squadron equipped with F4U Corsairs in late April 1943, it was back to Hawaii again. We came close to going to the forward area in the Central Pacific later in the year but lost out to the 45th Fighter Squadron because they had new P-40Ns. Next, in mid-1944, we were all set to go to Yap; our ground echelon was already aboard ship. The whole operation was called off, however, and the Yap invasion forces were diverted to participate in the Philippines invasion, but without us. The Fifth and Thirteenth air forces would be moving forward, and that precluded the need for participation by Seventh Air Force units. It was down in the dumps again.

Fortunately, we didn't have to wait long for new plans. As acting squadron commander, I was called to attend a highly secret meeting with the higher-ups, who said that we would be going to Iwo Jima. The 15th Fighter Group was to get ten P-51s in addition to our P-47Ds. We would use these P-51s to get each of our pilots checked out. In thirty days, a Navy jeep carrier loaded with P-51s was scheduled to stop by, pick us up, and head for the Western Pacific.

Three P-51s were given to each of the squadrons, and we started flying them from before daylight until after dark. We had a special maintenance crew working on them at night, to maximize their availability. Fortunately, things didn't go as quickly as planned, and the new aircraft came to us on land first. Even at that, we really didn't have enough time to achieve the level of qualification desired before we had to fly the P-51Ds down to Pearl Harbor to go aboard the jeep carrier USS *Sitkoh Bay*. I had been able to get 49 hours in that time period. This contrasted with 799:15 in the P-40 and 267:30 in the P-47. Many of our pilots had even less P-51 time.

The *Sitkoh Bay* took us to Guam. The initial plan was for us to be catapulted off the carrier. However, the Navy hadn't anticipated that we would have external tanks mounted on the aircraft. This messed up their parking plan, and in order to get all seventy-nine aircraft aboard, they had to foul the catapult. To use the catapult, they would have to push some of aircraft over the side. This would only be done if the carrier was attacked by Japanese aircraft. We had one Japanese airplane come near the ship while we were between Eniwetok and Guam, but he seemed to be too afraid of us to attack. It was noted on radar that his speed increased after he apparently sighted us. At Guam, the aircraft were lightered ashore. From there, we flew to Saipan and eventually to Iwo.

◆

The time had come. It was 0630 hours, April 7, 1945. I was sitting in the cockpit of my P-51 on Iwo Jima, waiting for the signal to start my engine. After years of impatient waiting, it sure looked like I would finally get to see some aerial combat. The six squadrons of the 15th and 21st Fighter groups were poised to take off from Iwo Jima for the first Very Long Range (VLR) fighter escort of B-29s to their targets in Japan. For all except the 531st Fighter Squadron, it was appropriate that this mission take place on the seventh day of the month, for all were at Wheeler Field on December 7, 1941. On this mission, we were going 750 miles, directly north to the Nakajima aircraft plant in the Tokyo area, escorting the 73d Very Heavy Bombardment Wing, which was based on Saipan.

As operations officer of the 15th Fighter Group's 78th Fighter Squadron, I, along with Major Jim Vande Hey, our squadron commander, had been involved in the trickle-down of briefings that had been given at VII Fighter Command headquarters, 15th Group headquarters, and in our squadron. Under the detailed operations plan, we would be using sixteen squadron aircraft for escort of the B-29s in the target area. An extra eight aircraft per group would also be launched. Four would come with us to about 200 miles and would fill in for anyone who had to abort the mission due to aircraft problems. Four others would make up one of the two flights that would provide protective cover for our B-29 navigation-escort aircraft and the rescue submarine at the post-target assembly point. The sub was to surface twenty minutes before the planned assembly time. It would attempt to rescue any B-29 or P-51 crewmembers who had to bail out or ditch after leaving the target area. Another submarine was at the halfway point, and a destroyer was about 200 miles from Iwo, also for aircrew rescue.

On this mission, we would be flying our oldest, most experienced pilots. The reason for this was twofold. One, we wanted to maximize the possibility of mission success, and, two, we wanted those who had waited the longest to get into aerial combat to get the first crack at it. Major Jim Vande Hey, who arrived in the command prior to Pearl Harbor, would be leading the squadron as well as the first section and Red Flight. Lieutenant DB Moore would be flying his wing, and Captain Hal Collins, with Lieutenant Al Sherren as his wingman, would be Jim's second element. Yellow Flight, in Jim's section, would be led by Captain Vic Mollan, with Lieutenant Leo Evans on his wing and Lieutenant Jerry Yellin and Lieutenant Don Gautsche as his element. I was leading the second section and Blue Flight, with Lieutenant Phil Maher on my wing and Lieutenant John Chambers and Lieutenant Bob Carr as my element. Captain Todd Moore was the Green Flight leader with Lieutenant Bob Roseberry on his wing and Captain Ernie Hostetler and Lieutenant Herman Beyl as his element.

We were to take off in two-ship elements, with close spacing between the elements. It was estimated that we would be in the air for close to seven and one-half hours, so we couldn't afford to dally getting the fifty-six P-51Ds airborne. The 15th Fighter Group was flying from Iwo's South Field, which was still pretty much like the Japanese had left it. The bomb and shell craters made by U.S. forces had been filled in, but it was still a short, wavy, narrow, dirt runway. We had become somewhat accustomed to it since our arrival at D+17—March 7, 1945. Although we had few takeoffs with both 108-gallon external tanks full of fuel, we had flown quite a few missions with two 500-pound bombs attached in support of the Marines on Iwo and interdiction of the neighboring islands of Chichi Jima and Haha Jima.

Since the P-51 had only a magnetic compass as its navigation instrument, after takeoff we were to climb to 10,000 feet and rendezvous with six B-29s that were to provide us navigation escort and rescue support to a point just south of Japan over Kozu Island. There we would join the assembling B-29 strike force at 18,000 feet. Our escort of the 73d Wing bombers would begin at this point and end when we reached our minimum fuel for return to Iwo. We were to drop our external fuel tanks as we approached the coast or prior to engaging Japanese fighters, should they come out to sea to meet us.

Contrary to the P-51 pilot's manual, we would do all of our combat maneuvering while burning fuel from the 85-gallon fuselage tank.

Aces At War

Under the section on prohibited maneuvers, the P-51 manual says: "Abrupt pull-ups should not be attempted with more than 25 gallons in the fuselage tank," and that "no aerobatics are permitted with fuel in the fuselage tank." The tank was aft of the pilot and the center of gravity, and it caused somewhat of a stick force reversal when you pulled Gs with more than 25 gallons. Nevertheless, if we were to do our mission, we had no choice but to fly with this configuration. We of course learned to live with the problem quite successfully. Our signal to terminate the mission and start the process of returning to Iwo was, ironically, the fuselage tank running dry. This left us with the 90 gallons of fuel in each of the two internal wing tanks, enough to recover and go home on. It was supposed to leave us with a small reserve on arrival at Iwo.

For me, it was the end of a very long wait. As I sat in the cockpit and looked for the signal to start engines, I wondered how we would do. It seemed certain that we would see Japanese fighters. The question really was how many. Would they be aggressive? Would they be well disciplined and go after the bombers, or would they prefer to engage us? Would our mutual-support formation, the Thach Weave, work as we had practiced it? As the squadron operations officer, I had been responsible for the training we had done. Would it prove adequate? Would this type of mission work? We had made a practice run from Iwo to Saipan and back. Too many of our aircraft had had to land at Saipan. There would be no opportunity to do so on this mission. There was only one airport around that we could land on—Iwo.

The signal finally came to start engines, and we were underway.

Everyone got into the air okay. The group leader made a big, sweeping, climbing turn toward Kita Iwo Jima, an island 35 miles to the north, where we were to meet up with our navigation escorts at 10,000 feet. The big turn made it easy for us to join up without having to use a lot of power and, therefore, gasoline. When we reached Kita, we immediately started on course to Japan. Our best long-range cruise speed was supposed to be 207 miles per hour indicated airspeed at 10,000 feet. This was compromised at 210, which was a better speed for B-29 engine cooling and easier for us to read. We used full throttle and controlled the air speed with the engine RPM control. The RPM had to be reduced as we burned off fuel, to compensate for the increase in airspeed due to the lighter weight of the airplane. The P-51 mixture control only had three positions, Idle cutoff, Normal, and Rich, so we didn't have to worry about it. We flew a very loose, easy-to-fly formation in order to conserve fuel.

At the last-chance-to-abort point, about 200 miles out, several people decided that their aircraft would not make it, and they had to return to base. The spares filled in, and we continued on our way. None of the 78th regulars aborted, but three of our spares got to fill in the formations of other squadrons.

As I settled back, a little bit of boredom set in. This gave my butt a chance to say that the seat was getting hard. We used a backpack parachute and sat on a survival kit that was attached to the parachute harness. It was something we had put together in the squadron. It was a compromise between comfort and survival gear. The "cushion" contained a one-man life raft with its CO_2 bottle, several cans of drinking water, a desalinization kit, a box of .45-caliber bird shot, a fishing kit, some emergency rations, dye marker, smoke flares, signal flares, and more. None of these things was soft, of course.

One the necessities en route was to use the relief tube. Those of us who had been on the Midway flight in 1942 were apprehensive. We had found on that flight that the relief tubes in our P-40s had become plugged up from lack of use. The funnel end filled up, and the only feasible course of action was to open the canopy and try to pour it out. No one was successful. The wind blew it all over the place. The P-51s, being quite new, did not present us with the same—or any—problem in this regard.

The weather en route proved relatively good. As we approached Japan, we began a slow climb to get to the escort altitude. There was a thin deck of scattered clouds just below us that merged in with the horizon ahead. All of a sudden, I realized that one of those clouds wasn't a cloud after all. It was snowcapped Mount Fuji. This was it!

We joined the strike B-29s as they proceeded to the northeast from the rendezvous point. The 15th Group position was on the right-hand side of the bomber stream. We were stacked up 2,000 to 4,000 feet above the bombers. From what we understood, they were flying at a base altitude of 18,000 feet, which was way below the altitude at which they normally flew on daylight missions. The 73d Wing was also all bunched together in one large, contiguous formation, which we never saw again on later missions.

I was aware that we were flying beyond the point where we were supposed to turn in to make landfall. I don't know if this was caused by the winds at our altitude, or whether it was a change in the bombers' plans. The B-29s finally did turn in toward the coast, and we dropped our external fuel tanks. We had already tightened our seatbelts and increased our power settings. Most important, we had turned on our N-9 gunsights and adjusted the reticle brilliance. The armament switch was in the gunsight-and-camera position.

As we got closer to Tokyo, the intensity of the flak increased. It seemed to be solid at the bomber altitude. It looked like they were laying down an asphalt highway for the B-29s. I thought, This is one time I'm glad I'm a fighter pilot. We also noted that there were many contrails on high ahead. The Japanese fighters were expecting the bombers to be above 30,000 feet; apparently that's where they all were. I was at around 22,000 at the time.

Shortly after we made landfall, I spotted a twin-engine, two-seat Imperial Army Kawasaki Ki-45 Nick fighter as it was diving toward the B-29s at a pretty steep angle. I figured that he would be going pretty fast, so I went after him with full throttle. We closed quite rapidly. When I got in to a range of about 1,200 feet and about 20 degrees off his tail on his right side, I began firing. I fired at the fuselage, right wing root, and right engine. The tracers indicated that all rounds were finding their mark. More significantly, the incendiaries were flashing on target. I noted we were not getting any return fire from the tail gunner, nor was the pilot doing anything to evade me. I don't think they were in condition to do anything about it. I was going too fast to stay behind the Nick and closed to near collision before breaking off the attack. No direct evidence of a kill was seen. But we weren't there to worry about kills, so we couldn't stay around to see what happened. Besides, we were closing on the B-29s, and they very probably would mistake us for Tonys.

As I pulled in to return to my previous escort position, I saw an olive-drab Imperial Army Kawasaki Ki-61 Tony coming down on an attack. This time, I decided to go after him a little slower. We closed on him from his left side, about 15 degrees off his tail. I started firing at about 1,000 feet and immediately got hits. This time we had a flamer. As we passed him on his left side at very close range, I could see the pilot sitting in the cockpit, which was aflame. Bob Carr, the number-four man in our flight, saw the pilot bail out and took a picture of him with his gun camera.

As we pulled up off the Tony, I saw a twin-engine Imperial Army Mitsubishi Ki-46 Dinah, which appeared to be initiating a head-on attack against the bombers. We had been told by our intelligence officer that it had been reported that Dinahs had been making frontal rocket and phosphorus-bomb attacks on bomber formations. The activity with the Nick and the Tony had brought us down to a lower altitude. Not being able to trade altitude for speed to the extent that I had with the other two, I poured the coal to it to close on the Dinah. As we went diving down through about 18,000 feet, the P-51's engine automatically switched to low blower, which seemed to stop us in mid-air. I saw that I wasn't going to close, so I attempted a shot from out of range. The attack had started from his front quarter, and by this time I was at the 90-degree point. I had to fly an almost-90-degree bank and develop a big lead angle, because the Dinah was going quite fast. As a consequence, the target became blanked out by the nose of my P-51. A few incendiary strikes were noted, but I had no confidence that I did any good.

The P-51s had an automatic high-blower system; as you climbed to altitude, a pressure-sensing switch at the carburetor intake caused the blower to shift to high between 16,000 and 18,000 feet, depending on the ram air pressure. There was a switch in the cockpit that you could use to override the automatic feature. But the problem was that the switch was spring loaded and you had to hold it. Being already short on hands to do things with, this was no good. Anticipating this problem, I had had all of the spring-loaded switches replaced before we left Hawaii. However, the Packard tech rep on Iwo found out about it and got VII Fighter Command to make us switch back. He argued that we would ruin the engines if we operated them at low altitude in high blower.

As we pulled back into escort position, a B-29 with his number-two engine afire was seen below us. It had left the formation and appeared to be taking the shortest route to the coast. I saw an unpainted Imperial Army Nakajima Ki-43 Oscar getting set to go after somebody, perhaps the burning B-29. We were not supposed to worry about cripples, but I rationalized that the Oscar represented a threat to the main body as well, so I started a 90-degree full deflection curve-of-pursuit pass. I started firing at 1,000 feet and 90 degrees and continued on around to very close range off his tail. I got hits all through the pass and observed pieces coming off the Oscar, but he never caught fire. The Oscar rolled into a steep descending spiral. Phil Maher observed the Oscar continue the spiral descent into the ground. When I returned home, we found gouges on each side of the canopy and on the left-hand engine cowling, and a piece of heavy glass was embedded in the right wing-root fairing. This apparently came from the Oscar's "bullet-proof" windshield.

Immediately after I broke off the engagement with the Oscar, I started looking around for other enemy aircraft. It had been drilled into us that you had to keep your head on a swivel, because the guy that shoots you down is the one you don't see.

As I pulled up off the Oscar, I saw six Japanese aircraft coming straight at us. Whether they were after us or we were simply between them and the bombers will never be known. I immediately turned head-on into them. As I faced them, those to my left were in a four-ship formation and appeared to be Imperial Navy Mitsubishi A6M Zekes. On the right was a two-ship formation of something else. Initially, I thought they were Imperial Army Nakajima Ki-44 Tojos, but I have since concluded that they must have been Navy Kawanishi N1K George high-altitude interceptors or some variant. What would two Army Tojos be doing up there with four Navy Zekes?

I picked the George to the right to go head-on with. I started firing at about 1,500 feet or so. This pass, of course, would only be a few seconds long. I observed flashes on the bogey's engine, fuselage, and left wing. I thought at first the latter was his 20mm cannon firing back, but I was a little puzzled because the flashes were too far out on the wing. As soon as we passed, the Japanese fighters made a hard left turn while I started a slow high-speed climbing turn. Our tactics called for avoiding turning-type dogfights, because that would be playing into the strong suit of the Japanese aircraft. I noted that one of the Georges was snap-rolling through the air. Phil Maher had observed that about six feet of the George's left wing had come off, and that the wing continued to disintegrate.

My intent was to get into position to come back after the five remaining enemy aircraft. This plan was interrupted by a radio call from Phil, stating that his fuselage tank had run dry. This was our signal to initiate recovery, so we headed for the rally point.

When the air-to-air activity started, our squadron formation had broken down into individual flights, as anticipated. It was amazing to me, though, that as we left the target area, all of the 78th Squadron P-51s just fell right into their proper squadron-formation positions. We had been in the target area from 1045 until 1130, but it seemed like only a few minutes.

The rally point was about 15 miles directly south of Cape Nojima. It seemed that everybody arrived there at about the same time, so we were able to proceed immediately for home. After we were beyond Japanese fighter range, we went into the relaxation mode. We were back down to 10,000 feet, cruising at 210 miles per hour indicated airspeed. We each loosened up the seatbelt, got the canteen out for a drink of water, had some candy, and found other ways to ease the tension of the fight. I looked over at Phil, and he had an elated look as he held up four fingers. To this point, I guess I had been too busy to realize what had been going on. It took a little while for me to figure out that he must have meant that we had gotten four Japanese between us.

We had been given "pep pills" to take prior to going into the target area, to make sure that we would be alert. After we started relaxing, the effect of the pills seemed to let us down even further than necessary. I never used them again; you didn't need anything to keep alert in the target area, as Mother Nature had her own built-in chemical for that purpose. And we didn't need any help relaxing once we started for home. However, the calm was soon disrupted.

With our load much reduced by this time, we were down to about 1,700 RPM required to hold speed at 210 miles per hour. This turned out to be too cool for a Packard-Rolls Royce Merlin engine burning the 115/145-octane leaded gasoline. Little globules of "lead" would form across the electrodes of a spark plug, thus shorting out the plug. You wouldn't think that just one fouled plug out of twenty-four could make the engine run so rough. The instrument panel would vibrate so badly that it was difficult to see the instruments. At this time, we didn't know what was going on, so it made it quite nerve-wracking for those few it happened to. This problem was solved on future missions by running the engine at 61 inches of manifold pressure and 3,000 RPM for one minute every half hour when operating at low RPM. Those of us who didn't have a rough engine to worry about became quite aware that our butts were objecting to having been sitting on hard objects for so long.

About 200 miles from Iwo, we began to hear faint Uncle Dog signals. Our VHF radios had been modified to include the AN/ARA-8 Homing Adapter. This was one the greatest gadgets in our bag, as it gave us a way to find things; we could home on any other cooperative VHF radio. According to plan, Iwo started broadcasting on a common frequency available on our VHF sets' button "D" for the mission. With our Uncle Dog turned on, we could hear a **U** when the nose was pointed to the left of the station, and a **D** when the nose was to the right of the station, inbound. It was the opposite outbound. This was our ambiguity check. With our noses pointed at that transmitter, we got a steady tone. When we had plenty of fuel, and the weather was okay, and we had a good strong signal, we would be able to leave the navigation escort B-29s. This mission set the precedent. We pushed the RPM up to a more respectable setting and dropped noses for a long high-speed descent to Iwo. This brought the airspeed up to around 400 miles per hour.

The traffic pattern over Iwo was something to behold. It was huge. Everyone was eager to get on the ground. Our standard low-level pitch-up was more or less dispensed with, and we all just tacked onto the end of the string of aircraft. Everyone seemed to ensure he had the right spacing, so he wouldn't have to go around again. All of the P-51s from the 78th made the trip okay. We landed at about 1430 after 7 hours and 30 minutes in the air. Lieutenant Gautsche won the squadron prize for least fuel, with 8 gallons remaining.

Once on the ground, debriefings began. Everyone was highly elated. The mission had gone smoothly. The 15th Fighter Group claimed seventeen Japanese aircraft destroyed, three probably destroyed, and five damaged. Only one aircraft was lost. Captain Frank Ayres ran low on fuel and was forced to bail out over the Lifeguard destroyer that was about 200 miles north of Iwo. The 21st Fighter Group also had a good day, but it lost one aircraft and pilot in the target area.

Brigadier General Mickey Moore, the VII Fighter Command commander, was ecstatic. He had started out on the mission but had to abort because of fuel system problems. When he came to the table where my flight was being debriefed, I told him that we would have had another claim if we hadn't taken out the non-spring-loaded supercharger switches, and I explained what had happened with the Dinah. He then and there made the decision to modify all the command P-51s to the non-spring-loaded switches.

In the end, thanks to gun-camera film and supporting testimony from others, Major Jim Tapp was awarded credit for four victories on his very first combat mission following three years' service in the war zone— the Nick, the Tony, the Oscar, and the George. On April 12, he achieved ace status when he downed a Tony over the Tokyo area. On April 19, Jim Tapp shot down an Imperial Navy Mitsubishi J2M Jack high-altitude interceptor over Atsugi Airdrome; on May 25 he downed a Tojo over Matsudo Airdrome, Honshu; and on May 29 he downed a Zero over Atsugi Airdrome.

Jim Tapp remained in the service after World War II and rotated between flying assignments and numerous important development jobs, beginning with the testing of improved fighter controls right after the war, to testing missiles and guns, to work on the Apollo space-flight program. He retired in 1970 with the rank of colonel.

PART II

At War Against Germany

MUSTANGS OVER DIEPPE

Flying Officer HOLLY HILLS, RCAF
414 RCAF Squadron
Dieppe, France—August 19, 1942

Hollis Harry Hills was born in Baxter, Iowa, on March 25, 1915, but his mother took him to Los Angeles in the mid-1920s in hopes that the mild climate would break the cycle of serious childhood illnesses that had plagued him since birth. Deemed too sickly to attend school, and left at home alone by his working mother, young Hills soon discovered a nearby airfield. There he met a World War I aviator, now selling private airplanes, who regularly took the boy aloft to demonstrate the safety of his wares. Before long, the veteran taught the youngster to fly—in order to demonstrate the ease with which his wares could be used. This early flying career came to abrupt end, however, when Hills's mother discovered how he was keeping himself occupied during his long days at home. He was 12 at the time, and he did not fly again until he decided to join the RCAF in mid-1940.

Hills entered the RCAF as a flying cadet in June 1940, but delays in the Empire Training Program kept him from entering pre-flight school in Toronto until mid-December of that year, and he did not resume flying until mid-January 1941. He earned his wings and the rank of sergeant pilot at Dauphin, Manitoba, on June 22, 1941, the day the Germans invaded the Soviet Union. Shortly, Hills was commissioned as a pilot officer and assigned as an instructor, but he managed to swap places with an underage pilot who had orders to an operational unit in England.

Pilot Officer Hills arrived in England in mid-August 1941 and took an operational training course in Wiltshire before being posted to 414 RCAF Squadron, which at the time was flying Tomahawks (Lend-Lease P-40s) from Croyden, near London.

414 RCAF Squadron received the new North American Mustang I ground-cooperation fighter in the first week of June 1942. The squadron commander, Wing Commander Doug Smith, and I made the first flights with our new planes on June 5. The landing gear retracting lever on the early Mustang was tricky to operate. A push, pull, and twist were required. Doug didn't get the knack and I had the dubious pleasure of beating him up on this our first operation. Lucky for me he was very tolerant of a junior officer that day.

The Dieppe operation started for our squadron on August 18, 1942. We flew our planes from our home base at Croydon, a few miles south to Gatwick. The following morning, in the pitch black, Flight Lieutenant Freddie Clarke and I, as weaver, took off on the first mission of the day for the Mustangs, four squadrons strong. Our task was a road recce of the route from Abbeville to Dieppe. We were to check on any movement of German armor. How I was able to find Freddie in the dark I'll never know. There were no navigation lights used and the join-up was on the deck. We set course for our penetration point a few miles south of the planned troop landing point. I was stepped up on Freddie as we were just a few feet off the water. About halfway across the Channel, an inverted cone of fire and searchlights at Dieppe hove into view. We later learned that RAF Boston bombers were attacking the heavy guns in the cliffs north of the beach. They had a terrible time of it. Our navigation problem was solved by all this action at the target. It also made stationkeeping with the other plane easy. That was a mixed blessing, for as soon as we crossed the coast Freddie's plane vanished in the inky black. I tried to finish the mission alone. It was much too dark and I could make out nothing on the ground. No roads, no vehicle traffic, nothing was visible. We both returned to Gatwick, alone and with no damage. That was the end of my first mission for the day.

My second mission later in the day was the same as the first—weaver for Freddie Clarke on the same road recce. Again we were to look for German armor en route to the battle site on the Dieppe beaches.

The weather had turned out fine and sunny, not a cloud in the sky. Visibility was unlimited, takeoff and rendezvous were routine, on the deck as usual. We set off on the same course we had covered not so long before. No other planes were sighted on the first three-quarters of the Channel crossing. That all changed as we approached the French coast. Starting at sea level and going all the way up to contrail level, the sky was full of fighters in one massive dogfight. I was busy, but in hurried glances I counted seven parachutes at one time.

A couple of miles short of landfall, I spotted four FW-190s off to our right at about 1,500 feet. Their course and speed were going to put them directly overhead when we crossed the beach. Radio silence was moot at this point, so I called Freddie with the Tallyho. There was no answer. Freddie, busy with the navigation, did not hear the warning nor see the 190s. He turned left underneath the 190s and headed up to intersect our target road. I wasn't all that thrilled by this procedure and called to warn Freddie again. No response; there was obviously no radio link between us. I knew things were going to get interesting.

We reached the road we were to recce in no time, and Freddie turned right, toward Abbeville. This put us in the ideal position for the FWs to attack. I had swung very wide to Freddie's left when we made the turn. This put me right over town, dusting the chimney tops. I believe the FWs had lost sight of me as I had stayed underneath them. My plan was to cut off the lead 190 before he could open fire on Freddie. My timing all went to pot when a crashing Spitfire forced me into a sharp left turn to avoid a collision. That gave the FW pilot time to get into firing position, and he hit Freddie's Mustang with his first burst. It wasn't a very hard hit, but it was obviously terminal. Glycol was streaming from the radiator, but there was no fire.

I was able to get a long-range shot at the leader, but I had to break hard right as the number-two man was having a go at me. He missed and made a big mistake when he slid by my left side. It was a very easy shot, and I hit him hard. His engine caught fire and smoked heavily. The cockpit canopy came flying off, so I hit him hard again. I knew he was a goner as he fell off to the right, toward the trees.

The last pair of 190s had vanished so I turned back toward Dieppe to look for Freddie's Mustang. There he was, heading for the harbor at 1,000 feet with the FW trailing behind. The 190 was a bit offset to his right and not firing. The glycol stream from the Mustang was very thin, so I knew the engine had little time left. Before I could get into good gun range of the 190, the pilot started to slide dead astern of Freddie. It is my opinion that he had held off firing up until then in the hope that Freddie would crash-land. An intact copy of the Mustang would have been a big bonus. In any case, I had to try to stop him, so I gave a short high-deflection burst at him. I was hoping to get his attention, and it worked. He broke hard left into my attack. Freddie was in controlled flight and heading for the harbor as I turned after the 190.

I now had my hands full with the FW. The fight seemed to go on forever, but of course that was not the case. I could outturn him, but I was able to gain the advantage only a bit at a time. Just as I would get into position to fire, he would break off and streak inland. It never entered my mind to follow him deeper into France then, nor would it now. He would come back at me as soon as I started for the coast, and we would start our turning competition all over again. During one of these circles, I had to dodge another crashing plane. This time it was a Bf-109. The FW pilot got his only shot at me then. The deflection was too great, but I was very impressed by the firepower that came out of his 20mm cannons. It was apparent to me that my opponent was highly competent, and so I was ready to call it a draw as soon as I could.

I had noticed that he was very concerned when his wingtips started to stream vapor trails during the high-G turns. As the entire fight had taken place in the treetops, a high-speed stall would have been the end of it. The planes of those days lost speed as a result of G forces applied during our ring-around-the-rosies. As our speed decreased, the other pilot would use the superior power of his BMW engine, breaking away inland. He could pull out of range before I could fire. The timing of one of these breaks was such that I could get my Mustang up to speed and head for the coast. This last break had given me a good start, and I headed for the south end of the harbor. I couldn't turn away from the ships assembled there as he would have caught me. All the ships were under attack, so they let fly at me. I don't blame them because, with all the smoke, there was no way they could recognize my plane. History records what kind of time they were having. The 190 did not follow my trip over the harbor and I was not hit by the fire.

Halfway across the Channel, I flew directly under a gaggle of Ju-88 bombers and Bf-109 fighters. They were the survivors of an attack on Southhampton and had taken heavy losses. We ignored each other, and the rest of the trip was without thrills. My Mustang was undamaged, and I kept telling everyone that Freddie should have made the harbor and ditched. I don't know how much I was believed. The action over Dieppe was very heavy, with mounting losses. There was talk of a third mission, this time as leader with Ray McQuoid as weaver. This did not come to pass or I would not be here to write these words. We later learned that the RAF fighters were under orders not to cross the coastline. It is no surprise that the heavy losses were sustained by the Mustangs as they tried to penetrate inland in pairs.

The squadron returned to Croydon the same day. We spent a very somber evening in the mess. Freddie was missing, our only loss. The two RAF Mustang squadrons had taken severe losses. The day had been a disaster for the Canadian troops. There was no cause for celebration. I went to bed in my quarters, a requisitioned house at the foot of the gardens of the mansion on Silver Lane in Purley that was our mess. About five the next morning, my door burst open. I was grabbed in a bear hug by what smelled like a huge clump of seaweed. It was Freddie Clarke, rescued by the amphibious forces, just as I had advertised on my return from the mission. His head sported a huge bandage that covered the severe cuts he had received in the ditching. We had been warned that ditching a Mustang could be hazardous to your health. Freddie had no choice. He was rescued, unconscious, by a brave soldier. The destroyer that brought Freddie back sustained heavy damage and losses while under savage attacks.

Freddie and I both saw the FW-190 crash, so the first Mustang victory was confirmed for me and 414 RCAF Squadron. The Mustang went on to great things.

So did Holly Hills. He left the RCAF on November 8, 1942, and transferred directly into the U.S. Navy. After returning to the United States in December, he was posted to a base in Florida for indoctrination and then sent on to a base near Miami for gunnery training. Next, Lieutenant (jg) Hills served as an instructor for three months before being posted to a newly formed fighter squadron, VF-32.

As a division leader with VF-32, flying from the USS Langley, *Lieutenant Holly Hills downed three Imperial Navy Zero fighters, and probably downed a fourth, over Truk on April 29, 1944. And he achieved ace status when he downed a Zero over Manila on September 21, 1944. The very next day, Holly Hills was shot down by ships' fire off Subic Bay. He was picked up by the submarine USS* Haddo *and remained aboard until she docked at Freemantle at the end of her war patrol.*

Hills received a regular commission after World War II and rose to the rank of commander before retiring in 1962. By his own reckoning, Holly Hills's most important accomplishment in twenty-five years of military flying was that no one who went out with him—be it in combat or peacetime—failed to return. Indeed, none of his pilots died while he was in command of two U.S. Navy squadrons later in his career. "You can well imagine," he says, "how very, very proud I am of those statistics, which were very rare in those days."

SLAUGHTER OVER CAP BON

Captain DARRELL WELCH, USAAF
27th Fighter Squadron, 1st Fighter Group
Cap Bon, Tunisia—April 5, 1943

Darrell Gail Welch was born on March 13, 1918, in Goldthwaite, Texas, and raised in Midland. He entered the University of Texas in 1935.

In the summer of 1940, I was making plans to return to the University of Texas in Austin to complete work for a petroleum engineering degree. My college career had been interrupted by a severe cash shortage. During the two years I attended, I had worked at two jobs but received only $15 per month in cash. The National Youth Administration (NYA) job paid twenty-five cents per hour, but was limited to $15 per month. My other job was waiting tables and washing dishes in a small family-style restaurant, where I received food for pay, but no tips. My NYA job was in the Journalism Building, where I helped the janitor sweep and mop from 5:45 to 7:45 each morning, before I attended my 8:00 class. During my sophomore year, I was promoted to the Geology Building, where I duplicated oil-well logs. My older brother helped me with enough money to buy books and pay tuition each semester, but at the end of my second year, he got married and my "student loan" program ceased. The nation was in the depths of the Great Depression and I had no other source of funds, so I started working and saving for my eventual return to college.

The gathering war clouds in Europe and the announced date of October 15, 1940, for registration for the Selective Service draft here at home caused me to rethink my plans. I had heard that two years of college credits met the educational requirements for the U.S. Army's Flying Cadet program. I had the requisite credits, and did not relish the idea of being drafted and marching with a rifle on my shoulder. Although I had never been in an airplane, flying suddenly seemed like a desirable alternative. The more I thought about flying, the more it appealed to me, and I also became convinced that I could succeed.

In July, my older sister was planning a trip to Austin, Texas, from Midland, where I had graduated from high school and was now living and working. I rode with her to Austin, then borrowed her car, and drove to Randolph Field outside San Antonio to get application forms for the Flying Cadet program. Looking back, I guess I did not know how to get the forms by mail, or I was in a hurry to get my application in.

I was soon sent to Fort Bliss in El Paso for my physical examination at the William Beaumont Hospital. I rode the Greyhound bus to El Paso, then early the next morning caught the city bus to Fort Bliss. All seemed to be going well until, at the end of the exams, I was returned to one of the many stations for a recheck. There, they again checked my blood pressure, heart rate, and rate of recovery after exercising and while at rest. During the recheck, I mustered enough courage to ask what the problem was. I was told that I had failed my "Snyder." Of course, I had never heard the term, and frankly have heard little of it since. Apparently it was a combination of a number of readings. When I returned to my hotel, I wasted no time getting directions to a doctor's office. Fortunately, a medical building was only a block away. Upon entering the building, I looked at the register, selected a name from several doctors listed, rode the elevator to the third floor, and was immediately ushered into the doctor's office by his receptionist. After hearing my story, he checked my blood pressure, and assured me there was no problem. He told me I was just over-anxious to pass the exams. He said he could give me a pill to insure that I would pass the exams, but it was not really necessary. He told me to eat a light evening meal and consume no coffee, alcohol, or meat. He also prescribed "early to bed." The next morning, I was to eat no breakfast and drink only a glass of water. I passed the tests with flying colors but was brought back a month later for a final check. Needless to say, I followed the doctor's orders again. On October 14, 1940, one day before the start of the Draft, I took my oath in Lubbock, Texas, and boarded a train for Glendale, California, where I entered Primary Pilot training at one of the Cal-Aero contract schools.

The cadets were housed in a building that was formerly a night club. We slept in the ballroom. The planes were hangared nearby, at Glendale Terminal, where I occasionally saw Wallace Beery and Jimmy Stewart when they came there to fly. Because the area was too congested for local cadet training, each morning the civilian instructors, with one cadet each in tow, would take the PT-17s across the San Fernando Valley, through Newhall Pass, to a wheat field from which we operated. The remaining cadets, along with box lunches, rode buses to the field. Once, while doing acrobatics over the San Fernando Valley, my instructor told me to put the plane into a spin. On about the second rotation, he called my attention to a house below us and told me it was the house of Robert Taylor and Barbara Stanwick.

On several occasions, I saw P-38 prototypes from the nearby Burbank Lockheed factory. The word was that they had only two YP-38s flying.

It was such a beautiful plane that I dreamed of flying it someday. My dream came true about nine months later.

My Basic course was at Randolph Field in San Antonio, where it had all begun six months earlier. Upon graduation, I expected to go across town to Kelly Field for Advanced training, but I was ordered to Barksdale Field near Shreveport, Louisiana, to attend the second class of twin-engine training. We flew B-18s, B-10s, and B-12s, because twin-engine trainers were not yet in the inventory. We studied bomb sights, too, so I fully expected to be assigned to a bombardment group upon graduation. I was surprised and thrilled when, on graduation day, May 29, 1941, five new second lieutenants (me included) were ordered to Selfridge Field, Michigan, and assigned to the 1st Pursuit Group. There I flew P-35s, P-36s, and P-43s for about two months before my squadron, the 27th, became the first in the Army Air Corps to be equipped with the new P-38 Lightning. In September, the 27th went on maneuvers in Texas, Louisiana, Georgia, and South Carolina. We lost one pilot in a mid-air collision while doing simulated combat with a P-40.

I was on leave in Midland on December 7, 1941, getting ready to take my bride of a few months back to Michigan. Two days later, when I arrived at Selfridge Field, the entire group had gone to the West Coast. At about the same time, another 27th pilot returned from his honeymoon. He was actually getting married while the Japanese were bombing Pearl Harbor, but he did not know until he emerged from the chapel. He and I were kept at Selfridge Field to ferry two P-38s that were undergoing repair to the West Coast. Unfortunately, he was one of the first three pilots from the group to be killed in North Africa.

The 27th Pursuit Squadron was stationed at Mines Field—later Los Angeles International Airport—where we flew dawn patrols, stood alert, trained, and experienced at least one false-alarm Japanese air attack. I flew one aerial gunnery mission against a towed target sleeve, and two ground-target missions while we were there. The ground targets were at Muroc Dry Lake—later Edwards Air Force Base—where we fired, landed on the lake bed, and scored our own targets. This now seems like very little preparation for combat against experienced German pilots.

In April, I was given command of B Flight and also promoted to first lieutenant. The other two flight commanders were also graduates of the twin-engine school at Barksdale Field. To my knowledge, we were the only twin-engine graduates ever assigned to the 1st Pursuit Group. How fortunate I was.

In early June, we left California for Bangor, Maine, to begin preparations for the first mass flight of fighter planes across the Atlantic. Since the P-38 had so little navigation equipment, the plan called for four P-38s to fly formation on one B-17. To measure that we could keep in formation in case of inclement weather, we practiced flying in heavy clouds. The first four ships of my flight were assigned to a B-17 of the 98th Heavy Bombardment Group piloted by Lieutenant Lipsky. He took us through some very dark clouds, but we were able to keep in formation by flying below his wing, so that a larger profile was visible. We never had a problem staying in formation en route overseas. I was later sorry to learn that Lipsky was killed on his second mission in North Africa.

On June 27, 1942, we completed the leg from Bangor to Goose Bay, Labrador. I still recall the Indians who lived near the base, but my most vivid memory is about the size and ferocity of the swarms of mosquitoes we encountered there.

On July 2, my flight made the first of three over-water legs. We flew to Bluie West-1 (BW-1), on the southwest coast of Greenland. The airfield bordered a fjord and lay between two mountains. The only runway was made of wartime pierced steel planking (PSP), and it sloped uphill from the fjord. All planes went into single-file formation and proceeded up the fjord, which became the base leg of the landing approach. The final approach was very short. It followed a 90-degree turn at low altitude just off the end of the runway. After the right turn onto the runway, stopping was easy, because the runway sloped fairly steeply uphill. There was some question about being able to abort a landing and make a successful go-around. I think the P-38 could have done so, but larger planes might not. The pattern was reversed for takeoff: a downhill run from the upper end of the runway followed by a left turn down the fjord was the only pattern available.

On July 6, B Flight left BW-1, climbed over the Greenland ice cap, and arrived safely at Reykjavik, Iceland. The next day, we moved to Patterson Field near Keflavik, where the 27th remained on local air defense for about six weeks.

On August 14, I heard a large aircraft over my Nissen hut billet. I rushed outside to see a German four-engine FW-200 Kondor reconnaissance plane flying directly over our base at only a few hundred feet altitude. The flight on alert, led by the squadron commander, Major Bill Weltman, took off in hot pursuit of the FW-200. P-39s from the 33d Fighter Squadron, which was permanently stationed in Iceland, joined in the chase. Major Weltman's guns jammed, so his wingman, 2d Lieutenant Elza Shahan, made the next pass. The FW-200 had already been set afire by a P-39 pilot, 2d Lieutenant Joseph Shaffer. Shahan later said he planned to fire his guns at close range, then fly underneath the big plane, but instead he fired and flew through it. As he was firing, the plane exploded in a giant blast that scattered debris over Reykjavik Bay. Shahan and Shaffer became the first U.S. pilots to shoot down a German plane in World War II, and both were awarded the Silver Star.

On July 26, all the officers of the 27th Fighter Squadron were assembled in our operations building. To our great surprise, we were joined by General George Marshall and Harry Hopkins, President Roosevelt's special advisor. They were returning to the States after a conference with Prime Minister Winston Churchill. For about an hour, they spoke freely to us about the conference and plans to prosecute the war against Hitler. I felt very fortunate to be that close to two of the most powerful figures on FDR's staff.

On August 22, we completed the final leg of our flight to England. We landed briefly at Stornoway on the Isle of Lewis, then on to Ayr, Scotland. Four days later, we flew to the Midlands to a Royal Air Force base, High Ercall, where we remained until September 15, when we moved to Colerne near Bath. The rest of the 1st Fighter Group was then in the southern part of England.

Orders promoting me to captain caught up with me at High Ercall, and I took my oath on August 27. While at Colerne, we trained with the RAF and escorted B-17s on daylight bombing missions over France. We saw German fighters, but had little contact.

On November 6, the 27th left Colerne for southern England in preparation for the flight to North Africa. Not until I attended a briefing on the November 8 did I learn that our destination was North Africa. The weather was bad. We made abortive attempts to leave on November 12 and 13.

Finally, on the fourteenth, we were successful. We used B-26s for navigation. Once again, it was four P-38s in formation with each B-26. I sat strapped in my P-38 for eight and a half hours enroute to La Senia Airdrome outside Oran. The trip down the Atlantic south from England, through the Straits of Gibraltar, then across the Mediterranean was uneventful for me except for one incident. At a point opposite Gibraltar, near Point Almina, Spanish Morocco, a burst of flak exploded between my plane and the B-26 on which I was flying formation. Fortunately, I was in loose formation, or I might have been an early casualty. I quickly took evasive action by changing speed, altitude, and direction away from land.

Upon arrival at La Senia, we found the runways damaged by bombs, so we were immediately sent to Tafaraoui Airdrome, 20 miles to the south. A week later, the 27th moved to Nouvion, a stubble field next to an old French Foreign Legion post 50 miles east of Tafaraoui.

After abortive missions to Sardinia on November 23 and 24, Tunis on the twenty-fifth, and Bizerte on the twenty-ninth, I finally completed my first bomber-escort mission in North Africa, to Bizerte on November 30. On December 2, we suffered our first losses with three pilots missing (all later confirmed killed) and one pilot hurt in a crash landing.

On December 14, the 1st Fighter Group moved to Biskra Airdrome, on the northern edge of the Sahara Desert. I slept in my pup tent one night, then moved into the Transatlantic Hotel in town. From Biskra, we escorted B-17s, B-26s, and B-25s, on bombing missions into Tunisia and Libya. Later, we did strafing sweeps against Rommel's equipment as he retreated west into Tunisia, where he made his daring attack at Kasserine Pass. One day, I flew a B-17 escort mission in the morning over Kasserine Pass, and that afternoon I escorted P-38s on a strafing mission against German Army tanks in the pass.

While staying at the Transatlantic Hotel, I often saw the famous *Life* Magazine photographer, Margaret Bourke-White. It was rumored that she flew in a B-17 on a combat mission. Ernie Pyle was also there, and he often came to our rooms in the evening to talk about the war and learn more about the life of a P-38 pilot. He published several articles about our group. When I moved into the Transatlantic Hotel, I had two roommates, Ted Runyon, the C Flight commander, and Bert Weil, but they were both shot down. Although injured, both survived and wound up in a German prisoner-of-war camp. Once alone, I did not like the odds, so I quickly recruited more roommates.

On January 18, 1943, I scored my first aerial victory, a Bf-109, that I shot down while on a bomber-escort mission to Tripoli.

The sand storms at Biskra got progressively worse, until we finally lost a pilot and his plane in take-off position when another plane landed on top of him. On February 13, we left the sand storms of Biskra for the mud of Chateaudun-du-Rumel, and traded our hotel room for a tent.

On March 23, I got my second victory, another Bf-109 confirmed. First Lieutenant John Wolford also got a 109, and thus became the first ace in the squadron. He was later killed in action.

On March 24, I took command of the 27th Fighter Squadron. Like many pilots during the war, I had gone from a new second lieutenant replacement pilot to a squadron commander in less than two years. In fact, I was to be promoted to major on May 5.

My most memorable mission occurred on April 5, 1943. I was nearing the end of my tour and expected to return to the States quite soon. I had been overseas almost a year, and in combat most of that time, yet I had only two aerial victories to my credit. Escort duty did not produce many victories, because our job was to protect the bombers. Had we been free to leave them, I'm sure we could have racked up many more kills.

The Allies knew that Rommel was receiving aerial resupply from Sicily in three-engine Ju-52 transports. On April 1, I had led the squadron on a mission to intercept them, but we were turned back by bad weather. The weather started to improve, and by the fifth was just about perfect. On that day, I was assigned to lead the 27th to attack the transports. First Lieutenant Sammy Sears was to lead the 71st Fighter Squadron and provide top cover against the fighters that always accompanied the transports. We were thoroughly briefed on the route they flew, their altitude, and their fighter escort. We were to accompany a B-26 group, which was to be escorted by the 82d Fighter Group (also in P-38s) as they conducted a raid against the fleet of ships that was also resupplying Rommel. At a certain point, I was to leave the B-26s and the 82d Group P-38s and try to intercept the Ju-52s.

I arose very early on the fifth, because I had to fly to the B-26 base for a combined briefing. The weather was continuing to improve, my P-38 seemed to run especially well—Sergeant Kischner always kept my plane in good running order—and I had a sense that this day held promise for a successful intercept of the transports. Of course, we had no radar or electronic means to find the enemy, only dead reckoning.

The combined briefing was very upbeat. We were definitely winning the North Africa campaign. My optimism continued to build. The 1st Fighter Group P-38s were to stay with the B-26s at a low altitude as we flew north to the Mediterranean, then we were to turn northeast and stay far enough out from Tunisia to avoid interception by German fighters.

After the briefing, the pilots from the 27th and 71st squadrons went to our planes and waited for the bombers to take off. After they were all airborne, and the 82d had started to take off, we cranked our engines and taxied to the runway just in time to start our takeoff in pairs. We quickly joined up behind the bombers and their escort. The first part of the flight across Algeria and the Mediterranean was uneventful. Best of all, the weather continued to improve. My anticipation continued to build.

About thirty minutes after we passed north of Tunis on an easterly heading, I beheld a sight I could hardly believe. Directly ahead of the B-26s was a large convoy of ships steaming south. At that time, and in accordance with my orders, I turned southeast so as to intercept the direct air route from Sicily to Tunis. I had not flown more than fifteen minutes before I again beheld another unbelievable sight. Directly ahead of me was a huge formation of oncoming transports, with fighter escort above them. They were about fifty feet above the water in huge V formation and looked like a swarm of locusts in the distance when I first saw them. Later estimates placed the numbers at seventy Ju-52s and thirty-one fighters.

I was elated that, after all the months in combat, I was finally in a position to engage in aerial combat without worrying about protecting bombers.

I called Sammy Sears, the 71st leader, who was to provide top cover, and told him we had found our target. I proceeded directly toward the lead aircraft and, in a head-on attack, simply knocked it out of the sky. As the Ju-52s droned on toward Tunis, we made beam attacks against them. A short burst of machine-gun and cannon fire would set the transports ablaze, and they would go into the water. Each time I circled for another pass, I could see the trail of crashed planes in the water behind us.

On my third or fourth pass, I saw tracer bullets coming from beneath my plane, toward the Ju-52 I was preparing to shoot down. At that moment, a P-38 flew into view below me, so close that I don't see how we missed colliding. I don't know how he missed seeing me, either, as I was just above him. He was obviously concentrating on his target. I aborted that pass and circled for another attack.

The air was filled with planes in a wild melee. In addition to the fighters firing at us, the Ju-52s each had a rearward mounted machine gun. My plane sustained several hits from them. Somewhere in there, I lost my wingman. Nobody saw him go down, but he never returned and was presumed killed.

As I started what turned out to be my final pass, Sammy Sears called to say it was getting too hot as more fighter planes were coming out from Tunis. He said he was exiting to the north, to our right. Despite this unwelcome news, I pressed my attack and shot down my third Ju-52. I had actually shot down four, but I claimed only the three that could be confirmed.

As the Ju-52 went down, I made what proved to be an almost fatal mistake. I had been attacking the left side of the Ju-52 formation, and was making left turns to position myself for the next pass. However, I instinctively turned left again, away from the direction I needed to go to exit the area. My last attack had carried me over land at Cape Bon, and I was alone in the midst of German planes. All the P-38s were now ahead of me and moving away. I knew I was in serious trouble. I was at full throttle, heading for the safety of the other P-38s, when I felt and saw the effects of a hail of bullets. I looked back and saw two Bf-109s firing at me from fairly close range. I knew I could not evade by turning, so I dived, zoomed, and skidded. I was avoiding most of their fire, but a lot of damage had already been done. The initial burst of fire had broken my cockpit canopy behind me, and a piece of Plexiglas had hit my right shoulder with great force. I assumed I had been hit by a bullet, as I had heard that in the heat of battle one could be shot and not realize it right away. Also, the supercharger on my left engine was knocked out, so I could get only partial power on that engine.

In those brief moments, a myriad of thoughts raced through my mind. I looked at the Mediterranean, lying so peacefully below me, and had a mental picture of me floating in my dinghy, waiting to be picked up and sent to a German prison camp to join many of my friends who were already there. I was genuinely miffed, because I had just become an ace and would not get back to base to claim my victories. I knew very well that with partial power, despite my evasive maneuvers, it was only a matter of time before the two 109s would land the crippling blow that would knock my plane out of the sky, set it afire, or force me to bail out. I knew that all my group's planes were out of range to help me. I had not called for them for help, nor was I going to do so; it was simply too late. I could not imagine anything that could save me now. I was resigned to my fate, but I continued my evasive actions.

At that instant, I saw the miracle that saved me. Above me, at the 11 o'clock position and heading directly toward me, were two P-38s. Because their propeller spinners were painted a distinctive pattern, I knew they were from the 82d Group, which had escorted the B-26s on the shipping sweep. After their shipping sweep, the 82d joined the Ju-52 "shoot" and chalked up fifteen airplanes destroyed. They barely missed me as they dove head-on into the two 109s that had me in their sights. To this day, I do not know if they shot down the 109s or caused them to break off their attack on me, but I do know that I received no more fire and was able to make it back to base. Also to this day, I do not know the names of the 82d pilots who saved me from being shot down or possibly killed. I have held a warm spot in my heart for pilots from the 82d Fighter Group ever since.

Our mission received wide press coverage, since we destroyed thirty-one German and Italian airplanes. My hometown paper told of my victories in banner headlines. Many people around the country sent clippings to my wife and my parents. On April 11, I flew to Algiers to make a radio broadcast about the mission on NBC's "Army Hour." And for leading the mission, I was awarded the Silver Star.

I led the group on another Ju-52 sweep on April 19, but we were unable to find any. However, our mission of the fifth was followed by other successful sweeps. On April 10, P-38s from the 71st Fighter Squadron shot down twenty Ju-52s and eight fighters. And, next day, P-38s got twenty-six Ju-52s and five fighters. We had put a serious obstacle in Germany's efforts to resupply Rommel's troops in North Africa.

I completed my combat tour exactly one month after my most memorable mission and was promoted to major the same day. Three days later, on the May 8, Captain Eddie Rickenbacker visited our group. He had been a member of the famous 94th "Hat in the Ring" Squadron during World War I, and became the leading American ace during that war. (In 1943, the 94th was one of the three squadrons of the 1st Fighter Group). Until Rickenbacker's visit, I do not recall any high-ranking American officer or civilian becoming emotional during talks to our pilots. Most approached our role in the war in a businesslike way. However, Rickenbacker exhorted us to go for Hitler's "jugular vein." Throughout his talk, he had "blood in the eye" and emotion ringing in his voice. It was too late for me, though; I was going home. However, I'm sure his speech inspired many of the newer pilots who would wrap up North Africa and go on to Italy and the larger war in Europe.

On May 10, four pilots bade farewell to Chateaudun-du-Rumel and the 1st Pursuit Group as we departed for the good old U.S. of A. Going home with me were 1st Lieutenant George Ross, the best wingman I ever had; Sammy Sears; and 1st Lieutenant Bob Sauer. We were transported to Algiers to receive orders sending us to the Fourth Air Force in San Francisco. After waiting in Algiers for several days, fully expecting to be sent home by boat, they announced we would travel by air. We rode C-46s and C-47s across Africa to Dakar, French West Africa, and crossed the Atlantic in an LB-30, the transport version of the B-24. We arrived in Florida eleven months after leaving Maine.

Following a series of assignments on the West Coast, Major Darrell Welch was ordered to the Panama Canal Zone and assigned to the fighter-defense command there. When the war ended, he requested release from the service so he could complete work on his degree. Welch graduated from the University of Texas in 1947 and was hired by Gulf Oil, but when he received a regular Air Force commission only five months later, he returned to active duty. He immediately applied for graduate school, was sent back to the University of Texas to complete work for an MBA in management, and graduated in 1950.

Overseas assignments took Welch, who was promoted to colonel in 1953, to Japan and the Philippines. He also served in the Pentagon and attended the Air War College both as a student and instructor. He retired from the Air Force in 1970 to teach business management for a decade.

BOMBER ESCORT TO PARIS

Major JACK PRICE, USAAF
84th Fighter Squadron, 78th Fighter Group
Paris—November 26, 1943

Jack Clayton Price was born in Grand Junction, Colorado on July 26, 1918, and raised on a small farm in a rural area east of the town. He attended Mesa Junior College in Grand Junction for two years, was accepted into the U.S. Army Air Corps Flying Cadet program in March 1941, and earned his wings and commission with Class 41-H at Mather Field, California on October 31, 1941. Second Lieutenant Price initially flew Curtiss P-36 Hawks and Curtiss P-40 Warhawks with the 14th Pursuit Group at March Field, California, and had approximately ten hours in the former and sixteen hours in the latter by December 7, when Pearl Harbor was attacked by the Japanese.

The 14th Group was transferred to Hamilton Field, California, in early 1942 and began flying Lockheed P-38 Lightning twin-engine fighters. When the group was split in two in order to create the new 78th Fighter Group, Price was posted to the 78th as a flight commander in the 84th Fighter Squadron, which began flying out of the municipal airport at Oakland, California.

In late 1942, the 78th Fighter Group was shipped to Great Britain, where it was posted to Goxhill Airdrome in East Anglia on December 1, 1942. Once established, the group continued training in P-38s, getting ready to fly escort missions in support of the U.S. Army Air Forces daylight bombing effort. In February 1943, however, P-38 groups in combat in North Africa had an urgent need for airplanes and trained pilots, so all the 78th Fighter Group's line pilots below the position of flight commander were sent with their aircraft to North Africa.

In time, our 78th Fighter Group cadre in England was reequipped with Republic P-47B Thunderbolt fighters, which few of us had seen on the ground before. New pilots were assigned, most of them fresh from fighter schools in the United States, but there was also a sprinkling of combat-experienced American pilots who transferred to the group from RCAF and RAF units. Also, a new P-47 group, the 4th, was activated in England to take advantage of the transfer to the U.S. Army Air Forces of Royal Air Force American Eagle squadron personnel.

The remanned 78th Fighter Group underwent several weeks of intensive training and was transferred to Duxford Airdrome in April 1943, and we flew our first operational combat mission on April 8. Early missions were for the most part uncontested fighter sweeps over the coasts of Belgium and France.

The heavily armed P-47B, with its 2,000 horsepower Pratt & Whitney Double Wasp radial engine, used so much fuel that all missions were fairly short fighter sweeps. There were no auxiliary fuel tanks available in England at the time, so the 4th, 56th, and 78th Fighter groups were able to escort the bomber force for only a short distance on penetration and then pick them up again for withdrawal support as they approached the English Channel.

My first clash in the air occurred on July 14, 1943, while we were escorting the bomber force on withdrawal in the area of Abbeyville, France. I shot down an FW-190 fighter out of a flight of four that was trying to position itself for an attack on the bomber force. I next destroyed two FW-190s on July 30, during withdrawal support of the bomber force returning from a raid on the Focke-Wulf assembly plant at Kassel, Germany.

The action on the July 30 mission was a first in many respects. It was the first time the entire VIII Fighter Command escort force was equipped with auxiliary fuel tanks, and it was the first time American fighters engaged a large enemy fighter force and came away with an overwhelming victory. We were outnumbered by at least three-to-one odds but were able to maneuver into attacking position with very little difficulty. The main reason for this success was that the German fighter pilots and *Luftwaffe* high command did not believe we could possibly be that far inland and were not expecting to see a defensive force at all.

Although seven P-47s were lost, sixteen enemy fighters were

destroyed by the 78th Fighter Group alone. In addition, eight others were destroyed earlier and later by members of the 56th and 4th Fighter groups. Captain Chuck London, of the 78th's Group's 83d Fighter Squadron, shot down two German fighters and thus became the first Army Air Forces ace in the European Theater. And the 84th's squadron commander, Lieutenant Colonel Gene Roberts, became the first VIII Fighter Command pilot to shoot down three enemy aircraft in a single action.

We continued to fly combat escort and sweeps over northeastern Europe, and on October 20, 1943, I damaged a Bf-109 over Dinant, Belgium.

During the months since our important July 30 victory over the Netherlands, the VIII Fighter Command had substantially increased the number of its operational fighter groups. Two P-38 groups had arrived in England, and several new P-47 groups were in place and operational. This permitted the Eighth Air Force to split its operations and bomb a variety of targets in different areas on the same day.

On November 26, the main VIII Bomber Command force of more than 350 B-17s and 77 B-24s was sent to Germany to hit submarine pens and industrial targets in the Bremen area. More than 350 P-47s and P-38s were assigned to support this operation into Germany. Enemy reaction was expected to focus on the main bomber force into Germany, while little or no reaction was expected against a raid against a ball-bearing plant in Paris. The 78th Fighter Group was assigned the task of providing target and withdrawal support for the VIII Bomber's Command's 3d Heavy Bombardment Wing, which was undertaking the Paris mission. By this time, I was a major in command of the 84th Fighter Squadron.

We flew a beefed-up squadron of twenty-four aircraft—eight more than usual at that time—and we took off from Duxford at 0930 hours. We made rendezvous with the bombers at approximately 1025 hours at 29,000 feet, so far according to plan. I was leading Bayland Red flight in the first section of eight aircraft. We picked up the bomber force in the Paris area as they were coming off the bomb run, They were not being attacked, but shortly after they had passed over Paris, bandits were reported below them and just above the clouds, the tops of which were at approximately 10,000 to 12,000 feet.

As we started down, a B-17 in the lower box of bombers blew up in flames. We could see five or six enemy fighters around the bombers. Lieutenant Colonel Gene Roberts, by then the group deputy commander, was leading our group. As he started down to attack the enemy aircraft, I saw two FW-190s flying parallel to the bomber force at about 20,000 feet. They were 1,200 to 1,500 yards ahead of me and heading for the front of the bomber formation in order to make head-on attacks. I started after them, pulling 47 inches of mercury (manifold pressure) and 2,600 rpm.

While growing up, I had frequently hunted and fished in the western Colorado area. As a result of this bird-hunting experience, I fully understood deflection shooting and could judge distances, speed of targets, and angle-off required to hit a flying target. This background greatly enhanced my ability to apply the correct geometry to air-to-air combat and deflection shooting.

I closed on the FW-190s very slowly. When I was 600 yards from the 190s, the second aircraft broke off and split-essed down. I continued to close on the first one, which was then about in position for a head-on pass at the B-17s. I saw that I was not catching him fast enough to stop him from making his pass, so I opened fire on him at about 500 yards. As I opened fire, I observed heavy strikes and flashes on the left wing root, close to the fuselage. I gave him a three-second burst, at which point he started turning to the left. I started giving him deflection and opened fire again. This time, I closed to about 100 yards and scored heavy hits. He stalled out, fell off to the right, and started down, spinning and trailing smoke. My wingman and element leader observed pieces falling off as the enemy aircraft spun down and trailed smoke into the cloud deck at 10,000 feet.

At this time, I looked around and discovered that I was headed almost head-on into the bomber formation, so I broke hard to the right and down to avoid flying through the bombers.

As I reformed my flight at the 11 o'clock position on the first box of bombers, I saw twenty-five to thirty enemy aircraft climbing up underneath us at 2,000 to 5,000 feet below us. They were slightly below my flight and directly in front of us at approximately 1,000 yards. I saw five Bf-109s in line-abreast formation trying to get into position to make head-on attacks on the bomber formation. I dove slightly below their level, hit the throttle, and closed to about 600 yards. At this time, the last 109 in the formation flipped over and split-essed away. I closed in on the next in line from dead astern and opened fire at 300 yards, giving him a two-second burst. The 109 blew up and later caught on fire. Meanwhile, the other three enemy aircraft split-essed away.

I looked around for my flight as I pulled up into a zoom climb. The second element was about 1,000 yards behind me and 1,000 feet below. About 4,000 feet lower, I saw, a Bf-109 was climbing toward them. I called them and told them to pull up. Then I looked around to see if there were any other enemy aircraft in the vicinity. When I looked back, the 109 I had seen beneath my second element was closing rapidly on the number-four man, 2d Lieutenant Wayne Dougherty. I called Dougherty to break hard left into the 109. The enemy aircraft must have come up out of a split-S, because of his rapid closing speed.

The 109 fired a very short burst and broke away before I was able to get my sight on him. Although Lieutenant Dougherty broke almost as soon as had I called him, I saw a puff of smoke from his aircraft. He rolled over and dived toward the cloud deck. He was not smoking then.

At this time, we were still in the 11 to 12 o'clock position on the bomber formation and there were no enemy aircraft in the area. I felt that we accomplished our mission to protect the bombers and drive away the German fighters.

We found out later that Lieutenant Dougherty recovered from his dive, but his aircraft was damaged too badly to fly. He bailed out and was a POW for the remainder of the war in Europe.

Jack Price, who on November 26, 1943, became the first Army Air Forces ace born in Colorado, flew eighty-two combat missions with the 78th Fighter Group before completing his combat tour on February 24, 1944. Instead of receiving orders to the United States for leave, however, he was ordered to report the VIII Fighter Command headquarters to serve as a combat operations officer. He spent six months in that job before finally returning home.

Major Jack Price returned to the United Kingdom in September 1944 and was assigned to the 67th Fighter Wing as a combat operations officer and the fighter wing representative on the Eighth Air Force

Combat Film Assessment Board. Six months later, in February 1945, Price was assigned to the 20th Fighter Group as deputy group commander. By the time the war in Europe ended, he had flown an additional 125 combat hours with the 20th Group, in P-51 Mustangs. Major Price was assigned to command the 20th Fighter Group, to bring it back the United States at the end of the war. He remained on active duty after the unit was disbanded at Camp Kilmer in October 1945.

Price was given a Regular Air Force commission in 1947 and continued to fly fighters for most of the rest of his years in the service. He commanded a Florida-based jet squadron during the 1963 Cuban Missile Crisis and retired from the Air Force in 1968 with the rank of lieutenant colonel.

A LONG WAIT

1st Lieutenant BOB CURTIS, USAAF
2d Fighter Squadron, 52d Fighter Group
Lorenzo Nuovo, Italy—February 19, 1944

Robert Charles Curtis was born in Syracuse, New York, on January 3, 1918. He dropped out of college in the summer of 1940 after attending for nearly four years.

In September 1940 I applied to both the Army and the Navy for flight training, hoping to eventually become a fighter pilot (called pursuit pilot in the United States until May 1942). The Army responded much more quickly than the Navy. I attended flight school from January 1, 1941, and received my wings at Craig Field, Alabama, on August 15, 1941, but I was assigned to duty as an instructor in advanced flying training. Not until January 1943 did I start fighter training, in the Bell P-39 Airacobra. In April 1943, I was sent overseas to North Africa and was assigned to the 52d Fighter Group (2d, 4th, and 5th Fighter squadrons), which, along with the 31st Fighter Group, had been equipped with Spitfires as replacements for their P-39s after they moved to Great Britain in June and July of 1942 to prepare for the invasion of North Africa in November.

I joined the 2d Fighter Squadron in early May 1943, about ten days before the end of the North Africa Campaign. I flew no combat missions during the campaign. Shortly thereafter, the 52d Fighter Group was taken out of the Air Support Command and put into the Coastal Command, which relegated us to flying convoy patrols, harbor patrols, and occasional scrambles against enemy reconnaissance planes. Enemy aircraft were seldom encountered.

Although now a fighter pilot, I was not doing what I considered a real fighter pilot's job—engaging enemy aircraft. Our dull work led some of us frustrated fighter pilots to call our squadron The American Beagle Squadron, a play on words reflecting our unhappiness about our situation as Americans flying Spitfires, like the pilots of the American Eagle Squadrons of the RAF, but doing "dog" work.

This work continued until December 1943, first at La Sebala airstrip, just north of Tunis, then at Bocca di Falco airdrome, on the outskirts of Palermo, Sicily. In December, the squadrons of the 52d were sent to Corsica. Our Spitfires, mostly Mark VCs, with a few Mark IXs, had bomb racks added so they could carry a 250-pound bomb under each wing.

From an airstrip at Borgo, about eight miles south of Bastia, on the northeast coast of Corsica, we flew dive-bombing and strafing missions against shipping, railroad traffic, motor transport, bridges, factories, and other targets in the coastal regions of western Italy, from Civitavecchia northward to Genoa. We also flew escort missions for medium bombers, B-25s and B-26s, that were attacking targets in this region. In addition to escort missions, harbor patrols, and scrambles against enemy photo-reconnaissance aircraft, we now flew occasional fighter sweeps, which were efforts to get the German fighters to come up and fight, or to intercept them when they were on missions. They seldom attacked the well-escorted medium bombers. During the "dog" days, from May to December 1943, we encountered enemy aircraft only twice during the missions I flew: first, in June, while on a patrol to protect British warships off Cap Bon, Tunisia; and again in August, on a patrol to protect warships that were shelling coastal targets east of Palermo, Sicily.

In the first instance, we encountered enemy fighters but did not engage them. When we saw each other, our planes dropped their belly tanks and the Germans jettisoned their bombs and departed. We did not chase them because, I presume, we were supposed to stay with the warships. There were about twelve of us and ten of them, six FW-190s with bombs, escorted by four Bf-109s. In the second encounter, four FW-190s made dive-bombing attacks on the warships, without success. Our lead planes chased them but could not catch them. I never even saw them.

In early November, I came down with jaundice (hepatitis) and didn't fly again until January 5, 1944, two days after my twenty-sixth birthday, rather old for a fighter pilot in those days. My clock was ticking!

My first personal encounter with enemy fighters did not occur until February 16, 1944, when I was in one of two six-plane flights on a fighter sweep in the region between Orvieto and Perugia, about sixty-five miles north of Rome. Our six-plane flight was in line-astern formation, with the planes about fifty feet apart and stepped to the right and down, slightly, so the pilots could easily see the planes ahead of them. I was leading the last two-plane element, and a veteran of the North Africa Campaign was my wingman.

I remember seeing six or so Bf-109s, flying line astern a few hundred yards to our right and about 3,000 feet above us. They were moving northward as we were, and nearly parallel to us at about the same speed. Our formation continued on course and no orders were given by the flight leader.

As I was watching the 109s, I saw my wingman make a sharp climbing turn toward them. This maneuver startled me, since I was the element leader, and he was supposed to stay with me. But I quickly recovered and immediately called him on the radio saying that I was following him.

As he climbed toward the 109s, one of them dived toward him. As it passed his plane I pulled my plane up into a vertical attitude in order to fire at it. I wasn't able to line up on it properly, but I fired anyway, out of sheer exuberance. I even thought of trying to ram it in the wing, a thought I immediately dismissed. I probably couldn't have done it even if I had tried, because my plane had lost so much speed I couldn't control it that well.

Then my plane stalled completely and fell a few thousand feet before regaining flying speed. This maneuver was undoubtedly a foolish thing for me to do, because it made my plane a good target for an enterprising 109 pilot. But I didn't care. I was so happy to be doing something other than sitting there waiting for the Germans—or our leader—to do something. I was completely in favor of my wingman's action, namely, attack them, and let *them* respond to *our* attack, rather than wait for their attack, then respond to it. Perhaps both flight leaders preferred to avoid a fight if possible. The Germans did not attack the remainder of the flight, probably because it dispersed and offered no easy targets.

The wingman of our flight leader also broke formation to follow my wingman. I didn't see him do so because he was ahead of me in the flight and out of my field of view. He and my wingman eventually caught the 109 and shot it down.

After regaining control of my plane, I was alone and could not see any other planes, so I called my flight, saying I was all alone. As I called them, I was surprised, then embarrassed, to hear the tone of fear in my voice, so I quickly shifted to a bantering tone, adding "and lonely." I think that "all alone and lonely" is a phrase from a popular song, but perhaps I was just improvising.

I then heard one of our pilots call in some FW-190s, so I knew they would not be able to look for me. I set course for base. A little later, I saw two Bf-109s a few thousand feet above me on my right, in close echelon formation. They tracked me for a minute or so, then started down. I thought briefly about taking them on but quickly rejected that idea, and dived my plane into a low overcast that was spreading inland from the Ligurian Sea. I flew on instruments in this overcast for fifteen minutes or so, until I was sure I was over the sea. Then I descended and flew just below the overcast the rest of the way to Borgo.

Although my wingman's action showed a lack of discipline, it also showed an unwillingness to wait "forever" for a leader to do something other than to wait until the Germans attacked. I decided that my wingman, far more experienced than I, had the right idea, and that the next time we encountered enemy fighters, I was going to wait only a short time before *telling* the flight leader that I was taking my wingman and attacking the enemy. As far as I knew, nothing official was said later about my wingman's action, so I felt free to do this. I learned after the war that the flight leader's wingman had been reprimanded.

Just three days later I took such action when I was again in a six-plane flight that encountered at least twelve Bf-109s north of Lake Bolsena near Orvieto. Again the 109s were above us, but behind us. After a short wait, I called the flight leader and said I and my wingman were going to attack the 109s. He acknowledged my message by simply saying "Okay."

I started a climbing 180-degree turn to the left. Just as I started the turn, I saw a 109 diving on our flight from behind. I immediately turned back, and after it passed me on my left and pulled up in a moderate climb, I was able to line up on it and fire my Spitfire's four .303-caliber machine guns and two 20mm cannons. Although I didn't have a gunsight—its light bulb had burned out—I lined up on the 109 as best I could. It immediately rolled over and dived. The German pilot probably knew he was in trouble because of hits on his plane by some of the .303 bullets from the machine guns. We did not use tracer ammunition, and hits by the .303 bullets seldom were visible, but hits by the 20mm cannon shells were easy to see.

The German pilot had made a basic mistake by not climbing steeply so as not to overshoot us. His plane, therefore, became a target, if only briefly. I was able to take advantage of this mistake, and of his next mistake—rolling over and diving instead of continuing to climb. I would have had a hard time staying with or closing on him if he had climbed steeply, because I didn't have sufficient speed after I executed a very tight 360-degree turn. After my turn was completed, his plane was still within firing range, but it was pulling away from me. It was something of a miracle of timing that I was able to fire on his plane and get some hits while it was still within range.

After the 109 rolled over and dived, I rolled over and followed it. The plane dived for about 1,000 feet, then pulled into a very tight left turn, rolled over again, and dived. It did this about three times.

The second time it pulled out of a dive and turned, I was about 75 yards behind and slightly above it, and turning with it. I was able to turn more tightly than it, so that it disappeared beneath the nose of my plane. I fired a two-second burst, and then pushed the nose of my plane down so I could see my target. I saw a cannon shell strike the fuselage about four feet behind the cockpit, and a little stream of white smoke was coming from the radiator under the right wing, which had been hit by .303 machine-gun bullets.

Shortly after the 109 was hit, its pilot jettisoned the canopy. I had to pull up to avoid overrunning the airplane. Then I rolled around and got back on its tail as it went into another very tight level left turn. I stayed in the turn with it, but I could not turn tightly enough to get another shot at it. Then it rolled over once more and started down, turning slightly to the left. I saw some small pieces flying off the fuselage, and the radiator was emitting a little more white smoke.

The 109 then leveled off at about 500 feet and flew a slightly weaving course southward. I thought that the pilot might be trying to bail out. I debated whether to give him some time, or to fire again. I decided that I couldn't wait, because someone might be lining up on me, so I fired. I saw cannon-shell strikes all over the 109. It flew on for a few moments then flipped onto its back and flew along, more or less straight and level, into a hillside. It seems to me that because the 109, after it flipped over, flew straight and level for a few seconds before crashing into the hillside, the pilot may have been trying to bail out but didn't know how close he was to the ground, or that there was a hill ahead of him. Perhaps his windshield was covered with oil, and/or he was injured and not aware of his situation.

I looked around for other aircraft, friendly or hostile. Seeing none, I headed back to base, with mixed emotions—elation over the victory, but also guilt over not giving the pilot more of a chance to bail out. I knew that someone in Germany would be unhappy.

When I got back to base, I did a victory roll, something I had long thought would never happen. After I landed, someone told me that a pilot in the other flight on this mission had been shot down. He was the flight leader's wingman who had been reprimanded for breaking formation on the sixteenth. After the war, he told me that he had wanted to attack the German fighters but had remained in formation because of the reprimand. His plane was hit by a 20mm shell fired by a 109 that dived on their flight. The shell went through the instrument panel and gas tank before taking out the engine. It started a fire and, after some trouble opening the canopy, the pilot bailed out. His chute opened before he hit the ground, and he was quickly captured. A short time later, he met the

German pilot who had shot him down, and the German said he had fired from far out of range and was surprised by the hit. One of the Spitfire pilots in that flight told me that the German had pulled up into a near-vertical climb to avoid overrunning their Spitfires, so clearly he was a cautious guy. This loss certainly illustrates the hazards of not being aggressive—or not calling a break soon enough!

More than a half-century after the event, I learned the identity and fate of the pilot of the 109 I shot down that day. He was *Oberleutnant* Rolf Klippgen, the newly appointed *staffel kapitaen* (squadron captain) of *Staffel* 7, *Gruppe* III of *Jagdgeschwader* (Fighter Wing) 53. A *Luftwaffe* report of the incident speculates that he was attempting a belly landing and was killed when the airplane flipped over.

I did not encounter another enemy plane until May 24, after we had given up our Spitfires and acquired P-51B Mustangs and started escorting B-17s and B-24s over southern and eastern Europe. Then, for two months, we encountered enemy fighters frequently and the squadron and group ran up a good score, including thirteen more for me. Thereafter, encounters became infrequent as German fighters were moved northward out of our area, to oppose the Allied forces invading Europe.

Bob Curtis's score indeed shot up with the advent of the 52d Fighter Group as a bomber-escort unit over southern Europe. On May 20, 1944, 1st Lieutenant Bob Curtis was made the commanding officer of the 2d Fighter Squadron, and on May 24 he downed one Bf-109 and damaged an FW-190 and two Bf-109s. He downed an FW-190 on June 6, and attained ace status on the morning of June 11 when he downed three Bf-109s on an escort mission to Romania. After that, he scored nine more victories, the final one being an FW-190 he downed on August 23, 1944. Curtis was promoted to the rank of captain on June 17, 1944, and to the rank of major on August 17.

Major Bob Curtis returned to the United States in September 1944 and served as the commanding officer of a P-40 squadron until August 1945.

LITTLE FRIENDS

Colonel MORT MAGOFFIN, USAAF
362d Fighter Group, Ninth Air Force
Near Kaiserlautern, Germany—April 24, 1944

Morton David Magoffin was born in Deerwood, Minnesota, on February 1, 1916. Following his graduation from high school, he sought and won an appointment to West Point in 1933 for just one reason—to pursue his life-long dream of flying military airplanes. Magoffin was commissioned a second lieutenant upon his graduation with the Class of 1937 and he turned directly to earning his wings, which were pinned on him at Kelly Field, Texas, on October 3, 1938.

By December 7, 1941, Captain Magoffin was serving in the headquarters of the 15th Pursuit Group at Wheeler Field, Oahu, and soon thereafter he was transferred to the headquarters of the Hawaiian Air Force and the VII Fighter Command. On March 1, 1943, Lieutenant Colonel Magoffin was appointed to command the new 362d Fighter Group, which was forming and beginning its training at Westover Field, Massachusetts, for eventual service as a ground-support unit in the invasion of northern Europe. The 362d Fighter Group, by then equipped with P-47s, arrived in England on November 30, 1943, as the first Thunderbolt unit assigned to the Ninth Air Force, a headquarters that had itself only just arrived in England following service in North Africa.

Colonel Magoffin aggressively sought every type of combat assignment for his P-47 group, and he won many a battle to gain combat experience for his pilots and keep his unit as well honed as he could. In the early days of the 362d Fighter Group's deployment in England, most assignments consisted of a routine fare of bomber-escort missions, and that sometimes meant air-to-air combat. In fact, following the 362d's combat debut on February 8, 1943—escorting a milk run to France—and its first actual combat on February 10, Colonel Magoffin's P-47 pilots began turning in victory claims at a slow but steady rate.

For the morning of April 24, 1944, we received a good mission, a deep escort of the heavy bombers on a full-scale strategic strike against important *Luftwaffe* airdromes in southern Germany. I felt I had to go.

Normally, the VIII Fighter Command assigned the most attractive missions to its own fighter units and left the dregs and milk runs for those of us in the Ninth Air Force while we waited for the invasion of France, which was our principal reason for being there.

I arrived on the flight line just in time for "Start engines," so I had to finish my pre-flight checks as we taxied out. To my dismay, I found that my electric gun sight did not work, but I planned to change the bulb en route to the target area, and so I let the matter ride. Nine times out of ten, changing the bulb would solve the problem, just as it does at your desk lamp or kitchen light. When it didn't, I shrugged my shoulders and said to myself, Well, I probably won't need it anyhow. I've never aborted the leadership and can't now for that piddling matter. So I promptly forgot about it.

Nothing eventful happened during our period of escorting a segment of the stream of B-17s, so after remaining with the bombers about five minutes overtime, I called for the group to head for home. However, within a very few minutes, we got word that some of the 2d Bombardment Division B-24s in the area were under attack by Bf-109s and would appreciate help from any "little friends" available. Following a quick calculation based on a stronger desire to see some action than a sense of what was prudent, I called out, "Everyone with one hundred eighty-five gallons or more who wants to, do a one-eighty and come with me; Turk [Major Charles Teschner, commanding officer of the 378th Fighter Squadron], take the rest of the group home,"

I figured that we could hurry back east for about fifty miles, get involved for a few minutes, and still have about two hours of gas to get home on. In retrospect, I was a bit foolhardy in not showing appropriate concern for the usual headwinds we would face all the way back to England.

Upon looking around, I found that my Red Flight of four was still intact and that four volunteers were following us as an additional flight.

After about ten minutes at increased speed back east, we could see the B-24s in the distance. Suddenly, several 109s dived right through us. I called out, "Drop extra tanks. Red Flight will attack. Yellow Flight, stay up for high cover." And down the four of us went, rapidly closing on the 109s.

I pushed my "Guns & Camera" toggle switch, but to my horror, no sight came on. And then a funny, fortunate thing happened. As I skidded about 30 yards off to the rear Jerry's right, I smiled and waved. He waved back and steepened his dive away from me to the left. What a break! The P-47 would outdive anything in the air, so I was a cinch to overhaul him again. On the other hand, had he hit his right rudder to skid over behind me, I might not be writing this account. Certainly, I'd have had to kick hard left rudder to dive under and behind him at full power to avoid being an easy target.

In no time at all, I found myself relentlessly pursuing a dodging target just above the trees. I hoped my wingman was protecting my tail as I fired two short, poorly aimed bursts at less than 100 yards. I was quite sure I didn't hit the 109, but my shooting caused the pilot to look back repeatedly, and he soon ran into a hill. Later on, I learned that in the skirmishing behind me, my number-four man, 2d Lieutenant George Kelly, had been hit and bailed out early. Also, my wingman, 2d Lieutenant Edward MacLean had shot a 109 off my tail while my number-three man, 2d Lieutenant Hayden, had gone past me in pursuit of another Jerry.

Reflecting that we'd done what we could and that perhaps we shouldn't even have gone back to help the bombers, I called out "Well, we're a long way into Germany. Let's go home." A quick retort from my element leader changed things. He said, "Piss on you, Colonel. You beat me to that last guy, and now I'm going to get this one if I have to chase him to Berlin." I replied, "Okay, Hayden, we're coming after you." Although I chuckled at his aggressive determination, I was concerned about the need to disengage him as soon as possible. For one thing, our gas supply was being exhausted rapidly in a high-speed chase, and for another, the P-47D, without paddle prop or water injection, was no match for the 109 at low level.

We were too late! As I closed to about a quarter of a mile, Hayden and the German went into a Lufbery Circle dogfight, and before I could fire, Hayden pulled too tightly and crashed in flames. The Jerry turned more or less into me, so I called to Lieutenant MacLean, "Red-Two. Turn left and I'll turn right. He'll have to choose, then the other can go after him."

The Jerry, who had victory markings on his plane, went after MacLean, and I quickly turned back to get a shot at him. Evidently, I was not in time to prevent him from hitting one wingtip of my wingman's airplane. When he saw me coming, he broke off and headed east.

My handicap of having no gun sight kept me from firing a parting shot. And the dreaded gas shortage caused me to cut the throttle and start a slow climb into the clouds as I headed west and called for Red-2 to tuck it in and save all the gas he could. I figured that we could surely get beyond the Belgian coast in two hours, but it would be nip and tuck to get home if the headwinds were strong. Although a high altitude was desirable for low gas consumption, it took more gas to climb up there, and then the headwinds would very likely increase proportionately. As I recall, I went to about 22,000 feet, as a compromise, and sweated it out. We began a long letdown as we crossed over Belgium. We lucked out and made it safely into our base at Headcorn, near Maidstone in Kent, in about two hours and ten minutes.

In the aftermath, I fretted a lot about this mission. Should I have gone or aborted? We lost two good men, though ultimately I felt better when we learned that Kelly was a prisoner. Surely we had helped protect the B-24s from the 109s by pulling some of them away on a diversion, and that was the main mission of escorting fighters. Hayden's tragic loss was largely his own fault, it's true, but I had caused it to some degree. Ultimately, it cemented our thinking on tactics to dive, hit, and run against more maneuverable enemy fighters at low altitude. Also, somehow my crew chief and armorer never seemed to pull guard duty thereafter when I was scheduled to fly a mission, and frequently there was a spare airplane available for me.

Colonel Mort Magoffin next scored against German fighters when he downed one Bf-109 and damaged another over Laigle, France, on July 8, 1944. On July 13, he shot down a pair of FW-190s over France, and he became the first and only original Ninth Air Force fighter group commander to achieve ace status when he downed another FW-190 over Beaumont, France, on August 7, 1944.

On August 10, while leading a mission against German Army ground forces near Falaise, France, Colonel Mort Magoffin was shot down by German flak. He was taken prisoner, but was liberated in Paris when that city fell into Allied hands.

Colonel Mort Magoffin remained in the service after World War II and was medically retired in 1958.

ALL FOR ONE

2d Lieutenant DWAINE FRANKLIN, USAAF
5th Fighter Squadron, 52d Fighter Group
Northern Italy—June 9, 1944

Dwaine Robert Franklin was born on November 12, 1920, in Guda Springs, Kansas, and raised in a succession of small oil towns in Texas and New Mexico. Franklin was inducted into the U.S. Army as an infantryman on August 3, 1942. He went through basic training at Camp Roberts, California, received additional training as a combat wireman, and served with an infantry heavy weapons company at Camp Buckner, North Carolina. Shortly after passing tests to gain entry to the Army Air Forces as a pilot trainee, Franklin was ordered to begin flight training. He graduated from Marianna Field, Florida, with Class 43-J on November 3, 1943, and was ordered to a P-47 replacement training unit at Millville, New Jersey.

When 2d Lieutenant Franklin arrived in Italy in March 1944, he was assigned to the 52d Fighter Group's 5th Fighter Squadron, which had just transitioned from Spitfires to P-51s. As soon as the transition was completed, the 52d Fighter Group was transferred to Madna Airdrome, Italy, to begin bomber-escort missions over southern Europe.

For my fourth combat mission, we were to escort some of the 500 Fifteenth Air Force B-17s and B-24s dispatched to Munich on the morning of June 9, 1944. I hadn't seen a German airplane on my first three missions, but Munich was reputed to be a heavily defended target. On this mission, the 52d Group was to pick up its section of bombers just before Munich, escort them to the target, and then take them back on the first leg of the withdrawal. Captain Tim Tyler, of the 4th Fighter Squadron, was leading the group, and I was flying wing on 2d Lieutenant Peewee Holloman, who was leading our flight. On this mission, the 5th Fighter Squadron formation was flying low and behind the other two squadrons.

The group, which hadn't picked up its bombers yet, was up over northern Italy, still just a little short of the Alps, when someone in my squadron called out that the B-24s behind us were getting clobbered. Tim Tyler said, "We can't worry about it. We have our own work cut out for us." We flew on, but somebody soon called out again, "There go some more B-24s," meaning that others had been shot down.

Our dilemma was that we had bombers of our own to escort; we hadn't rendezvoused with them yet, but we couldn't abandon them just because another fighter group had failed to protect the bombers charged to its care. But neither could we just leave those B-24s behind us to the enemy fighters. Finally, Tim released two flights of 5th Fighter Squadron P-51s to go back and see if we could help the B-24s that were under attack.

All eight of us dove into the fray as soon as we arrived over the B-24s, which were climbing through 18,000 or 20,000 feet. There were 109s all over the damn place! It looked like a Cecil B. DeMille production. There were airplanes going up and shooting, and there were airplanes going down and burning. There were parachutes all over the place. And there were many planes burning all over the ground.

The 52d Fighter Group had evolved unique tactics during its Spitfire days. The main idea was to get all guns working, rather than having half the pilots following someone else around a sky full of enemy fighters. In other units, I would have had to stick with Peewee Holloman while he chased the enemy fighters. But here, with the 52d, everyone was to get into the fray with as much mutual protection as possible.

The closest 109 I could see was just a little bit lower and coming from my right rear to my left front, going from my 4 o'clock position to my 10 o'clock position. As soon as I started chasing the 109, the pilot split-essed, and I followed him around. As he came through the bottom of the maneuver, I started firing. I was dead on him. I noticed that my guns didn't sound quite right, but I was intent on getting hits on the 109. As I was firing, he pulled up pretty close to level, rolled over, and split-essed again. I followed him through the maneuver. As he came through this time, I tried to pull my nose in on him, to get my guns to bear. I saw some decent strikes on him, on the left wing. I was very close behind the 109 by then, but my gun camera didn't register the few hits I saw on him.

As I fired, I noticed that my guns *really* didn't sound right, like all of them were not firing. But I kept following the 109. He rolled over and split-essed a third time, and we came out right on the deck. I pulled in on him and hit the trigger again. Nothing. The guns were jammed. I got some beautiful pictures of the 109, though, flying along right on the deck.

Soon, I noticed that an airfield was coming up. I could see the grass strip and some gun emplacements, and there were some guys running out to the gun emplacements. So I said, Well, I better get the hell out of here. I turned off to the left at about 90 degrees and then broke back 90 degrees to the right to come parallel with the 109. As I climbed, I looked over at the 109 and saw this big ball of flame rolling across a field. The 109 was cartwheeling and falling to pieces. The pilot just panicked and tried to belly in at high speed.

I went back up to 15,000 or 16,000 feet. The rest of the bombers were long gone and we had broken up the 109 attack on them. I found Peewee and joined on his right wing. No sooner had I taken position on his wing than here comes another 109, going about our way but a little lower and a lot faster. Peewee kept motioning for me to go after this 109, but I kept motioning back that I couldn't. I waved my arm and shook my head, but Peewee kept motioning for me to get on the 109. Finally, I decided to give it one more go. I checked all the circuit breakers and did everything I could think of to rearm the guns. Then I flew off after the 109.

This 109 was going home. It was in a shallow dive—really smoking. The pilot probably knew I was there, but he took no evasive action; he was going home as fast as he could get there, with no detours. I got into position behind him and took some more good pictures. He still hadn't reacted to me, so I broke off and motioned to Peewee that nothing was coming from my guns. Peewee finally pulled up behind the 109 and fired, but he had only one gun working. He probably fired ten rounds in all before the gun quit, but he put a few of the bullets into the 109; I could see the strikes. Well, just like that, the pilot bailed out. He hadn't take any evasive action from the time we first saw him until he left the airplane. Peewee's couple of strikes probably hadn't caused much damage, and there was nothing more we could do to harm him. He could

Aces At War   125

have flown on home, or he could have come on back and done us a world of hurt. He must have been petrified.

When we got back, we learned that other 5th Fighter Squadron pilots who had turned back with us to protect the B-24s had shot down three other 109s. And we later learned that the pilots of those 109s were Italians.

My guns had jammed because bullet belts in the feed chutes in the wings had become kinked when I pulled into my high-G turns to stay with the first 109 as it split-essed away from me. This turned out to be a common problem with the B and C model P-51s, because the guns had to be laid over at a 45-degree angle due to the thin profile of the wing. We eventually solved the problem by installing electric booster motors to get the ammunition belts over the rough angle. The six-gun D models we eventually flew had redesigned wings that were just thick enough to stand up the machine guns in their normal position.

Peewee tried to get me to take half the credit for the 109 the pilot had bailed out of, but I hadn't done anything except take some nice pictures, so I declined. I never claimed the 109 I had chased into the ground, either, but at least I knew that there would be one less 109 and one less enemy pilot to grapple with the next time we went out.

On June 30, 1944, 1st Lieutenant Dwaine Franklin shot down a Bf-109 and an FW-190 near Lake Balaton, Hungary; and he shot down an FW-190 on July 2 near Budapest. On July 16, Franklin achieved ace status when he downed two Me-110 twin-engine fighters (and probably shot down a third) in action over Austria; and on August 25, 1944, he shot down a pair of FW-190s near Zeltweg, Austria.

When ordered home at the end of his combat tour in the late winter of 1945, Captain Dwaine Franklin had flown 74 combat missions totaling 374 combat hours. He trained replacement fighter pilots until the war ended. Franklin declined the offer of a Regular commission, but he opted to remain on active duty as a Reservist. Franklin flew jet fighters out of Munich during the Berlin Airlift, stayed active in fighters and interceptors, served in numerous flight and staff positions over the years, and retired from active duty in 1965 with the rank of lieutenant colonel.

DAYLIGHT RANGER

Flight Lieutenant CLARENCE JASPER, RCAF
418 RCAF Squadron
Off Rostock, Germany—June 27, 1944

Clarence Murl Jasper, who started flying in his native Long Beach, California, in 1938, joined the Royal Canadian Air Force in Vancouver in May 1940 because, at 25 years of age, he had not attended college for two years and thus did not qualify for pilot training in the U.S. Army Air Corps. He earned his wings in March 1942 and was assigned as an instructor in Canada for fourteen months. Asked why he did not transfer to the U.S. Army Air Forces along with many other American-born RAF and RCAF pilots, Clarence Jasper replied, "Transferring to the U.S. forces was purely optional. Some of my friends who transferred got some lousy postings, so I stayed put."

Jasper attended the RCAF's first Mosquito course, in Nova Scotia, in October 1943, and in December 1943 he was assigned to combat flight duties with 418 (City of Edmonton) Squadron, the RCAF's first Mosquito unit. On March 12, 1944, flying a Mosquito VI fighter-bomber, he damaged a Junkers Ju-86 medium bomber on the ground and scored his first victory in the air, an FW-190, on April 12. His next victory, on April 16, was a Caudron Goeland, followed on the same day by the destruction of two other Goelands on the ground. On May 14, 1944, Flight Lieutenant Jasper destroyed an He-111 medium bomber in the air and a Ju-87 Stuka dive-bomber on the ground. These three aerial and four ground victories earned him a Distinguished Flying Cross.

The Mosquitoes of 418 Squadron were flying "Flower" Night Ranger intruder missions over occupied Europe from our bases in 11 Group, in the south of England. Unlike night-fighters, which were in the business of intercepting the enemy bombers over England, our missions, among others, were to intercept the enemy bombers as they were returning to their respective bases and hopefully to keep the enemy night-fighters on the ground when the RAF was bombing Germany. We also did Night Rangers to areas where there was reported activity, and we did Daylight Ranger operations to various parts of Europe.

On the Daylight Ranger mission of June 27, 1944, I was flying lead in a two-plane element. My wingman was Squadron Leader Russell Bannock, who was on his first Daylight Ranger mission. My observer was Flight Lieutenant O. A. Martin.

We took off from Coltishall at 1545 hours, flew to Europe across the North Sea through broken thunder clouds with showers and lightning. We made no contacts over Germany and, at 1749 hours, we recrossed the coast at Graal. At 1752 hours, Martin, my observer/navigator, spotted a Ju-88 from our position at 54°17'N, 12°05'E, about two miles out to sea north of Rostock. The German twin-engine bomber was at 800 feet and traveling southeast on course 135° about two miles to the seaward of our position.

We were at 300 feet when the sighting was made, so I climbed and maneuvered to a position below and behind the 88 at an indicated air speed of 290 miles per hour. Before I got into firing position, however, we were spotted by the crew of a large passenger liner of about 10,000 tons that was slightly farther out to sea. The ship began sending up flares and the Ju-88 pilot responded by maneuvering almost directly over the ship, which was well equipped with 40mm self-destroying ack-ack. The ship was 2 o'clock from our position, the Ju-88 was at 12 o'clock, and the coast was at 3 o'clock.

Though extremely mindful of the ack-ack, I closed the throttle and maneuvered to a position behind and below the bomber. This obliged me to fly directly over the ship. At 150 yards, I pulled up into a 20-degree climb and continued to close on him.

At gunnery school, we had been told, "It will be to your advantage not to open fire, when using cannon, at a range less than two hundred yards." These words of wisdom flashed through my mind as I opened fire with a two-second burst of my four 20mm cannon and four .303-inch machine guns from about 75 yards.

I saw strikes on both wing roots, and the port engine burst into flames, followed almost immediately by the starboard engine. A violent explosion then took place; the Ju-88 exploded in a huge cloud of flame, and flaming pieces fell into the sea over a wide area. I pulled through to starboard, but I could not avoid flying through the flames and debris. After emerging, I looked at my left wing, which was burning like a Yule log, and thought, "Jas, you stupid bastard, you really blew it this time."

We were too low to bail out, and ditching in the Baltic Sea is very nonhabit-forming due to the temperature of the water.

In a very few seconds, the fire burned out, but the rudder pedals were vibrating badly. I thought of heading to Malmo, Sweden, which was about 70 miles away, but after checking the engine instruments and seeing that everything was working normally, I elected to head for home.

Crossing 300 miles of the North Sea gets your attention. That water is rough even in good weather. We flew on to our squadron's base at Holmsley South and landed at 2113 hours. After touching down, I found directional control a little tricky. By using light touches of brake differentially, I managed to keep the airplane in a straight line.

After getting out of the airplane I could see why I had had problems. The fabric was burnt entirely off the rudder, as was a large strip of fabric on the port side of the fuselage and a smaller piece of the port wing. Fortunately, control surfaces other than the rudder were metallized.

Flight Lieutenant Clarence Jasper scored his fifth, and last, aerial victory—another Ju-88—on July 27, 1944. In addition, he destroyed three V-1 buzz bombs in the air and three more enemy aircraft on the ground.

UNBALANCED*

1st Lieutenant BOB GOEBEL, USAAF
308th Fighter Squadron, 31st Fighter Group
Budapest, Hungary—July 2, 1944

Following his graduation from high school, Robert John Goebel, a native of Racine, Wisconsin, enlisted in the Army Air Forces as an Aviation Cadet. He was called to active duty on April 4, 1942, and commissioned at twenty years of age on May 23, 1943. After six months' service in the Panama Canal Zone, 2d Lieutenant Goebel was transferred to the Twelfth Air Force and assigned to the 31st Fighter Group, then about to transition from Spitfires to P-51s.

Bob Goebel's first aerial victory was a Bf-109 he downed over Wallersdorf, Austria, on May 29, 1944. Thereafter, he downed another

---

* Goebel, Robert J. *Mustang Ace: Memoirs of a P-51 Fighter Pilot*. Pacifica, California: Pacifica Press, 1991. Used with permission of the author.

Bf-109 near Bucharest, Romania, on June 23, and an Me-110 over Hungary on June 27.

My mother used to say that there was no rest for the wicked. I didn't think I qualified as being wicked, but there was no rest for me or any of us in the squadron. In quick succession we went to Bucharest; to Blechhammer, Germany; and then back to Budapest, with only one day off in between to go swimming. There was no action on any but the last mission, on July 2.

It was my forty-first mission, and I had begun to get careless. Maybe not careless, but, well, jaded. Incautious, perhaps. I knew that it was a damned dangerous business, this flogging the air all over Europe in a single-engine plane. But going out almost every day as I did, I think I began to get complacent, to lose that sense of hazard that makes one careful. However, this mission, by the time it was over, got my attention. And, having been brought back to reality, I don't think I ever again lost my focus or grew contemptuous of danger.

With the full 85 gallons of fuel in the fuselage tank, the aft center of gravity in a maximum-rate turn caused a stick reversal; the plane tended to wrap the turn tighter without any back pressure on the stick. In short, the plane behaved like a pregnant sow. The standard procedure was to burn the fuselage tank down to about 30 gallons immediately after takeoff, even before going on the external tanks. That way, if the external tanks had to be jettisoned unexpectedly, you were already in a condition from which you could fight.

On July 2, we were taking the B-24s of the 55th Heavy Bombardment Wing up to Budapest to hit the marshalling yards and industrial areas. The route was familiar to me; I had been there twice before, and fuel had not been a problem. Why, then, did I leave more than 50 gallons in the fuselage tank on the climbout? I don't know. I suppose I thought I was getting some kind of edge in the hunt for victories, being able to hang around the bombers in the target area longer. I glossed over the aerodynamic effect. That was for new guys to worry about.

Our assignment was to provide close escort for the penetration, target area, and withdrawal of the bombers. The rendezvous point was over northern Yugoslavia, at 0916 hours, with a planned bomb release at 1014.

That was a long time to be providing close escort. Because of the 100-mile-per-hour difference in speed between the heavily laden bombers and the fighters, it was not possible to just fly along above them. Nor was it a good idea to pull the throttle back to stay with them; at that speed the Mustangs would be at a tremendous disadvantage if forced to defend against enemy fighters. The standard tactic was to split into flights, crossing over the top of the bombers as we scissored from one side to the other, so that no part of the bomber formation was ever uncovered at any time.

We approached rendezvous on time, but the bombers were obviously late. The group leader elected to make a very shallow 360-degree turn, to kill time and keep the three squadrons more or less intact.

Rendezvous was finally made at 24,000 feet at 0925. As we split up to begin our escort duties above our assigned bombers, I noted that the sky was a clear, brilliant blue. In the distance to the north, however, were several thin layers of cirrus at about our altitude.

The run to the Initial Point (IP), east of Budapest, seemed to take forever. After thirty to thirty-five minutes of monotonous patrolling, it became progressively easier to lose your edge and get complacent. Finally the bombers made their left turn off the IP and began the assault from east to west. As the first bombs began to fall, the lead squadron broke radio silence by calling out fifteen to twenty Bf-109s away to the northwest and high, at 32,000 feet. Everyone stayed with their part of the bomber stream, which had gotten strung out. Although the bombers were not attacked, everyone sat up a little straighter in the cockpit and redoubled their vigilance.

The increasing cloudiness above and below our altitude made doing our job progressively harder. Scattered clouds lying below the bombers allowed them to bomb visually, but the clouds above occasionally caused us to lose sight of the B-24s. In addition, the clouds were a potential screen for lurking German fighters.

Quite suddenly, without anyone calling them out, we collided with a formation of eight to ten Bf-109s. It didn't seem like a bounce; it was more like the two formations just blundered into each other. I don't think anyone even called a break. It was instant pandemonium. The radio was useless, absolutely saturated by a half dozen pilots trying to transmit at once. I broke sharply, without even looking back; got my tanks off and my guns on; and went to full power. In the vertical turn the Mustang felt a little rubbery. I immediately remembered the fuselage tank, but it was too late to worry about that now; I was going to have to play the hand I had dealt myself. A lot of airplanes—both kinds—were going in all directions. In the brief instant I looked around, I couldn't pick out the rest of my flight.

What I did see was a 109 close on the tail of a 51 below me at about 10 o'clock, 600 to 700 yards away. A string of tiny smoke puffs strung out behind the 109 told me the German pilot was already firing. As I took after them, I could see that the 51 was doing a lot of jinking. It hadn't been hit. Not yet. I was about 450 yards from the 109. With the spread harmonization the group used, I was still too far away to shoot—the inboard guns crossed at 250 yards and the outboard at 300. But waiting for a proper shot might prove fatal for the Mustang pilot. I tried to make a guess where the rounds would go at that range and snapped off as good a shot as I could get. The one-second burst produced one or two hits on the German's left wing, enough to make the pilot break off. Just as he did, I got off another burst, again getting a few strikes back in the tail area. Now he was turning hard! I tried to follow, but no way. My P-51 started shaking immediately. When I tried to force it into a tighter turn, it quit flying and fell out. The recovery was easy enough, I just let it go and it started flying again. The 109 was still there, above me now and still turning, almost opposite me. I thought I could see a thin streak behind him. Coolant! Was it my imagination? Was I merely seeing something I desperately wanted to see?

Reef it in! We became locked in a plain old-fashioned turning duel, a Lufbery Circle. I was working hard, sweating. My heart was pounding as I tried to outturn him, playing the stick just to the point of a high-speed stall. Was it enough? He seemed to be closing on me a little, but then I saw that thin streak again. He really was losing coolant! But could I hang on long enough to get some help or until he overheated?

He was definitely gaining on me. One-third of the circle was between his aircraft and mine, two-thirds between mine and his. In my semipanic I pulled the stick back hard again. Again I literally fell out of the sky and had to direct my attention to regaining control of the plane. Nose down, ease the stick. We were flying again. Now where the hell was he?

He was gone, and so was everyone else. Several sharp turns confirmed it. I switched the fuel selector to "Fuselage," eased myself into a cloud bank, and burned off the fuel in my fuselage tank as fast as I could. I was still pretty excited and not doing a very good job flying on instruments. The needle and ball went their own separate ways; the only time either one was in the middle was when it was passing from one side to the other. I was all over the sky. I just concentrated on keeping the wings level and dropped the nose slightly until I came out into the clear. I was still alone.

It didn't take long to get the fuselage tank down to 20 gallons, at which point I reduced power to normal cruise and went looking for the rest of my flight. I spotted the 24s straightaway. Since the radio traffic was down to normal, I arranged for a meeting with the other three members of my flight and used the bombers as a marker. In a surprisingly short time, we reformed.

I unhooked my mask momentarily and wiped the sweat from my face with my sleeve. My heart rate and breathing had slowed almost to normal. Finally, my aircraft was ready to fight, but I wasn't. Fortunately, no one was left to fight with—all the enemy airplanes were long gone.

Later, when I was telling Lam, the group intelligence officer, the substance of the encounter, as well as I could piece it together, I said I wasn't sure what kind of claim to make.

"If you hit him and you saw glycol, why not claim a probable?"

That was fine with me; Lam's offer was more than generous. A bit much, perhaps, almost getting my ass hammered and still making a claim. But who could resist an offer like that?

Bob Goebel rebounded from his July 2 scare the very next day, when he downed a Bf-109 near Bucharest; and he achieved ace status on July 20, 1944, when he shot down yet another Bf-109 over Villaorga, Italy. On August 3 Goebel shot down a Bf-109 over Austria, and on August 18 he shot down three more in the vicinity of Ploesti, Romania. His tenth confirmed victory was a Bf-109 he downed on August 22 over Troppau, Austria; and he scored his eleventh and final aerial victory on August 28, 1944, when he shot down yet another Bf-109 near Vienna.

Captain Bob Goebel went on Reserve status at the end of the war and completed a degree in physics on the GI Bill in time to return to active career status during the Korean War. Lieutenant Colonel Goebel retired from the Air Force in 1966 following many years of service with the NASA Manned Space Program.

LAST MISSION

Captain BUD FORTIER, USAAF
354th Fighter Squadron, 355th Fighter Group
Lechfeld Airdrome, Germany—July 24, 1944

Norman John Fortier was born in Pelham, New Hampshire, on May 30, 1922, and raised in Nashua. While attending St. Anselm College in Manchester, New Hampshire, he completed both phases of the Civilian Pilot Training program, then dropped out of school in January 1942 to enlist as a U.S. Army Air Corps Flying Cadet.

Fortier attended flight school as a member of Class 43-A. He was commissioned at Spence Field, Georgia, on January 14, 1943, and assigned to the newly formed 355th Fighter Group's 354th Fighter Squadron in Orlando, Florida. The group initially trained in P-40s, but was reequipped with new P-47 Thunderbolt high-altitude fighters before being shipped to England and assigned to the VIII Fighter Command in July 1943.

On March 6, 1944, 1st Lieutenant Bud Fortier joined two other pilots in the downing of a Bf-109 near Dummer Lake. Then, shortly after the group transitioned to P-51Bs, he shot down a Bf-109 and shared in the downing of another near Munich on April 24. On May 13, Lieutenant Fortier downed a twin-engine bomber (probably a Ju-88) near Landsberg, Germany, and an FW-190 near Bremen. On June 6 he shot down a Ju-87 near Chartres, France, and Captain Fortier achieved ace status on July 20, 1944, when he downed a Bf-109 near Oschatz, Germany.

The business of shooting down airplanes in "aerial combat" is, to my mind, much over-rated. In many instances, there was no aerial combat involved; the victim was totally unaware of being attacked until it was too late. Some of those "victories" were training aircraft, caught in the act of taking off or landing. Billy Hovde got one of those and said, "My daughter could have gotten that one!" One of mine was a Ju-87 Stuka dive-bomber, hardly an even contest!

I know there were many victories gained in the course of exciting dogfights, and I had a few of those, but I would guess that for every one of them, there were maybe three in which the victim was a sitting duck. Today, I suppose, it's possible to become an ace without ever seeing the enemy aircraft involved—not quite the same as in World War I.

The strafing of heavily defended airfields in the heart of Germany exacted a much greater toll than did air combat. All German airfields bristled with antiaircraft guns, and a high-speed, minimum-altitude attack left little room for error. It took skill, guts . . . and luck!

One bit of trivia: I flew "tail-end Charlie" on the 355th Fighter Group's first combat mission, as a second lieutenant, and I led the group on its last mission, as a major.

♦

I pushed aside the blackout curtains and looked out at the dark gray morning. Light rain was slanting down from low, ragged clouds; the whole English countryside was soggy and dripping.

Captain Jim Duffy, my roommate since flying school, had completed his combat tour two weeks earlier and was already back home, catching up on home cooking and other things. I had one more mission to go, and I was on today's schedule.

I walked through the cool drizzle to the orderly room to catch a ride to the flight line. The damp, heavy air muffled the spluttering drone of the Mustang engines being readied by ground crews across the field. What a lousy day for a mission, I thought. Especially the last.

Three hundred hours was the magic number. After three hundred hours of combat flying, you had a choice: go back to the States for reassignment, or sign up for a second combat tour and go back home for a thirty-day rest-and-recuperation leave. I had signed up for another tour, but I was really looking forward to that R&R.

Six or seven pilots were already waiting in the weapons carrier. I hopped in the back and joined in exchanging the usual ribald observations on the previous evening's activities. A few more pilots got in, and we lurched on our way. The drizzle turned to rain again, and the conversation in the carrier ebbed. We sat staring at the rain, each of us wrapped in his own thoughts.

The drive to the flight line led through a centuries-old village—a narrow, twisting road lined with thatched-roof cottages. Rumbling through the ancient rain-washed streets, I felt curiously detached from this scene, no more a part of village life than the glistening fighters a few hundred yards away. Our passing broke the tranquility of the old village, but only temporarily. It was here long before we came, it seemed to say, and would be here long after we left.

By contrast, our ready room bustled with movement and high spirits. The record player filled the room with Benny Goodman, and a fast-moving ping-pong game drew a loud and boisterous audience. The smell of coffee and spam-and-eggs revived my sagging spirits. Fresh eggs were a luxury in England, but one of our enterprising non-coms operated a thriving black market, trading our gum, candy, and cigarettes for eggs and milk. By the time I finished breakfast, the rain had stopped and the sky seemed a little brighter as we headed for the group briefing room.

Like most of our buildings, Group Headquarters looked like a huge oil drum that had been split down the middle and laid on a cement slab. The end pieces were flat, but the arch was corrugated for structural strength. Nissen huts, we called them. The briefing room was filled with wooden folding chairs; a large map covered the semi-circular endwall. England was squeezed into the upper left side; Norway and Denmark stretched toward the top of the curved ceiling; Russia sprawled on the far right; Spain and Switzerland formed the bottom. A low stage in front of the map enabled the briefing officer to reach all these places with a long pointer.

A low hum of conversation filled the briefing room. About half the chairs were occupied, and more pilots were straggling in behind me. I looked at the flood-lit map and felt that familiar twinge just below my navel. A thick red string stretched like a taut nerve from a spot just southwest of Cambridge, England, to a spot just south of Augsburg, Germany.

The chalkboard on the left side of the stage gave the mission details: start-engine time, take-off time, headings, time to different checkpoints, communications information, and the target: the airfield at Lechfeld. No bombers this trip; this was a strafing mission: high-speed, just a few feet above the ground.

The chalkboard to the right of the stage gave the rest of the story—the weather. The mission profile revealed thick, unbroken clouds all the way to the target.

I slouched down next to our squadron intelligence officer. "How in hell are we supposed to find it?"

He shrugged. "Maybe they'll scrub it."

The group operations officer opened the briefing with a weak joke about the weather; he wasn't going on this flight. He spelled out the details of the route, timing, and all the other items that make up a combat mission. Pilots wrote the essentials on the back of their hands.

"The Germans," he went on, "have been developing a jet-propelled fighter, the Me-262. Most of the work has been going on at the Messerschmitt factory at Lechfeld. We know they've been flying experimental models. We believe they are now building production models—combat-ready, operational fighters." He paused and looked around dramatically. "Jet fighters can change the course of this war. Our job is to destroy them!" I half-expected to hear a trumpet fanfare.

The intelligence officer was next. He showed sketches of the 262, then recited the types and numbers of guns that would make up our reception committee at Lechfeld. I was only half listening. He didn't have to convince me that it would be no picnic. We all knew that strafing losses were three to four times higher than those in air-to-air combat. On a strafing run, the only thing that mattered was luck—or fate.

It was the weather officer's turn. The top of the overcast was about 15,000 feet over England and a little higher over all of Europe. "There's a fifty-fifty chance," he said, "that you'll find breaks in the overcast in the target area or just east of it." And if we don't, I thought, this would be a monotonous, five-hour milk run. Somehow, I was not dismayed at *that* prospect.

Finally, Captain Billy Hovde, who would be leading the group on this mission, took over the pointer. Hovde was a young, aggressive West Pointer. I knew if there was any way at all of finding that target, he would find it. The 358th was the lead squadron, then the 357th, and I would be leading the 354th, bringing up the rear.

Our tactics were simple. Dive down east of the target on an easterly heading, as if headed for Munich, until we were below radar-detection level, then double back at tree-top level, hoping to catch the Lechfeld defenders by surprise. Well, I thought, *he* might catch them by surprise, because he would be the first flight across the field; but by the time the 354th got there, everybody and his brother would be firing at us—with rifles on up. Our luck could wear thin.

Back in our ready room, I went over the mission with the other pilots. My wingman and number-four man were newly assigned, so I had to be sure they knew what was expected and what to expect. This was one helluva mission for a newcomer, I thought, but in this business, there was no easy way to learn. One more quick trip to the latrine, then into the weapons carriers again for the ride to the airplanes.

Exactly on time, the lead squadron's engines sputtered into life across the field, followed by the 357th farther to the left. Our turn. Controls set . . . energize . . . engage. The prop turned through four blades . . . ignition on. The engine coughed once, then settled into a smooth idle. I checked the engine instruments and gave the crew chief the thumbs-up signal to pull the chocks. Eleven red-tailed Mustangs followed me to the end of the runway.

The last pair of fighters from the first two squadrons began to roll down the runway. I taxied on to the runway and my wingman rolled into position at my right wing. Leaning forward as a signal for advancing power, I released brakes and eased the throttle full. With full internal fuel and a 108-gallon external tank under each wing, the Mustangs lumbered clumsily down the runway the first few hundred yards, then swiftly gathered speed and lifted off. Gear handle up; I felt the landing gear coming up and felt that soft thump beneath me as the door covers closed—like a nice reassuring pat on the ass.

After takeoff, I stayed below the ragged clouds in a slow right turn to let my second element catch up. My wingman slid into position on my left wing. The second element leader eased inside my right wing with his wingman tucked tight to his right. I would be flying instruments through the overcast, but they would be flying tight formation, close enough to see me in the thickest clouds.

The overcast was a dark gray, gloomy world as we began our climb. All my attention was focused on the instruments, but out of the corner of my eye I could see the other Mustangs in the wispy clouds, wings interlocked, only inches apart. As we climbed the clouds became brighter, and at 16,000 feet we were skimming the silvery cloud tops and suddenly we were in the clear. The brilliant sunlight lifted our spirits. Tension eased and the formation loosened up. High above, stark white against the deep blue, a single contrail streaked toward the southeast, like a huge chalk-mark pointing the way to the target.

The group leader saw my flight coming out of the overcast and radioed his position. Then my other two flights popped out of the clouds and I circled back to pick them up. In a surprisingly short time, the group's thirty-six planes were in formation, climbing toward Germany.

We leveled off at 25,000 feet and spread out in combat formation. My squadron, three flights of four, was high and to the right of the group leader.

We were navigating by dead reckoning, flying an assigned heading for the specified time, but we did get some navigational help from German flak batteries. We knew when we crossed the enemy-held coast, because of the sporadic, almost casual, black puffs of antiaircraft fire a few thousand feet below us. It wasn't close and it looked harmless, but we knew better.

As soon as the flak appeared, the leader of my third flight called, "Falcon Leader, this is Blue Leader. My engine's running rougher 'n hell. Feels like it's shaking right off the mounts. I'm returning to base."

I suspected he just didn't like his odds if we did find the target. I felt like saying, "My engine's running rough, too. They all run rough when flak comes up." But I didn't. I just said, "Roger," and watched his flight bank sharply to the right. I could almost hear four sighs of relief. They were out of sight in seconds. That left eight of us.

There was no sound now save the almost hypnotic drone of the big Merlin engine, nothing but the deep blue of the sky and dazzling white of the clouds below as far as we could see in all directions. The Mustangs seemed suspended, motionless, in a silent, empty sky.

Suddenly, the sky erupted with orange-red flashes and greasy black puffs of smoke. This was the heavy stuff, the big guns. And it was close. Too damned close! We had apparently blundered too far north of course, probably over the Ruhr Valley, dubbed "Flak Alley" by bomber crews.

Mustangs bobbed and weaved, trying to keep the enemy radar from getting a good track. The radio came alive.

"Flak!" an excited, high-pitched voice. "No kidding!" calm and sarcastic. Another voice, "Let's get the hell out of here!"

The group leaders's calm voice, "Uncle here, turning forty-five degrees right." I could barely see the lead squadron through the heavy black barrage. I banked into a climbing right turn, hoping to get above the explosions and the hot jagged shrapnel.

"Falcon Leader, this is Yellow Three. I've been hit!" I looked behind me. Yellow-3 looked all right. There was no smoke, and the airplane appeared to be under control.

"Yellow Leader here. I'll check him out." I watched as Yellow Leader slid over to his number three. The flak was lighter now; we were getting out of range.

"There's a hole in the leading edge of his left wing, just outboard of the guns," reported Yellow Leader. "Looks okay otherwise, but I'd better take him back." It might have been my imagination, but I thought he sounded relieved.

I watched Yellow Flight disappear behind me. And now there were four of us. It probably wouldn't make much difference, but if we did manage to find the target in all this lousy weather, we'd be the last flight across.

The flak stopped and we returned to our briefed heading. The radio fell silent. Again I had that eerie feeling of hanging motionless between sky and clouds. Below was an unbroken sea of glaring white. Every now and then, bursts of flak jarred us back to reality, but for the most part, it was like a dream world . . . twenty-eight Mustangs, destined to fly forever between earth and sky.

Gradually, I became aware of mountain peaks thrusting through the clouds ahead. I snapped back to reality. Those were the Alps. We were getting close. I checked my watch. If our navigation was anywhere near accurate, we should be somewhere near Augsburg.

As if in confirmation, flak mushroomed all around us. It was not nearly as heavy as the Flak Alley variety, but we took vigorous evasive action. Even a little flak could be hazardous to your health.

There was still no sign of a break in the overcast. A milk run after all?

"Looks like a big hole to the south," said an unidentified voice. The group leader turned right and I felt that twinge again. There it was—a hole in the overcast about five miles across. As we got closer, I could see the ground and what looked like a slender silver ribbon running north and south—the Lech River.

"Uncle here. Drop babies." That was the code for getting rid of our wing tanks. I pushed the release button and felt the lurch as the tanks dropped off. The Mustang seemed relieved to be rid of the burden and surged ahead—clean, smooth and responsive.

One after the other, six flights of four dove through the opening in the clouds. So much for the element of surprise. Even the lead flight could expect a warm reception. I turned on the windshield defroster, flipped the gun switch on, and followed in a spiraling dive toward that thin ribbon far below.

The Mustang seemed to come alive as the airspeed built up rapidly. Gone was the sensation of hanging motionless. We were moving! Streaking down the walls of cloud, my pulse quickened with the excitement of high-speed flight. Below, I could see the lead flight level off above the river and head for the target, which was still blanketed by clouds.

We leveled off just above the trees and headed north, straddling the river. Almost immediately, we were beneath the overcast in a light drizzle that sharply restricted visibility.

With the throttle wide open, doing better than 400 miles per hour, I was straining to find the target in the sunless gloom. I knew the field was west of the river, so if I held this heading . . .

A large hangar, dead ahead. Big brick buildings to the left. "There it is!"

I pulled up to about 300 feet to get a better angle for firing the guns and find a target worth shooting at. Of course, this also made us more vulnerable, because now the gunners could see us, and we had to maintain a steady, shallow dive to the target—no evasive action—just like flying down somebody's gun barrel.

I spotted a row of hangars on the far side of the field and what looked like Me-262s scattered around in sandbagged revetments. Some were burning, the black oily smoke merging with the low clouds. I picked out an airplane parked at an angle, half inside a small hangar, and lined it up carefully in my gunsight. There would be only one pass. It had to be good.

I was aware of small white puffs from exploding 20mm shells all around my airplane. I could hear the soft popping of near misses. I forced myself to concentrate: keep that pip steady on that airplane!

I squeezed the trigger on the stick. The four .50-caliber machine guns in the wings hammered, jarring the airplane as if it had been hit. Instantly, like a string of firecrackers, orange flashes appeared on the fuselage of the 262. Then a small yellow flame licked up around the cockpit and flashed into a red-orange explosion as the fuel tank blew up.

I was almost too close. I pulled back on the stick and cleared the hangar roof by inches. As I did, a bright flash behind me reflected off the clouds and lighted the whole area. Something had exploded. I banked left a few degrees to avoid flying over Augsburg and skimmed the trees until well out of range of those airfield guns. I had seen enough of those for one day.

I scanned the engine instruments and checked the plane over for damage. That's when I noticed the large chip in the "bullet-proof" windshield. A shell had apparently hit the windshield on a slant and been deflected off. Somewhere on that strafing run, I had been only six inches from having my head blown off!

I checked the rest of the flight. Red-3 and -4 both had minor flak damage. "Where's Red Two?" I asked.

"He went in. Right on the airfield, replied Red-4 in a faltering voice. I knew they were roommates. I remembered that bright flash. Of the last four planes on that strafing run, the German gunners had shot down one and hit the other three!

I signaled the other two into a tight formation and we started the long climb through the heavy overcast.

It was a long, silent flight back to England. I kept staring at that chipped windshield and thinking about Red-2. The difference between life and death had been a matter of inches, or perhaps a few miles per hour one way or the other. This was my seventy-fourth mission—his second.

Bud Fortier returned to the 354th Fighter Squadron following his home leave, and was in command of the squadron with the rank of major when the war in Europe ended. In his 112 combat missions and 457 combat hours, his aircraft sustained damage only once—on the July 24, 1944, mission.

Fortier returned to school after the war, then flew war-surplus aircraft for several civilian non-scheduled airlines. Within three months of joining Northwest Orient Airlines, he was recalled to active duty in 1947 to take part in the Berlin Airlift. Bud Fortier remained in the service until retiring with the rank of lieutenant colonel in 1964 and thereafter served his community as a school teacher and principal.

THE RESCUE

2d Lieutenant DEACON PRIEST, USAAF
354th Fighter Squadron, 355th Fighter Group
Franco-German Frontier—August 18, 1944

Royce Whitman Priest grew up in San Antonio, Texas, the lap of Army Aviation. From his earliest youth, he admired the men who flew the fabric-and-wire pursuit planes of the day and dreamed that he might someday become one of them. In response to his youthful queries, the Army pilots he knew told him that a Military Academy graduate would qualify for pilot training, and they also suggested that he pursue a Presidential appointment from the enlisted ranks. Without hesitation, he entered the Army as an infantryman in 1940. Shortly thereafter, he transferred to the Army Air Corps as an aviation mechanic trainee, but within months, World War II began and further opportunities opened up. Priest gained entry into glider pilot training as a noncommissioned officer and was later selected as an aviation cadet. He finally graduated from pilot training as a second lieutenant with Class 43-J in November 1943.

Following additional training in P-39s, Priest shipped out for England and the Eighth Air Force in May 1944. Then after P-51 transition training, he was assigned to the 355th Fighter Group's 354th Fighter Squadron, which was based at Steeple Morden, and he flew his first combat mission just after D-Day.

It was the summer of 1944, and I was a happy young fighter pilot, flying combat in one of the world's best fighters, while being given the privilege of participating in man's greatest adventure. At least, that's my general recollection of the way I saw myself at the time. The fact of the matter is that, at the ripe old age of twenty-one, I had an unwarranted abundance of youthful exuberance and conspicuous audacity that had kept me in some sort of trouble with my superiors a good part of the time—and had probably led me into more close scrapes in combat than clear insight and good judgment might have otherwise permitted.

My combat unit was the 354th Fighter Squadron, 355th Fighter Group, VIII Fighter Command, Eighth Air Force. Our base, RAF Steeple Morden, was situated in the beautiful English countryside, little more than an hour's train ride north of London. The village of Steeple Morden was located in the general vicinity of the ancient university city of Cambridge.

We flew the P-51 Mustang, then a new long-range fighter which had only been introduced into combat some months earlier, in the spring of the year. Our predominant combat role was to provide long-range, high-altitude fighter escort for our heavy bombers, to protect them from attack by enemy fighters during their massive bombing raids against major strategic targets deep in the enemy's homeland. At the same time, however, our primary standing orders required that we "seek and destroy the enemy in the air and on the ground." Accordingly, a substantial part of our combat time was spent at low altitude, operating against ground targets that offered a worthwhile return. Sometimes the targets were prebriefed fixed locations, such as airfields, bridges, antiaircraft gun emplacements, or known concentrations of rail or barge traffic and the like. At other times, we might sweep a given area, looking for "targets of opportunity" known or suspected to be in the region. There were other days when enemy fighter opposition along the target route was light or nonexistent. If so, we could bring the bombers out to a point at which they were relatively safe from attack, then "hit the deck" and strafe our way home, sometimes hitting specific objectives previously identified as potentially rewarding targets for attack as circumstances permitted and, at other times, attacking anything that appeared to be of military value.

To those not initiated in the aerial warfare of the day, the ground attack activity may at first appear to be a "piece of cake" and great fun, whereas merely surviving an aerial dogfight could almost be seen as an act of valor. While there were certainly significant differences between air-to-air combat and air-to-ground attack, any such generalizations betray a somewhat inaccurate perception of the air battle we fought over Europe at the time.

On any given day, an air-to-air engagement with enemy fighters could result from any of a variety of scenarios. However, no matter how it began, aerial combat usually came down to a one-on-one affair, with the initial advantage generally held by to the pilot who saw the other airplane first. By the same token, since neither combatant could exploit some built-in advantage such as physical size or choice of weaponry, the outcome more often than not hinged upon the skill and determination each could bring to bear upon the engagement—unless the unfortunate loser never even saw the winner.

The ground target, on the other hand, was fixed or, at best, slow moving, unable to evade the attack on it. The problem facing the attacker, however, was not one of being able to hit the target; it was the probability of surviving the ground fire coming from any direction, the better part of which was not even aimed at him specifically. Indeed, many of us considered the strafing of a heavily defended German airfield to be the most dangerous fighter mission of all. The most effective counteraction for the attacker was to fly as low and as fast as possible in the target area. Even then, the risk of taking a hit was high. While our fighter group absolutely excelled in the ground-attack role, we paid a high price. In fact, attacks against ground targets accounted for about forty percent of our combat losses.

The action at hand took place some ten weeks after the start of the D-Day invasion of Normandy. The enemy was heavily engaged in the ground movement of troops and supplies in response to the urgent demands of intense fighting along the battle front. Our assigned task that day was interdiction of the battle zone, in the classic sense of the term. Our specific objective was to destroy, or limit to the extent possible, the enemy's ability to move his personnel and supplies in support of his front lines.

We had been briefed to attack a crowded railway marshalling yard located north and east of Paris, in the general vicinity of the German border. I was flying the position of Falcon Red-3, element leader in the flight led by my squadron commander and the mission leader that day, Captain Bert Marshall.

Bert Marshall was not only my boss, he was my hero and my friend. As a kid growing up in San Antonio, I had admired Bert as a top high school football player out of Greenville, Texas. Later, his exploits as a 147-pound all-star quarterback at Vanderbilt University had raised him even higher in my esteem. And now, here he was, big as life and leading me in combat! To make matters even better, I had come to know Bert well enough by then to realize what a superb, kind, and gentle man he was, as if to further complement his remarkable prowess as a star athlete and military aviator. To say I was merely happy to be where I was at that time would be an understatement.

It was the middle of the afternoon on a bright, clear midsummer day as we approached the pre-assigned target. We could see it was indeed crammed with rail traffic, apparently a perfect setup for realizing a high return on the effort. Yet, strangely, there was no ground fire from the target area. As we moved in closer, we could see why. Most of the rail cars were marked with large red crosses, the international symbol for medical shelter or medical transportation facilities. Bert directed that we hold fire and bypass the target, stating that we would sweep the region for other targets of opportunity. After all, it was only a couple of months after D-Day and we were aware the Germans were frantically repositioning troops and supplies in an effort to accommodate the ever-changing requirements of the battle on the ground.

We had not gone very far before Bert called out a new target, a fat little railroad marshalling yard packed with rolling stock that appeared to be loaded with war materials. As we positioned for attack, heavy ground fire was already beginning to come up at us. Bert immediately warned the group that the target was "hot" and to remain out of range until he could assess the defensive situation.

Our tactics called for a flight to make its initial attack run in a spread-out formation, with each pilot selecting his own particular target. As our flight of four closed on the target area, I selected a heavily loaded flatcar. At about the instant I opened fire on the flatcar, I was amazed to see the sides of the boxcar next to it suddenly fall away, exposing a large-caliber antiaircraft weapon. This was a first for me! I instinctively slid my aiming point onto the big gun and held the trigger down. As I observed the pyrotechnics of my .50-caliber rounds hitting the gun mount, I became fascinated by the spectacle of what appeared to be little orange golf balls floating lazily up in my direction. Along with instant realization that heavy-caliber cannon fire was coming straight at me, I sensed rather than heard the sound of an explosion somewhere just ahead and to my left. I shifted my vision enough to see Bert turning away from the guns, trailing fire from a bad hit in the lower fuselage. I told him that he was on fire and quickly shifted my attention back to the antiaircraft weapon, which now appeared to have ceased firing.

After completing my firing pass, I turned back hard to my left, craning to get a line on Bert's whereabouts so as to quickly rejoin and assist him in any way possible. He wasn't hard to find. He had used his attack velocity to gain some maneuvering altitude and was heading generally in a direction away from the target, still trailing fire and smoke. Almost certainly, he had only limited or no engine power, and he was too low to use his parachute.

The gravity of his situation was obvious. His airplane was on fire and going down—for sure!—and he couldn't bail out. The best he could hope for was a survivable crash landing. His immediate pressing problem was to pick out a suitable touchdown area that he could reach with no engine power. The very last thing he needed at that instant was outside intrusion that could divert his focus on the urgent problem of survival. Yet I was compelled to blurt out the suggestion that he attempt to put the airplane down somewhere that would permit me to land alongside and pick him up. His response was in the negative, to put it very mildly. In precise, emphatic terms, he instructed me to take the squadron and go home.

I maintained radio silence and observed Bert as he lined up on a plowed field that was obviously his best bet. Having identified potential landing sites as I quickly scanned the immediate area, I now knew enough to inform the two wingmen in Red Flight of my intention to land and the need for close cover. They responded immediately. When Bert overheard the exchange between the wingmen and me, he exploded over the radio. My recollection is that his precise words were, "Goddamn' Priest,

I told you to go home, and that's a direct order. Now get the hell outta here!" Again, I maintained discreet radio silence as Bert stretched for the plowed ground, his windmilling propeller now slowly winding down.

By the time Bert's airplane had come to a stop, I was maneuvering overhead at low level, trying to get in as close as I could in order to assess his physical status. To my great relief, he was busily flailing away at his harness and chute, trying to get away from the burning airplane as quickly as possible. As he scrambled over the side, I watched as he tossed a thermite bomb into the cockpit and started running. I then took a quick look around for any enemy activity that might have been attracted by all the commotion, but I saw none. I still felt somewhat uneasy, though, considering we were not all that far from the target we had just attacked.

Knowing better than to attempt a wheels-down landing in the plowed ground where Bert had gone down, and realizing the imperative of staying close enough for him to get to my aircraft, I had selected what appeared to be the most acceptable landing area in relatively close proximity to Bert's crash site. It was a wheat field about half a mile away, which was at the time occupied and being worked by a number of people, along with a team and wagon and some pieces of heavy equipment. Much of the field was still uncut, and most of the remainder consisted of shocked wheat bundles sitting in geometrically precise rows, but in one corner there was a small cleared area where men were loading shocks onto the wagon. I reasoned if I could full-stall the airplane into that small clearing and then keep it aimed between two rows of shocks, along with fair braking action, the combined effect would not only get me down safely, it would also clear a runway for takeoff.

By now, Bert was running in the direction of where he had seen me drag the wheat field, busily shedding personal equipment as he ran. With landing gear down, at very low level, and heading in the direction I needed Bert to run, I waggled wings at him as I flew directly overhead. From there, a burst of high power, a quick pull-up, and a couple of steep turns effectively set the Mustang up for a minimum-airspeed, power-on approach to my little cleared space. Lining up on short final, I could see that my flight path would take me into somewhat close proximity to the men at the wagon and, as one might expect, they were running in all directions as I began to close in on where they were. After all, a warplane landing in the midst of a group of working wheat farmers wasn't exactly to be expected.

The landing worked out fine. With full flaps, minimum airspeed, nose high, and power on, the airplane was sort of hanging on its propeller as it came over the field boundary. As I eased power all the way back while holding the nose up, the Mustang gently *whomped* down and went clattering off between the neatly stacked rows of wheat shocks. In fact, nature's arresting gear was so effective that I decided to lengthen my runway a little before turning back to look for Bert. I could now see that a haystack I had all but ignored in the air was somewhat larger than I had perceived it to be and, indeed, could become a factor on takeoff.

For whatever reason, up to this moment I had not really given much thought to the people working the field. Now, in retrospect, I can only reason that I must have mentally categorized them as being of no particular consequence to my immediate problem, which was to find Bert, get him in the airplane, and get out of there as quickly as possible. As I taxied back toward my touchdown area, I noted that they were observing me with obvious curiosity. I wondered whether they might be hostile. After all, we had been working within a relatively few miles of the border, and I could be in Germany, not France. I couldn't see whether they were armed, but they all had long pitchforks.

With the airplane rolling through the wheat stubble, I unbuckled and pulled myself up to a more-or-less standing position in the cockpit in an attempt to see whether Bert was anywhere in sight. As I strained to get a glimpse of him, I was chilled by what I saw. At a distance of little more than a city block, there appeared to be a truckload of German troops approaching along a little dirt road beside my wheat field.

Struggling in a half panic to get my headgear on, I called the wingmen to kill the truck. My wingman immediately responded that they had the troops in sight and were rolling in to attack at that instant. To my overwhelming relief, I saw clouds of bullet dust in the dirt road. As I gunned the engine fairly hard to get the airplane rolling fast in a direction away from the road and toward the location where I thought Bert should show up, my last impression of the area in which I had seen the enemy vehicle was one of dust, smoke, and scurrying people.

Deliberately taxiing the airplane at high speed on the surface of the wheat turned out to be unwise—and almost disastrous! As I approached the field boundary, rolling at a fairly high rate, I barely discerned a wide, deep ditch. It was almost totally concealed by a heavy growth of vegetation bordering the edge of the field, and rapidly coming up directly ahead of me. Heavy braking only seemed to make me go faster on the ice-slick wheat stubble. Instinctively, I slammed full rudder and stood on the brake, which broke the tail wheel out of its centering detent and sent the airplane into a wide skidding turn. It came to a lurching stop just feet short of putting a wheel in the ditch, which would have meant the end of the affair.

Somewhat shaken, I stood up in the airplane once more to search for any enemy activity possibly ensuing from the truck incident on the road, and to crane for a glimpse of Bert, whom I expected to be showing by now. There was smoke in the direction of the truck, but Bert was not in sight yet. However, much to my consternation, I could see the field laborers walking toward the airplane, pitchforks in hand. I didn't know what to do. I was armed with my issue weapon, but common sense convinced me that using it would be a bad decision, regardless of whether they were friendly, hostile, or neutral.

Having similarly dismissed the notion of calling the wingmen in on the civilians, I slowly sat back down in the cockpit and pondered my situation. I could still get out of there, but I just as quickly dismissed that thought, also. I couldn't abandon Bert without certain knowledge that he had somehow become incapacitated—not after having come this far, and not after having risked the lives of others. No, I would wait for him to show, and that was that.

As I sat there, with the engine ticking over in a quiet idle, trying to think of something to do about the laborers, my glance fell on the engine-coolant temperature gauge. It was well into the red, telling me that I had an overheating problem that could well blow the coolant and leave me stranded for sure. As I applied power to get some cooling propwash air back into the large intake scoop on the belly of the airplane, I could see in my rearview mirrors that my propeller blast was stirring up a cloud of dirt and wheat debris. I glanced back toward the laborers, who were now even closer to the airplane, and a thought struck me. I immediately turned the tail of the airplane toward them and continued to observe them in my rearview mirrors. As they came in a little closer, I ran the engine up to high power and watched as the flying dirt and debris flew into their faces. They turned around and ran back and off to one side, away from the direction of my propwash. I promptly pointed the tail at them again and blasted more debris.

Knowing this charade couldn't last much longer and wondering what in the world to do next, I pulled myself up again to search the horizon for any sign of Bert. I was almost overcome with joy and relief when I saw him in the near distance, running toward me just like the star quarterback he had been only a few years earlier. He reached the field boundary, disappeared into the deep ditch I had narrowly avoided, and came charging back out toward my airplane, which I taxied back to the edge of the field to get as close to him as I could.

I set the airplane's brakes and climbed out onto the left wing just as he reached the trailing edge. Red-faced, with sweat running from every pore, clad in a soaking wet flying suit and muddy boots, and heaving for air, he greeted me with a firmly expressed string of highly vituperative invectives, the gist of which was that I was to get back in the airplane and go home before I got both of us killed or captured. Bert adamantly refused to get in the airplane with me and raged when I suggested that he take the airplane home and let me stay—though in all honesty, I believe I regretted that youthful impulse even before getting it all out.

So there we were: me standing on the wing, wondering again what to do next; the two wingmen overhead, duly providing close air cover; the German truck, still billowing black smoke; a real possibility that armed enemy stragglers were hiding from the view of the wingmen; the now-forgotten civilian bystanders gawking at us, as if uncertain of what they might do next; the airplane's engine contentedly chuckling away; and Bert standing on the ground, beating on the trailing edge of the wing and yelling at me. I was in a true quandary; he wouldn't get in the airplane, and I was determined not to leave him there.

Then, from out of nowhere, it occurred to me that my parachute, dinghy, and associated survival equipment were taking up too much room in the cockpit to permit both of us to fit in and be able to close the canopy; we needed the space provided by an empty bucket seat. Without giving further thought to the matter, I lifted the bulky gear out of the seat, dropped it on the wing, pulled the parachute ripcord, and tossed the ballooning mess onto the ground.

Bert's face took on a look of surprise and disbelief, and I believe I probably shared the same thoughts in that instant. Shaking his head in resignation, Bert climbed up on the wing and we immediately entered into a spirited exchange about who would fly the airplane. I wanted him to fly; after all, he was the boss, with far superior skill and experience. And besides, I had never even heard of this trick being tried before—at least not in the P-51! (The sudden realization that the two of us in the single-seat cockpit might take up so much of the available space that the various controls couldn't be operated satisfactorily shook me somewhat.) Bert firmly insisted that he would get in the seat and that I would sit on his lap and fly the airplane. At this point it occurred to me that I was already guilty of more than one charge of gross insubordination while under fire in the face of the enemy, and that maybe I had better do as I was told, for a change.

As we fitted ourselves into the cockpit, it became obvious that my face would end up near the gunsight, access to certain cockpit controls would be awkward or difficult, and full rudder travel would be restricted to a degree, as would full elevator and aileron control. However, access to the throttle quadrant seemed reasonable enough, and judgment seemed to indicate that if I pressed back hard enough on Bert, I would have enough stick travel to at least get us up and down in one piece. I had considered removing my flotation life vest for added comfort and space but discarded the idea, reasoning that, since it didn't seem to interfere with the controls, it could keep us afloat for awhile, should we be forced to ditch in the sea on the way back and manage to survive impact. The fact that the airplane's seat belt and shoulder straps would be useless didn't even occur to me.

I lined up with my "runway" between the wheat shocks, closed the canopy, and eased on take-off power. But I realized at that instant that I had not done even a perfunctory cockpit check before releasing the brakes. It was too late to worry about it; we were on the roll and getting out of there! Besides, I couldn't get my head down low enough to see the instrument panel, and even if I could have, the very idea that some engine temperature or pressure indicator might deter me from taking off was preposterous.

As these trace thoughts flickered through my consciousness during the initial take-off acceleration, they were soon replaced by the jolt of being struck squarely on the forehead by the front edge of the canopy as it slid back out of the closed position. In my haste within the overcrowded cockpit, I had obviously failed to get the canopy control properly set in the locked detent. Bert reached around me and managed to get it closed and locked. Meanwhile, the combined effects of full take-off power and increasing airspeed brought the realization that I was having difficulty trying to override the combined effects of torque and trim tabs, which had not been properly set for takeoff. Under normal circumstances, this would present little more than an annoying distraction. In this case, however, rudder-pedal travel was being limited by my inability to extend my leg at the knee in the crowded cockpit, and Bert's left leg was in the way of ready access to the rudder trim controls. Elevator trim was also well out of adjustment, having last been set during my nose-high, power-on approach to the wheat field. I forced the tail off the ground with considerable forward pressure on the stick, but directional control was developing into somewhat more of a problem, with the nose gradually trying to drift left, more toward the direction of the haystack.

I recall pressing back hard on Bert in order to extend my leg a bit more, also applying aileron to the extent that I was able, while at the same time holding firm forward pressure on the stick to keep the nose from coming up too far, too soon. In this weird, cross-controlled, semi-stalled condition, the superb flying machine got itself airborne, after which it was a simple matter to lift myself off Bert's left leg long enough to reach back and adjust the trim tabs.

My wingman later told me that he thought I had clipped the haystack on takeoff. In fact, I had managed to put the airplane into a slight right bank at liftoff and actually missed the haystack, passing just above and to the right of it. I made our climb-out from the target area using maximum power in order to gain altitude as quickly as possible, hoping to minimize the threat of being hit by ground fire.

Since we were unable to use the oxygen system, I cruised at about 14,000 feet until we approached the French coast, and then I slowly descended into a pleasant, uneventful flight back to Steeple Morden, where the beautiful Mustang gracefully landed itself in a gentle, easy touchdown.

Upon landing back at Steeple Morden that late afternoon, I did not taxi directly to my assigned parking revetment, but turned off the runway early and let the Mustang roll across the airfield to a gentle stop in the open grass facing our squadron hut. My reasoning was that, after what Bert had been through that day, he would no doubt prefer the removal of my bony frame from his weary legs as quickly as conveniently possible. It had also occurred to me that he might appreciate the opportunity for a brief moment in retrospection before having to face people.

As Bert and I stood on the wing after having gingerly extricated ourselves from the cockpit, we simply looked at each other in silence for a brief instant, each of us cognizant that the other was fully aware of the momentousness of the episode that we had jointly experienced and survived that day. He shook my hand and in a gentle, subdued voice, quietly and sincerely expressed his sentiments concerning the events of the day, as well as his feelings toward me. I stood in silence and listened. When he had finished, I offered a sincere apology for my breach of discipline and for any problems he might incur as a result. And I took the opportunity to express my own appreciation of him as a man, and of the standard of excellence he set for all of us. I also told him, for the first time, about the inspiration he had provided for me back when I was a ragtag kid who needed a hero he could relate to. Now, thinking back on our continuous friendship over the many long years prior to his ultimate sad loss in 1979, I cannot recall either of us ever again even mentioning the incident to the other. There was, after all, nothing more to say.

As for my associates, relatively little was made of the incident. There were congratulations, along with expressions of gratitude for the fact that we had managed to return safely. There were certainly no backslapping salutations, and quite properly so. Fellow professionals living a similar day-to-day experience in a life-threatening environment tend to share a common insight and appreciation regarding the significance of sheer good fortune in the outcome of any related enterprise.

To my relief and satisfaction, I was back flying combat missions in the same airplane within a couple of days. The airplane had not been damaged, although the ground crew ended up spending quite a few days getting the wheat debris out of its nooks and crannies. As luck would have it, however, I eventually was forced to land that very airplane, wheels up, in a muddy field just behind the British lines.

This narrative would be far from complete without the accordance of due and proper tribute to the two wingmen who flew overhead and provided close air support during the entire episode. It is practically certain that the rescue would not have been successful without their timely attack on the German troops approaching my position in the wheat field. In fact, they probably saved my life. Indeed, for that matter, they may have saved Bert's life as well. Be that as it may, the fact is that they were there, in the direct line of enemy fire, doing what they could to protect us. I will be forever grateful for their selfless dedication.

Bert's wingman was 2d Lieutenant Thomas Wood, of Macon, Georgia. My wingman was Flight Officer Marion Woolard, of Richmond, Virginia. As far as I know, Wood survived the war. Woolard, however, came to a tragic end. After I became his flight commander, he regularly flew my wing in combat. We even shared a Nissen hut as living quarters, and became close friends. His chain of misfortune began on November 16, 1944. The group had broken escort over Belgium, returned to central Germany, and was working at low level in the Marburg area, having excellent results strafing railway locomotives and "goods wagons" while flying in and out of snow squalls and intermittent rain showers. In the course of this action, Woolard's aircraft took a direct hit from a flak gun and caught fire. He pulled up, rolled over to inverted flight, and bailed out of the burning Mustang at about 2,000 feet above ground level. Woolard survived the episode, but was captured and taken prisoner. After spending a number of months in captivity, he managed to escape from prison camp, and by April 1945 he had made his way to the forward area of the battle zone, where he was mortally wounded in an American artillery barrage while trying to cross through our front lines—a tragic victim of the unpredictable fortunes of war.

For his brave and audacious act on August 18, 1944, Lieutenant Deacon Priest was awarded a Distinguished Service Cross. On September 11, 1944, 1st Lieutenant Deacon Priest shot down a Bf-109 near Kassel,

Germany, and on September 27, he downed an FW-190 near Eschwege, Germany. His next aerial victory was over a Bf-109 near Naumberg, Germany, on November 2, and he achieved ace status when he downed two FW-190s over Misburg, Germany on November 26, 1944. In the same period, he participated in the last shuttle mission over Warsaw, flying in close escort of the bombers dropping supplies to beleaguered Polish fighters, then on to Russia, Italy, and back to England. And October produced a close call when he belly-landed his flak-damaged Mustang in France, just behind British lines, in a muddy field that had not yet been cleared of German land mines.

Captain Deacon Priest returned home in December 1944, after flying 310 combat hours in 67 missions over enemy territory. After the war, he made the service his career and retired with the rank of colonel in 1968.

NEVER SMOKE IN THE COCKPIT

2d Lieutenant HARLEY BROWN, USAAF
55th Fighter Squadron, 20th Fighter Group
Near Saarbrucken, Germany—August 28, 1944

Harley Lee Brown was born on April 1, 1922, in Humboldt, Kansas. His first flight experience was at the age of four, when his barnstorming uncle used him as a shill to entice people to fly in the uncle's biplane. At fourteen, Brown went into show business full time with his parents—a career that ended when he graduated from high school in 1941. After enlisting in the Army on September 16, 1942, he was selected for flight training in the Army Air Forces, graduated with Class 44-B from Foster Field in Victoria, Texas, and made his way through the replacement system to England, where he joined the 20th Fighter Group.

On Lieutenant Brown's first combat mission—August 25, 1944—he was credited with damaging two Ju-88 medium bombers during a ground-strafing attack. Nothing happened on his second mission, on August 26, and on August 27 he was involved in an airfield strafing attack. Ground fire that day claimed four 55th Fighter Squadron P-51 pilots, including the group commander, who was Brown's element leader.

♦

The 20th Fighter Group was famous and known as the "Loco Busters," for destroying 400 locomotives and damaging 122 during World War II. My first loco busting mission was my fourth combat mission. It was flown between Bad Kreuznach and Saarbrucken, on the German frontier, during the afternoon of August 28, 1944. That day, I flew on the wing of 1st Lieutenant Joseph Ford, who was leading our flight.

On most missions, the 20th Fighter Group joined the bombers near the front lines and escorted them over the target area and back to the front lines. On some of the shorter missions, when we had enough fuel and ammunition, after leaving the bombers the group would drop down to the deck and look for targets of opportunity. Not like the old saying—"Grandmothers in tennis shoes pushing baby buggies"—but military targets, with locomotives being our main objectives. Destroying locos was one of our favorite sports. After one or two passes with good concentrated hits with our API rounds, the boiler would explode and shoot steam 40 or 50 feet into the air, like Old Faithful.

On most missions, we wore oxygen masks for four to six hours. After that length of time, the mask seemed like it was glued on. Descending through 10,000 feet, I would almost have to peel it off. Next in order, I would unbuckle or loosen my safety belt and shoulder straps, which I always kept very tight and snug, ready for any dogfight with the Nazis, since these usually required very violent maneuvers. How good it felt to feel free and regain my circulation.

Now I was ready for that much wanted, relaxing cigarette, which was hard to get to with all the winter clothing we had to wear to keep halfway warm at 30,000 feet. Those first few puffs would taste about as good as they did during a rest period after having fun in bed.

On that fourth mission—the heavy bombers were grounded that day by bad weather—I was tooling along 200 or 300 feet above the ground, enjoying my cigarette and looking for any military target. Our flight was in line-abreast formation as it passed over a small hill, and all of a sudden I spotted a train sitting in a deep valley. When fighter planes were in an area, trains would try to hide in deep valleys or tunnels.

This train was fairly close to me, so I had to push the joystick quickly forward. With my seat and shoulder straps loose, this violent maneuver threw me up with my back against the top of the canopy. My dinghy, which I sat on, turned edgeways and pinned me against the canopy, jamming the joystick forward, keeping my P-51 in a steep dive.

All of a sudden, that great-tasting cigarette became a great problem. I was having no luck getting that dinghy back in place with one hand, so I jammed that cigarette between my lips to free both hands. My Mustang's nose was heading for that locomotive like I had given it free reins and it was heading home.

I was fighting that dinghy like mad. The locomotive was getting closer and closer and bigger and bigger. Just as I thought I was ready to buy the farm, the dinghy slipped into place, allowing me to grab the joystick and pull back with all my might.

I passed over the top of the locomotive, barely missing it by about five yards. With my getting so close to it and not firing my guns, I bet the engineer thought, "Those crazy Yankees are turning into kamikaze pilots, but this one chickened out."

As I gained altitude, I gave a great sigh of relief, regained my composure, and tightened my seat and shoulder straps. I then made a 360-degree turn for another pass. This time, with a good long burst from my six .50-caliber machine guns, those APIs lit up the locomotive like a Christmas tree, and steam spurted up like Old Faithful. Later, Lieutenant Ford and I shared in destroying another loco. The entire group was credited that day with destroying twenty-five locos, ten freight cars, four trucks, a radar station, and a power station—a pretty good day's work.

For the rest of my fifty-seven missions, I never loosened my safety belt or shoulder straps and *never* smoked a cigarette in the cockpit. All these years later, I still don't know what happened to that damned cigarette! I hope I didn't swallow it.

Second Lieutenant Harley Brown did not get into the scoring column until November 2, 1944, when he downed two FW-190s and a Bf-109 near Halle. He next downed an FW-190 near Koblenz, and after promotion to first lieutenant, Brown achieved ace status when he downed two Bf-109s over Magdeburg on January 14, 1944. Brown remained in the reserves after the war and retired as a lieutenant colonel. He is also a retired United Air Lines captain.

SAVE THE BOMBERS

1st Lieutenant FRANK GERARD, USAAF
503d Fighter Squadron, 339th Fighter Group
Annaberg, Germany—September 11, 1944

Francis Robert Gerard was born in Belleville, New Jersey, on July 11, 1924. He graduated from high school in June 1941, and on October 22, biked from his home in Newark to the recruiting station in Lyndhurst. It was his intention to enlist in the Marine Corps, but he was arrested at the entrance to the building by a sign depicting Uncle Sam pointing his finger and emblazoned with the question, "Can You Fly?" A crack athlete and a top scholar, young Gerard said to himself, Why not?, and proceeded to the Army Air Forces recruiter. He passed the written exam with ease, but when he returned for his physical the next day, he could not get the recruiter to commit to an early departure for training, so he threatened to join the Marines. At this point, the teenager was ushered into the office of a full colonel, who questioned him on various aspects of his life. At last, the colonel promised to have the young pilot recruit sworn in on October 26 and on his way as soon as possible. The colonel's word was golden—Gerard was sworn into the Army on October 26, 1942, and on his way to training on December 18.

Second Lieutenant Frank Gerard, age nineteen, emerged from flight training with class 43-H at Craig Field, Alabama, on August 30, 1943. After completing his training with a replacement training unit, he was assigned to the 339th Fighter-Bomber Group, which had been formed as a light dive-bomber unit in mid-1942 and now was undergoing training as a P-39 fighter-bomber unit at Rice Field, California.

The group was shipped to England in March 1944 and there it transitioned to P-51s for escort duty with the VIII Fighter Command's 66th Fighter Wing. The group flew its first mission, a fighter sweep ahead of the heavy bombers, on April 30, 1944.

First Lieutenant Frank Gerard scored his first aerial victory, a Bf-109 he downed with only 42 bullets, while escorting bombers near Gotha, Germany, on August 16, 1944.

♦

I flew my entire combat tour as a member of the 503rd Fighter Squadron, 339th Fighter Group, based at Station 378, Fowlmere, England.

On September 11, 1944, we were awakened early by the many B-17s and B-24s droning overhead to complete their join-ups in the murky weather prevalent in England at that time of the year. I remember so well that it was pretty foggy that morning, and so I hoped that I would be able to sleep a little while longer. That was not to be, so my five Nissen hut buddies and I donned our damp flying suits and sloshed through the mud to have our sumptuous breakfast. Afterwards, we bicycled to the briefing hut to receive our mission for the day.

It was a typical briefing at the start, but when it came to the type of tactics that the bomber boxes were to employ that day enroute to Grimma, Germany, and how we were to effect the rendezvous and the escort procedures, I could sense the perking interest of my fellow pilots and operations officers. En route to the target near Leipzig, we were told, we would not use the normal formation of boxes in trail. Rather, the bomber boxes would fly basically line abreast into Germany and then wheel into trail at a designated point before the Initial Point (IP). We could only conclude that this method of approach was to confuse the German air defenses. And it did cause confusion, no doubt about it, but mostly on the part of the Eighth Air Force escorts, both P-51s and P-47s. When the time came for the Fortresses to wheel into position toward the IP, the 503d Fighter Squadron, with a total of fourteen Mustangs, was the only fighter unit in the proper position to offer protection to the many boxes of bombers.

While we were still en route to the target area, the Germans sent up several decoy Bf-109s to entice our fighter units away from the bomber force. Our squadron was led by Major John Aitken, an experienced fighter pilot. We stayed with the B-17s, ignored the decoys, and maneuvered toward the front of the scattered bomber formation.

When we were in the vicinity of Annaburg, I called in a mass of bandits, and Major Aitken gave the order to drop our external fuel tanks. It certainly was a frightening spectacle to spot the two gaggles of fighters approaching the bombers. The gaggles were composed of more than fifty enemy aircraft each, and the sight of them raised the hackles of my hair, as I am sure it did to the thirteen other Mustang pilots in our formation. I thought, This is it! However, we pressed on even though our instincts warned us that we would not return from this mission. But it was our duty to protect the bombers to the best of our daring and skill.

As the enemy aircraft approached the bomber force, we dove down and began the attack. At first, I didn't think of anything except trying to distract the 109s from their goal of destroying the B-17s by getting them to mix it up with us. To this end, I fired a burst in their general direction, but I was firing from out of range. This premature action had no effect upon the deadly determination of the 109s and 190s.

I was flying as the element lead in Major Aitken's flight, and initially I was slightly ahead of the others, in the nearest position to the enemy gaggles. After my futile attempt to distract the enemy I said to myself, Steady, boy. Concentrate on one at a time. Then I picked out a 109 that was about 300 yards out and crossing in front of me at about a 40-degree angle. He was the tail-end charlie of a flight of 109s.

I put all my football-passing and skeet-shooting experience to good use then. I gave him a good lead while aiming a little high, because of the distance. Then I gave him a short burst from my six .50-caliber machine guns. He blew up with coolant and flames streaming out. My wingman, 2d Lieutenant Raymond Mayer, saw him spin out with his wheels down and pieces flying off, so it was a confirmed victory. Scared as I was at the time, my lucky hits gave me a lot of confidence and elation.

I pressed on through the melee, and as we reached the American bombers, I maneuvered frantically to get in position while protecting my tail. All hell was breaking loose around me, and there were so many aircraft involved that it was difficult to distinguish friends from enemies, but thank God there were so many of them and few of us. I finally picked out an FW-190 that was in a slight dive. I got on his tail and gave him a short burst, and he immediately exploded. Captain James Robinson confirmed this kill. I then damaged another 109, but in the confusion of diving through the bomber formation—I swear that I could hear the rapid fire from the heavy armament of the B-17s, and the sky around me was filled with parachutes and pieces of debris flying through the air—I wasn't able to follow him to confirm this kill. Much remained to be done to assist the bomber crews and their aircraft.

Opening to max throttle, I attacked another 109 that was going down in a dive, but as I was positioning on him, I spotted two more 109s coming in on my tail. As we were already getting into a sort of Lufbery, I accelerated my turn and got it in so tight that I thought my G-suit would break me in half. (We were one of the pioneer groups to test the pneumatic G-suit, and I said at the time that I never wanted to fly combat in a fighter without wearing one.) Because of the benefits of the G-suit, I was able to twist my head without blacking out, and I was able to outmaneuver the two 109s. I was determined that they would never fight against our valiant bomber crews again.

I put that P-51 through every gyration it was designed for, and more. In fact, I snapped it around so forcefully that I was concerned about the wings coming off, but I gave it a go.

After two or three turns, I was on their tails. Though I was pulling a lot of Gs, I lined up on the nearer of the two 109s and gave him two or three short bursts. The pilot must have been amazed at this turn of events, for his previous target was now the aggressor—and was scoring hits all over his airplane. He blew up and started his final descent. I followed him in a steep dive and saw him spin into the ground.

While I was in this steep dive, Major Aitken passed me. He was on the tail of another 109, and he was getting serious strikes all over it. I pulled up because my speed was excessive, and this afforded me the opportunity to bounce another 109. I pressed the attack for what seemed like quite a while before I was in a position to fire. This 109 pilot was aggressive. He tried to lose me with various maneuvers and tactics, descending all the time. However, I was determined not to let this one fight another day. It was crazy up there at the time, but I got into position for a good deflection shot. When I was close enough I gave him a short burst, and he blew up and entered a crazy spin. As I pulled up in a tight turn to clear my tail and look for other enemy aircraft, I saw my 109 hit the ground. When he hit, he was still spinning.

Next, I spotted six more 109s break for the deck. I rolled after them, but I had only 110 gallons of gas left, so I broke off the attack, climbed to 15,000 feet, and began my long and lonely flight back to Fowlmere.

It had been a long day. The mission was seven hours and forty minutes, but adding the time for the fog-delayed takeoff, I was strapped into that Mustang for more than nine hours. My muscles and my mind were sorely challenged. I thought of a lot of different things that day, but most of all I was proud to be part of the 503d Fighter Squadron and thankful for the wisdom of Major Aitken for not being lured by the decoys, and for his dedication to protecting the bomber crews by following orders and not chasing across the skies for personal glory.

We did our best that day, but it was not good enough. Twelve B-17s went down in flames before other American fighters finally arrived to protect them on the flight home. I do not think I had the courage to be a bomber pilot over Germany. I had—and still have—the utmost respect for the valor and dedication of those brave crews.

The 503d Fighter Squadron shot down fifteen German fighters in that action, and we damaged many others. The 339th Fighter Group was awarded the Presidential Unit Citation for its achievements on September 10 and 11, 1944, and I was awarded the Silver Star for "Gallantry in Action."

Frank Gerard was awarded four confirmed victories for the twelve-minute September 11 fight over Annaburg; he was a five-kill ace, and only a month past his twentieth birthday. He went on to down two Bf-109s, and damage a third, near Magdeburg on March 2, 1945; and shortly after being promoted to the rank of captain, he scored his eighth and final victory on March 18, 1945, when he downed an FW-190 near Dummer Lake.

After World War II, Frank Gerard served with the New Jersey Air National Guard while completing college. He earned his law degree in 1949, but his legal career was cut short when he was called to active duty during the Korean War. Thereater, he divided his time between various civilian pursuits, the New Jersey Air National Guard, and numerous stints on active duty with the Air Force, including a tour during the 1962 Berlin Crisis. He flew jet fighters until 1976 and retired from the Air Force several years later with the rank of major general.

Rudy Augarten,
Israeli Air Force

Lieutenant Commander
Tom Blackburn, USN

Major Jack Bolt, USMC

1st Lieutenant John Bolyard, USAAF

Vice Squadron Commander Charlie Bond, AVG

Lieutenant Guy Bordelon, USN

Lieutenant Colonel Jerry Brown, USAF

2d Lieutenant
Harley Brown,
USAAF

Captain Jim Carter, USAAF

Captain Tink Cole, USAAF

Major Niven Cranfill, USAAF

1st Lieutenant Bob Curtis, USAAF

Captain Bud Fortier, USAAF

1st Lieutenant Herman Ernst, USAAF

1st Lieutenant
Cecil Foster, USAF

2d Lieutenant Dwaine Franklin, USAAF

1st Lieutenant Frank Gerard, USAAF

1st Lieutenant Bob Goebel, USAAF

Lieutenant (jg) Connie Hargreaves, USN

1st Lieutenant Ivan Hasek, USAAF

Lieutenant Colonel Ed Heller, USAF

Flying Officer Holly Hills, RCAF

2d Lieutenant George Hollowell, USMC

Flight Lieutenant Clarence Jasper, RCAF

Major Jim Kasler, USAF

Major John Loisel, USAAF

Colonel Mort Magoffin, USAAF

Ensign Jojo McGraw, USN

Ensign Don McPherson, USN

1st Lieutenant Larry O'Neill, USAAF

Lieutenant Jim Pearce, USN

Major Jack Price, USAAF

2d Lieutenant Deacon Priest, USAAF (*left*)
and Captain Bert Marshall, USAAF

Major Ed Roddy, USAAF

Major Jim Tapp, USAAF

Captain Darrell Welch, USAAF

PREY

Captain JIM CARTER, USAAF
61st Fighter Squadron, 56th Fighter Group
Langensbold, Germany—November 18, 1944

James Richard Carter was born in Pullman, Washington, on May 2, 1919. He attended Washington State College for three semesters after graduating from high school in 1937, and then he transferred to the University of North Carolina's pre-med program. Family problems forced Carter to return to Pullman in 1940 to work on the family farm, but there he became enamored with military flying when a neighbor's son serving in the Army Air Corps occasionally flew over the region in a B-17 bomber. Carter was accepted into the Flying Cadet program in March 1941 and was called up for flight school in November. He graduated from Kelly Field, Texas, with Class 42-F and was assigned directly to the 56th Fighter Group, which had begun the long job of taming the new P-47 Thunderbolt fighter in Stratford, Connecticut. He was one of the famed 56th's stalwarts for nearly the entire war.

First Lieutenant Carter's first combat was on August 18, 1943, and he damaged a Bf-109 over the Netherlands. He was promoted to the rank of captain in December and became the 61st Fighter Squadron's operations officer under Major Francis Gabreski—the beginning of a successful partnership that lasted until Gabreski was shot down and captured in July 1944. With Gabreski and other 56th Fighter Group leaders, Carter was responsible for hammering out many of the group's—and the VIII Fighter Command's—most successful fighter tactics.

Captain Carter scored his first confirmed victory on January 11, 1944—a Bf-109 he downed near Osnabruck, Germany. On January 30, he downed an FW-190 over the Netherlands, and he shot down an Me-110 over Steinhuder Lake, Germany, on February 20, 1944. Thereafter, Carter flew fewer of the promising missions. When the extremely aggressive Gabby Gabreski moved up to become the group operations officer, he took Jim Carter as his assistant, but only one of them was permitted to participate on a given mission, and Gabreski managed to post himself to more of the promising missions than Carter. Neverthe-

less, Carter downed another FW-190 over Hoperhofen Airdrome, Germany, on May 22, 1944, and he achieved ace status on July 4 when he downed a Bf-109 over France. So far, including other German aircraft he probably destroyed or damaged, Captain Jim Carter had never failed to hit an enemy airplane at which he fired.

On November 18, 1944, the Eighth Air Force mission was given to VIII Fighter Command aircraft that were assigned to strafe oil storage depots, airdromes, and rail traffic in Germany. More than 400 P-47s and P-51s were directed against these targets. The 56th Fighter Group was assigned to hit an oil storage depot at Langensbold, northeast of Hanau, Germany. The weather forecast was for clear skies and ground haze in the target area, and it was as predicted.

Major Harold Comstock was the group leader that day, and he flew with the 63rd Fighter Squadron. I was leading the 61st, and Captain Mike Jackson was the 62d Squadron leader. Each squadron formation was composed of sixteen P-47s. Except for flight leaders and element leaders, the 61st pilots were mostly newcomers, and this was only the first or second mission for most of them.

As we arrived over the target area at about noon, Major Comstock was unable to locate the target due to the ground haze, but I could see it from my position. Harold told me to attack the oil storage target while the 62d Squadron gave me top cover. Harold then took the 63d on to Gross Ostheim Airdrome, where they strafed Bf-109s and He-111s, claiming five destroyed and one damaged. Unknown to me, the 62d Squadron zipped over to join the 63rd in its turkey shoot, which left me with no top cover.

The half-buried oil tanks were dispersed in a wooded area and they were well camouflaged. Our first pass was a low-level attack, but due to the haze, we missed the target to one side. It was unsuccessful. I reformed the squadron at 8,000 feet over the target and proceeded to dive-strafe the oil tanks. We made several diving attacks, and set five or six of the tanks on fire.

On recovery from my last dive, I spotted a Bf-109 and made almost a 360-degree turn to get behind him. He was at 1,000 feet, flying parallel to the railway track from Hanau to Gelnhausen and on the south side of the tracks, heading east. I fired from about 300 yards with small deflection and got a few meager hits. My K-14 gunsight didn't seem to be working, so I switched it to "fixed" and fired quite a long burst, which blew pieces of the canopy and cockpit metal off. The 109 crashed and burned. I saw the parachute of the pilot about ten yards to the right of the airplane, unfolded but not open.

We reassembled our four flights and headed up and back to the target. My number-three man had a K-25 camera in his aircraft, and I wanted him to get some pictures. Just south of the target, at about 8,000 feet, I started a right turn to the north to cross over when I saw—and heard reported—that sixteen or more FW-190s were coming in on us from the northeast, at about the 5 o'clock position. At first sight, I had thought they were our top cover—the 62d Fighter Squadron—because the Germans were flying a formation very much like ours and had evidently come down from not more than 2,000 feet above us. When I realized that these were enemy fighters, I called the 62d to come and help. Meanwhile, the 61st broke into the FWs, and the fight started.

Three or four of the FWs took turns firing at me from 90 degrees and narrower angles, and finally one hung on to me. The 47s and 190s appeared to be all over the sky, but this one joker stuck tight to me, firing mostly at too great an angle or from out of range. I out-turned him several times, making him stall, but he could accelerate faster than I could on recovery, and he kept coming back at me.

During about the fifth such turn, I felt that my airplane was on on the verge of snapping. He only had about a 70-degree deflection, which seemed too little to me, so I rolled it over and hit the deck with the water injection on. My thoughts were that God was seeking quick retribution for my downing of the 109 pilot, and I sure hoped the armor plate behind my seat would stop the 190's 20mm shells from hitting me in the head.

As I kept flying straight, I slowly increased my lead from the 190 to more than 1,000 yards, so his 20mm shells were bursting behind me. I kept to the deck with full power on and prayed that he would either run out of ammo or get tired. Just when I thought he would do neither, he pulled up and away. I was so relieved to see him go, I do not think I'd have tried to catch him even if I'd had the fuel. My P-47 sure put out for a long stretch at full power.

I climbed to 15,000 feet and, except for an occasional burst of flak, made it home to Boxted Airdrome without further mishap. The good news I learned then was that, before the 62d Squadron joined the fight, the 61st's youngsters had claimed eight 190s destroyed, two probably destroyed, and two damaged. When the 62d finally arrived, they got an additional four. The bad news was that two of our pilots were missing. One was seen as he bailed of his airplane after being attacked by an FW-190. The second got separated from the rest of the squadron during the encounter, but he later reported by radio that he was all right. He returned after the war from a prisoner of war camp.

Altogether, between mid-1943 and 1945, Jim Carter flew 137 combat missions and 435 combat hours over western Europe. He remained in the service after the war and retired in 1968 with the rank of colonel. Much of the 56th Fighter Group's astounding success in World War II is owed to Jim Carter's technical, tactical, and planning prowess.

Colonel Jim Carter passed away in 1996.

OUTNUMBERED

Major NIVEN CRANFILL, USAAF
368th Fighter Squadron, 359th Fighter Group
Near Merseberg, Germany—November 27, 1944

Niven K. Cranfill was born in Ft. Worth, Texas, on July 23, 1920. As a boy, he built model airplanes, and he often saw military aircraft based at Army Air Corps bases in Texas. From an early age, he was simply in love with the idea of flying. As a result, he attended the University of Texas through the first semester of his junior year, leaving as soon as he had the college credits required and was old enough to be accepted into the Army Air Corps Flying Cadet program.

Cadet Cranfill began Primary flight training at King City, California, took the Basic course at Taft, California, and graduated with his commission and wings from Luke Field, Arizona, on December 12, 1941. Though originally assigned to train in A-20 light bombers, Cranfill was sent to the 20th Pursuit Group in the immediate wake of Pearl Harbor and the onset of the Pacific War. While serving with the 20th, Lieutenant Cranfill trained in P-40s. In fact, he took his first flight in a P-40 the day he checked into the 20th Group at Hamilton Field, California, on December 24, 1942.

After serving briefly with the 20th Group, Cranfill was tabbed as an instructor in P-39s, P-40s, and P-43s, and he took part in accelerated service tests on early P-47s. Finally, in March 1943, he was transferred as a flight commander to the 359th Fighter Group, which was then being formed at Westover Field, Massachusetts. The 359th, in P-47s, moved to East Wretham Airdrome in England in October 1943 and became part of the VIII Fighter Command. When the unit became operational in December 1943, Captain Cranfill became the 369th Fighter Squadron's operations officer.

Cranfill damaged a German fighter in January 1944 and, following his promotion to the rank of major, shared in a credit for a probable Bf-109 in May. The group transitioned to P-51s in April 1944 and was used in a strike and ground-support role before and after D-Day. Cranfill was awarded a Silver Star for penetrating heavy flak and skipping two 500-pound bombs into a rail tunnel near Conches, France, on June 10, 1944. On August 16, he downed a Bf-109 near Einbeck, Germany, his first official victory.

Following a leave in the United States during September and October, Major Cranfill was moved up to command the 368th Fighter Squadron.

The 359th Fighter Group was based at Station 133, East Wreatham, England, which was located halfway between Cambridge and Norwich in East Anglia. My duty was Commanding Officer, 368th Fighter Squadron, whose call sign was Jigger. November 27 was the sixth mission of my second combat tour.

My airplane on this mission was a P-51D-15-NA. The Army Air Corps number, 44-14857, was painted on the vertical stabilizer. The 368th Squadron identifier was CV-Q, which was painted on each side of the fuselage. The engine was a 1,610 cubic-inch liquid-cooled V-12 Rolls Royce manufactured under license by Packard Motor Company. Armaments for this mission were six .50-caliber machine guns with 300 rounds each. The fuel load was approximately 279 gallons in internal tanks, plus two 105-gallon drop tanks. This quantity of fuel allowed us to escort the bombers for up to three hours to and from Berlin or further.

The mission leader on November 27 was Colonel John Randolph, the 359th Fighter Group commander. Our briefed mission was a strafing sweep of the airfield at Ehmen, Germany. This was a minimum effort of thirty-six P-51s, twelve per squadron; a normal effort at this time was forty-eight aircraft, sixteen per squadron. My takeoff time was 1021 hours.

Weather over the Continent was variable, with large masses of clouds at all altitudes and some clear areas where we could see the ground. En route to the target, we climbed to about 28,000 feet. My squadron was to the left and above the squadron led by Colonel Randolph, who was down sun, per our usual tactics.

The weather caused doubts that we would be able to attack our primary target, but all doubts were removed when our leader was instructed by radio by MEW (Microwave Early Warning), our control station located on the Continent, to turn to a southerly course and advised that many enemy aircraft directly ahead.

The group commander ordered the group to drop tanks and prepare for engagement. Since I could not see any aircraft ahead, I countermand this order: "Jigger Squadron, hold tanks." This order was too late, however. Only my wingman, 2d Lieutenant Richard Daniels, complied; everyone else dropped their tanks.

The "enemy" aircraft turned out to be friendly P-51s, apparently en route home to England. Shortly, most of our group departed for England due to their low fuel supply.

I was continuing on our assigned heading with Lieutenant Daniels when I heard Captain Ray Wetmore, of our group's 370th Squadron, call in 100-plus bandits near Hanover. I soon saw this very large group—200-plus, we agreed later—apparently attempting to form up in a large clearing in the weather.

I dropped tanks then and selected a Bf-109 that was at about 23,000 feet. As I attacked, the German pilot saw me and began a sharp left turn. I followed, closing, and tracked his aircraft with my new K-14 computing gunsight. I fired a burst but scored no hits. I fired again, and no hits again. I caged the gunsight to the manual position to which I was accustomed and, while still in a tight left turn, I led the 109 and fired another burst. This time, I hit it in the tail section. The rudder and most of the tail came off. As the 109 went out of control, the pilot bailed out, flying no more than 20 feet to the left of my plane. I later saw his chute open.

At this moment, my attention shifted to a diving FW-190, and I immediately gave chase with full throttle (70 inches manifold pressure and 3,000 RPM engine speed) Next, Lieutenant Daniels called, "Jigger Leader, there is a one-owe-nine coming around behind us." I called back, "Take care of him." I could not see a 109 on my tail, but Daniels did take care of it. He claimed one Bf-109 destroyed, but he was awarded only a probable by the review board because he did not see it crash.

The dive continued and I began closing on the FW-190. My bullet-proof windscreen—one-inch-thick glass—iced up on the inside as we entered warmer air from the intense cold at high altitude. As we leveled out on the deck at about 50 feet, I lost sight of the FW-190 because the two side panels of my windshield assembly also frosted over. I tried to wipe the iced windshield with my gloved left hand, but to no avail. While doing this, I saw another P-51 joining up with me—a pilot apparently lost from his group leader. I tried wiping the frost from the right side of the windshield with my left hand while flying the aircraft with my right. When I could clear the panel enough, I saw the FW-190 immediately in front of me. I fired a good burst without the benefit of gunsight and saw .50-caliber bullets hit both sides of the fuselage forward of the tail assembly. I was very close to him. Our six machine guns were harmonized to converge at 750 feet, but he was nearer than that distance. My windshield panel frosted up again, so I pulled up from the deck to look around and clear the windshield as the ice was beginning to melt. I could not find the FW-190, but the pilot who had joined me saw the plane crash as result of my gunfire, and he confirmed it as destroyed when he returned to his home base. (This claim was also confirmed many years later by the German pilot himself.)

At this time, I saw another German aircraft, a Bf-109, ahead of me and turning toward me in a right turn. We were about 2,000 feet above the ground. This was an even fight, in a tight right-hand turn, each of us directly opposite the other in the circle. I saw the wing flaps of the 109 extend partly to enable a tighter turn. I had not seen nor heard of this tactic employed by the Germans. Then I said to myself, "I had better go to work." I extended my flaps to the combat position—20 degrees—applied full engine power, and quickly out-turned the 109 to where I could get a shot at about 40 degrees deflection. Still using my gunsight in the manual position, I established a lead on the 109 and fired a good burst. I saw a concentration of hits at the cockpit on the right side of the airplane. The 109 immediately rolled over into a dive and exploded upon hitting the ground.

The elapsed time from dropping the external fuel tanks to this part of the engagement was 13 minutes. My new wingman was still with me, and he accompanied me to the English coast. We never did have radio contact. I noted his aircraft identification and reported this to the squadron intelligence office during debriefing.

I landed at 1511 hours. After the flight, while we were still debriefing, our intelligence officer received a telephone call from the other pilot's group intelligence officer, who said that he had confirmed two aircraft destroyed. These, along with the one who bailed out, totaled three for the mission.

Captain Ray Wetmore, of our group's 370th Fighter Squadron, entered the fray with a flight of four P-51s. He shot down three, Lieutenant Robert York shot down three, and another pilot in the division shot down one. Altogether, six P-51s from our group attacked an estimated two hundred FW-190 and Bf-109s, and we shot down ten, plus two probables, without loss.

I was proud of my marksmanship on this engagement. I expended only 515 rounds of the 1,800 we carried in our six guns. My early years learning to shoot flying birds and small moving animals on the outskirts of Abilene, Texas, paid off on this mission. I was later awarded a second Silver Star for this day's action.

The rest of my second tour was not remarkable. I did destroy four locomotives on a mission the day the Allies performed the aerial assault over the Rhine River en route to Berlin. Again, we were on an area patrol to shoot anything that moved toward the U.S. Army drop zone. All four locomotives were pulling freight cars in that direction.

I shot down one Me-262 jet fighter and damaged another in a brief engagement near Leipzig on March 19, 1945. I finished my second tour in April 1945, having been promoted to lieutenant colonel the month before.

Lieutenant Colonel Niven Cranfill accepted a regular commission at the end of World War II and remained in fighters for most of the rest of his career. He commanded fighter squadrons, a fighter group, and a fighter wing with a nuclear delivery capability.

During the Korean War, Niven Cranfill served as a shift chief in the combat operations center at the Tokyo headquarters of the Far East Air Forces. He was promoted to the rank of colonel in 1953, During the Vietnam War, he served as the assistant commander for air operations at the Saigon headquarters of the Military Assistance Command, Vietnam. He retired in 1970.

SHOT DOWN

Captain TINK COLE, USAAF
55th Fighter Squadron, 20th Fighter Group
Stendal Airdrome, Germany—February 25, 1945

Charles Harold Cole, Jr., was born in St. Joseph, Missouri, on September 27, 1920. It was Charles Lindbergh and his epic flight to Paris in 1928 that sparked young Tink Cole's passion to become a flier; from then on, he read every dime novel about flight he could get his hands on. When Cole was fourteen, his focus on flight took on new dimensions when he learned details of Army Air Corps pilot training; from then on, only an Air Corps career would suffice.

Cole was getting ready to go back to college when the entrance requirement for Air Corps pilot training was lowered from four years to two. He was within weeks of having the requisite sixty college credits when he enlisted as an Air Corps Flying Cadet in April 1941. He graduated from St. Joseph Junior College in May, and reported to Fort Leavenworth, Kansas, for his physical in June.

When it turned out that Cole was two pounds underweight, but acceptable in all other details, the Army flight surgeon gave him a week to put on the extra weight. When Cole returned after eating all the bananas and drinking all the water he could stuff inside himself, he was four pounds heavier, and thus qualified.

Cadet Cole was sworn in at Fort Leavenworth on October 31, 1941, and assigned to Primary flight training at Thunderbird Field in

Glendale Arizona. Basic was completed at Minter Field in Bakersfield, California, and he completed Advanced training at Luke Field, Arizona. There, on May 21, 1942, Tink Cole graduated with Class 42-E and pinned on his second lieutenant's bars and Silver Wings.

Lieutenant Cole was assigned to Luke Field as an instructor in AT-6s, where, toward the end of his tour, he helped train Nationalist Chinese Air Force pilots in AT-6s and P-40s. After sixteen months at Luke, he was transferred to the Central Instructor School at Randolph Field, Texas. In the autumn of 1944, Captain Cole was shipped to England and assigned to the 20th Fighter Group's 77th Fighter Squadron, a veteran P-38 unit that was just transitioning to P-51s. He flew his first combat mission on October 9, 1944, and was credited with his first victory, a Bf-109 he downed near Perleberg, Germany, on January 14, 1945.

It was a dull, dreary, high-overcast day that Sunday, February 25, 1945. The 20th Fighter Group had been assigned to the Magdeburg area for strafing and targets of opportunity. This was to be my first mission with the 55th Fighter Squadron. The week before, Colonel Robert Montgomery, our group commander, had called me into his quarters and told me that he was transferring me from the 77th Fighter Squadron, with which I had flown some 240 combat hours, to the 55th, as their new operations officer. I voiced my objection, but in vain. I was to report to the 55th the next day and, in addition, the colonel said I was flying too much and I was to cut down on missions, flying only one in four or five.

I had been on the ground all week, so I decided this Sunday would be a good time to break in with the 55th. I set up the squadron flight with me leading the lead flight (Sailor White), 1st Lieutenant Schuyler Baker leading Yellow Flight, Captain Dick Fruechtenicht leading Red Flight, and Captain Ron Howard leading Blue Flight. Typically, a squadron on a combat mission was made up of four flights—white (lead) flight, a yellow flight, a red flight, and a blue flight. There were four aircraft in each flight, making a total of sixteen aircraft in the squadron. White and Yellow flights made up the lead section, and Red and Blue flights made up the second section.

In ground strafing, we cruised around at low altitude, looking for any movement or, in the case of trains, looking for smoke. When we saw the smoke from a train, we approached it from a 90-degree direction, which enabled us to move in fast, strike, and get out. We did this because the Germans had been known to put one or two flak cars on the train, and if we approached the train lengthwise, they would drop the sides of the flak cars and start shooting. This could be disastrous, so we made the first pass 90 degrees to the train and then, if there was no resistance, we made subsequent passes along the length of the train until the boiler blew and the train engine was out of commission.

We did find a couple of trains while cruising around at 1,000 feet above the ground, and we did put them out of commission. However, due to the poor visibility, Fruechtenicht and his entire two-flight section lost me and my lead section while we were strafing trains and other ground targets.

While still looking for targets, we came across a German airdrome with four FW-190 fighters on the take-off roll and the rest of the squadron lined up waiting to get airborne. I let the four aircraft get airborne, and then I went after the leader. His two-ship element had broken off to the left and his wingman followed them, so the leader was alone.

In a few seconds I found myself in a tight Lufbery Circle at 500 feet above the ground, staring across the circle at the German pilot and wondering how I could get the advantage and enough lead on him to shoot him down. For the moment, we were evenly matched, but then I remembered that if I lowered 10 degrees of flaps, I could increase my angle of attack and turn my P-51 in a tighter circle. This I did, and sure enough, I began to turn a tighter circle and started to get a lead on the FW.

Apparently the German saw what was happening and decided to try a reversement. I saw his ailerons move and knew what he was going to try. I was ahead of him. When he completed the reversement, I was waiting and had a good lead on him. I gave a short burst with my guns and either I hit him or the FW-190 was a snap-rolling airplane, because he never recovered from the reversement but kept snap-rolling into the ground. Of course, we were only 500 feet above the ground and this is not much room for maneuvering a fast fighter aircraft.

I turned and dropped my left wing so I could get a clear view of the crashed FW-190 and take pictures with my hand-held camera for confirmation. As I completed the turn and looked up, another FW-190 suddenly appeared in front of me. All I had to do was grip the trigger to activate the guns, which I did. I apparently caught the FW-190 in the converging cone of my guns, which I had set at 2,000 feet. The plane just blew up. Having just taken off, they must have had a full fuel load, and with the main fuselage tank situated mid-airplane, beneath the pilot, a hit in this area would be disastrous, which it was.

I flew through the debris of this plane and was about to pull out when I saw another FW-190 about to belly-land in a field. I couldn't resist not helping him belly in. All I had to do was drop my nose, line up my gunsight, and give him a burst, which I did. He crashed.

I had started a turn and climb to gain some altitude and get away from this area when another FW-190 appeared in front of me. I turned to get a lead on him and fired my guns. Again, I must have hit the pilot. As he started to turn away, the FW went into a snap-roll and snap-rolled into the ground. After I shot him down, I looked around and could see nothing but large German crosses on airplanes. I decided it was time to get the hell out of there.

I could not see or find any of my squadron. I set course for England and was thinking about my good fortune when my instrument panel just blew apart, leaving nothing but twisted metal and broken glass.

My first reaction was to bail out. I didn't know how badly the airplane was damaged, or how much time I had to leave it. I opened the canopy, unhooked my belt, and stood up to dive over the side. It was then that the connecting cord on my headset jerked on my head and caused me to think, Wait a minute! I then realized that the aircraft was still flying and the engine sounded okay. I thought, Hell, settle back down and fly this bird out, which I started to do.

I looked around, but there wasn't any other aircraft in the area. This was a phenomenon that always mystified me. I had been in dogfights before where one minute the air was full of airplanes, or so it seemed, and in the next few minutes there wouldn't be an aircraft in the sky. Where they all went so quickly, I'll never know. Not having a compass or any other instruments, I guessed at a heading that would get me back into France or England. About this time my wingman, Major Maurice Cristadoro, a green member of the 20th Group staff, joined me, and we kept flying in a westerly direction.

After about ten or fifteen minutes, I noticed sparks coming from underneath the cowling, and then I realized the burning sensation that I had on my face was coolant that had flowed back into the cockpit. The coolant caused a stinging sensation where glass from the instrument panel had hit me in the face. It was shortly after this that the engine froze up and I shut it down to prevent a fire. I looked around, found a field that looked good, set up a straight-in approach, and belly-landed the bird.

After the bird came to a stop, I stood up to get out, and it was then I realized I had not refastened my safety belt after my attempt to bail out. I got out of the cockpit, took off my chute, and left it and the dinghy in the cockpit. All this time, Major Cristadoro was circling overhead. I thought he was waiting for me to clear out so he could strafe the bird and burn it up, so I left the plane and headed for the woods. Then I saw Cristadoro heading for England. I wasn't about to go back to the bird and destroy it, but I did dig a hole and bury my G-suit and .45. I didn't want the G-suit to fall into enemy hands because it was new in our service and I didn't know whether or not the Germans knew anything about it or how it worked.

I got my little escape compass out and checked it to see if I was headed in the right direction. I was, and I thought as long as I was in this forest, I would keep going and then, during the night, maybe I could hook a ride on a train headed west. I kept walking. As long as I was in the forest, I was safe. After awhile I came to the end of the forest. There was nothing but small scrub cedars between it and another forest about 2,000 yards away. I got down on my hands and knees and started to crawl through the scrub bushes.

After about fifteen or twenty minutes, I stood up. Don't ask me why; I had been very careful up to this point, and I don't know why I stood up. As I looked around, I saw two soldiers to the east. As soon as I saw them, I dropped back to the ground, but it was too late. They saw me, and I heard their motorbikes start up. In a few minutes, I heard them right above me, telling me, I guess, to come out with my hands up, which I did.

I later found out these two soldiers were Home Guards. They took me to a small village and locked me up in what I guessed was the local jail. As we entered, I noticed a parachute on a table in front. I suppose it was my chute. This was about four or five in the afternoon. At about 7 or 8 in the evening, they loaded me in the back of a truck with two guards in *Luftwaffe* uniforms. After about thirty or forty minutes, the truck stopped and I was motioned to get out, which I did. I found out that I was on some kind of military installation, which I later learned was Magdeburg Airdrome.

I was led into a room in which a group of German officers was sitting behind a table, like a jury. The one that seemed to be in command said something to me in German, to which I replied, *"Nicht verschtaen."* The officer said something else, which I guessed to be, "If you don't understand German, why did you reply in German?" And I said, in English, "I only know a few German words, like *eine, zwei, drei."* Then I gave my name, rank, and serial number. This seemed to satisfy them, and I was taken to a cell and once again left alone.

After a short time, another German came in and looked at my forehead and cheeks, which had been nicked by flying glass when the instrument panel disintegrated. He dabbed some liquid on my cuts, which stung a bit. I assumed he was a doctor or medical orderly, and that the liquid was something like iodine or merthiolate. Then I was left alone until the following day.

In the morning, two Germans came to the cell and motioned me to follow them, which I did. We got into the back of a truck and left the base. When we stopped and got out, I saw we were at a train station. A large sign hanging from the roof and another in front of the door spelled out "Magdeburg." After a short wait, a train pulled in and we got on. I was glad that I was dressed the way I was—wool khaki shirt and pants, and an Army field jacket—as I was very inconspicuous.

Progress was slow. The train would run for about two or three hours and then stop. The engine would leave the cars on a siding, and there we would sit for a time, sometimes for three or four hours. Then the engine would come back, hook up to us, and we would be on the move again. I began to realize just how badly the Army Air Forces had disrupted the German transportation system. It took us almost five days to go about 300 kilometers, from Magdeburg to Frankfurt.

We arrived in Frankfurt early in the morning, left the train, got aboard a trolley car, and rode on it for about twenty minutes. We left the trolley car and entered what I later found out was the *Luftwaffe's* central interrogation center. I was photographed, strip-searched, given back my clothes, put in solitary confinement, and left alone.

The only food I had had since bellying in was some black bread and ersatz coffee at Magdeburg, and more of the same from the guards on the train. Shortly after noon, a guard came in with a bowl of something that looked like thick, gummy oatmeal. It looked awful, but it was warm and I was hungry, so I started to eat it. I had only taken two or three bites when another guard came in and motioned for me to follow him. I did, and he led me to an office and motioned me to enter. There was a German officer sitting behind the desk. I noticed that on the desk was my 16mm hand camera and some small pictures. The camera, I must explain, was the result of our group photo sergeant and me getting together and rigging up a 16mm gun camera on a P-38 pistol grip and fitting the camera with a long cord so I could plug it into the 24-volt DC outlet in my P-51 and shoot pictures. This was the first mission that I had taken the camera on, and I had shot pictures of my wingmen on the climb-out, and then I took pictures of the aircraft that I had shot down for confirmation purposes.

I didn't show any recognition or acknowledgement of the camera, nor even that the Germans had it and had developed the film.

The officer—I guess he was an officer, but a better term would be "interrogator"—had on the uniform of a *hauptmann,* a captain. I guess this was because I was a captain. He opened the conversation with, "How is our old friend, Captain Robert Riemensnider?" I knew then that the information they had was very old and out of date, because when I took off that Sunday, Bob Riemensnider was a major and had finished his tour. The German asked me what mission I was on. I replied with my name, rank, and serial number. He asked me some other questions, to which I again replied with name, rank, and serial number. After a time, he picked up the camera, pointed it at me, and asked what it was. Again, I replied with my name, rank, and serial number. After a few more questions, I said, "Look, if you want to keep hearing my name, rank, and serial number, just keep asking the questions. As for that camera, any photo enthusiast would know what it is and why I had it. That's all I will say." This seemed to satisfy him, and he called the guard and I assume told him to take me back to my cell.

Of course, when I got back, the gruel was cold and even more gummy and thick. I ate what I could because I was hungry, but it certainly was not the best lunch I have ever had. I was left alone the rest of the day and night. The evening meal was black bread and a cup of ersatz coffee. Then, for the first time in a long time, I got a good night's sleep.

The next morning, I was awakened by the guard bringing me my daily ration of black bread and ersatz coffee. I was left alone the rest of the morning, and shortly after noon, the guard came in with a bowl of the thick, gummy substance. Once again, I had only taken a few bites, while it was hot, before another guard came in and motioned for me to follow him. I did, and once again he led me to an office and motioned me to go in, which I did. Sitting behind the desk was another German officer, dressed the same as the officer the day before. He was holding the camera and had it pointed at me as I came in.

I sat down and waited for the *hauptmann* to say something. He started out with, "I am a camera enthusiast. I wish we could have met under other circumstances, like in Switzerland, so we could take pictures of the Alps and other parts of the country." I replied, "I do, too." Then he showed me two pictures that I had taken of my wingman on the climb-out. Each picture showed two large, 150-gallon fuel tanks. The *hauptmann* asked me what kind of mission I was on and what kind of bombs those were under the wings. I replied with my name, rank, and serial number. He said, "Now you know, Captain, we can't let you go from here until you give us the information we want."

In the interrogation room was a war situation map of England and Europe. It was similar to the one I had seen in our briefing room back in England. The German map had lines drawn on it almost like the ones we had on our map. As the *hauptmann* spoke, I studied the map, and when he said they could not release me from the interrogation center until I gave them the information they wanted, I replied, "Good! It looks like General Patton and his troops will be here in a few days, and then I will be returned to Allied control and you all will be the prisoners."

There was no comment from the *hauptmann*. Evidently, he decided that I wasn't going to give them any information, so he summoned the guard and had me taken back to my cell. And once again, when I returned, the gruel was colded and gummier than ever, so I left it.

In about an hour, a guard came in and motioned me to follow him, which I did. He led me to the toilet, handed me soap, a towel, and a razor, and motioned for me to get cleaned up. It felt good to get rid of the beard that I had grown. In fact, I felt like a new man and not a prisoner, but shortly the guard came and led me back to my cell, and once again the realization that I was a POW came upon me. It wasn't too much longer before a guard came and motioned for me to follow him, and I began to wonder what it was this time. But any fears I might have had were soon laid to rest.

The guard led me to another room in the center, opened the door, and motioned for me to go in. In this room there were a lot of American soldiers, mostly officers, pilots, and bomber crewmen. I don't remember whether I had heard it in the past, at one of our briefings, or whether one of the officers came up to me and said, "Don't go talking about your mission; Jerry has been known to put a plant in with the POWs in order to gain information." This seemed like good advice.

I sat down, leaned against the wall, and tried to get a little sleep. The rest of that day and night was spent in silence, staring at the four walls of the room. But it still felt good to be out of solitary and in the company of Allied troops.

The next morning, all of us were marched a short distance and found ourselves in a compound filled with other Allied prisoners. This we found out was *Dulag Luft*. The senior Allied officer, a colonel, briefed us on what would happen to us. The first thing was the news that this camp received Red Cross food parcels that were meant to go to each POW. They had a staff of POWs set up to pool the parcels and provide meals for all the POWs in the camp. He also told us that, at most, we would only be there three or four days before being shipped out to a permanent POW camp.

We ate well—three meals a day—and had a good night's sleep every night. It was so good that those of us who had been in the separate room together talked among ourselves and wondered how we could become members of the staff and spend the rest of the war right there in *Dulag Luft*.

Just as the colonel had predicted, on the evening of the third day at *Dulag Luft,* fifteen or twenty of us were singled out, formed up in a column, and marched out of the compound. We had no idea where we were going, but it soon became clear that we were headed for a train station. It was night, and snow was on the ground. Most of us were a bit cold.

We waited about three hours, but no train arrived, so the guards formed us up and marched us back to a barracks for the night. But they did not put us in with the other POWs; we were put in a separate barracks, all by ourselves. The reason why become clear the next day when, after roll call and breakfast, along about mid-morning, the guards formed us up again and marched us back to the train station, where we were put aboard a boxcar to which the door was shut and, I assumed, locked.

After a short period of time, we felt the car being hooked onto a train, and then we pulled out. We had no idea where we were headed or what was in store for us. I don't remember how long this trip took, but one incident is still vivid in my mind. It was shortly after noon that the train dropped our car off at a siding. The door was unlocked and opened, and the guards motioned us off the train. At this time, we heard air-raid sirens and assumed the village or city we were parked close to was under attack by our people. The guards motioned for us to follow as they headed for what looked like an air-raid shelter. We were just about to enter the shelter when one of the civilians who was also headed for the shelter grabbed a grease gun—a German machine pistol that looked like the grease guns we used back in the States to grease cars. The civilian pulled the slide back to chamber a live round, pointed the gun in our direction, and yelled in German. I assume he was strictly against our going into the air-raid shelter when it was our planes conducting the raid. This German civilian was only about ten feet from me, and I was the one he was pointing the gun at. Needless to say, we did not go into the shelter but headed in the opposite direction and back to the boxcar. This was the one time that I was really scared. It wouldn't have taken much for that irate civilian to squeeze the trigger and eliminate a few of the enemy, namely *us*.

As it turned out, the air raid was someplace else, and we heard no more about it. Sometime later, the train stopped and once again dropped our boxcar off on a siding, which we were to find out was on the outskirts of the permanent POW camp, just southwest of Nuremberg. We were escorted into the camp by our guards and turned over to the senior

Allied officer. Once inside the camp, we could relax. We were assigned to a barracks and given bunks. These bunks were standard German two-tier wooden bunks with a thin straw mattress and a couple of thin blankets.

Right away, we missed *Dulag Luft* as we had no Red Cross parcels and we were back on German rations of ersatz coffee, black bread, and the thick oatmeal-like substance. A few days of this, and we began to feel weak and hungry.

One evening guards came in, formed us up in groups of thirty or so, and marched us to a building that turned out to be a shower house. We were ordered to take a shower, and then we were given long American GI overcoats, which were most welcome. I don't know to this day what prompted me to do what I did next, for I am not an overly religious individual. But I felt it was my duty to talk to the troops, and I did. I called the gang together and read from the little pocket Bible my grandmother gave me when I started flying for the Army. I read Chapters 6 and 7 from the Book of St. Matthew—part of Christ's Sermon on the Mount—and then asked the group to join me in reciting the Lord's Prayer. Call it a coincidence, or fate, or something else, but the very next morning the Germans delivered our first Red Cross parcels. The parcels changed our way of living as POWs. I don't remember all the food that was in the parcels, but everything sure tasted good.

Four of us—three other fighter pilots and I—pooled our parcels, and from that time on we cooked together, ate together, and worked together as a unit. We had started playing contract bridge on the train from *Dulag Luft*, and we continued this game each day until we got back to the States.

I think probably the most important item in the Red Cross parcel was the one-pound can of a powered substance called Klim—milk spelled backwards. We used it in the food we cooked, used it to drink, and we even learned to use the empty cans, along with some of the other cans, to make our little cookstoves called "smoky joes."

Following his release from captivity, Captain Tink Cole was assigned to Luke Field, Arizona, and he was promoted to major in 1946. He flew P-80 jets at Williams Air Force Base, Arizona, served a two-year exchange tour with the RAF, and thereafter undertook a variety of staff and flying positions. In 1960, he was sent to Vietnam, where he served as the chief advisor to the commander of the Republic of Vietnam Air Force. Following several more assignments in the United States, Tink Cole retired with the rank of lieutenant colonel in 1966.

NIGHT STALKER

1st Lieutenant HERMAN ERNST, USAAF
422d Night Fighter Squadron, Ninth Air Force
Rhine River Area—March 2, 1945

Herman Elliott Ernst was born in Philadelphia on January 2, 1918, and raised for the most part in Chattanooga, Tennessee. His interest in aviation stemmed from his participation in his high school model airplane club and a school shop project that involved the rebuilding of a real airplane. Whenever Ernst could save two dollars from his lunch money, he spent it on fifteen minutes worth of flying lessons at the local airfield.

At the end of his first year at the University of Chattanooga, Ernst and fellow school bandsmen traded in their band uniforms for GI olive drab—a one-year enlistment in the local National Guard field artillery band. The musicians were halfway through their Army basic training when the Japanese struck Pearl Harbor, and plans to return to college were put on indefinite hold when their artillery unit shipped out to Camp Roberts, California. At that time, Private Ernst applied for flight training, and he was assigned to a Pre-flight course at Anaheim, California, after passing the Air Corps two-year college equivalency examination.

Cadet Ernst attended Primary Flight training at Oxnard, California; Basic at Gardner Field in Taft, California; and the Advanced multi-engine school at Stockton, California. He earned his wings and commission at Stockton on May 20, 1943, and immediately volunteered for night-fighter training.

As a preliminary to night-fighter school, I was assigned to Mather Field, California, to check out in B-25s. This was to prepare me to fly the P-70, a two-place, radar-equipped night-fighter version of the Douglas A-20 Havoc light bomber. At the time, the P-70 was the only night fighter in the Army Air Forces inventory. From Mather, I went to Williams Field,

Arizona, for gunnery training, and then on to Orlando, Florida, to begin the night-fighter course.

At Orlando, I was teamed with a radar observer, 2d Lieutenant Jimmy Londeree, and we began night-fighter training together, as a permanent team. We did a lot of instrument flying and took part in many hours of training in the Link flight simulator. During the various phases of our training, we flew out of air bases at Orlando, Kissimmee, and Dunnellon, Florida. Then we returned to Orlando, where we were assigned to the newly formed 422d Night Fighter Squadron. At the time, the 422d was equipped with P-70s but it had also received four new YP-61s, the pre-production, in-service test model of the North American Black Widow twin-engine night fighter. Our job, among many others, was to help work out the bugs in the P-61.

On December 24, 1943—Christmas Eve—I flew one of the YP-61s for a few hours, and then we landed and changed airplanes to an A-20 in order to take our turn as a target for another crew flying a YP-61. While we were flying target for the YP-61, we were hit by a third airplane, a P-70 that none of us had seen. Apparently the P-70 pilot, who was in a night-fighter training squadron, was looking the YP-61 over and did not see my A-20 in time to avoid hitting it. The P-70 took off my right wing, right engine, and the tail. I was able to parachute out, but Jimmy Londeree and another man who was riding with us were lost, and so was the crew of the P-70, which spun in. The accident left me without a radar observer, but 2d Lieutenant Eddie Kopsel had lost his pilot in another flying accident, so we were teamed up.

At the conclusion of our training, the 422d Night Fighter Squadron was shipped to England, where we received our P-61s. When we joined the Ninth Air Force just before the invasion of France, the P-61 was still unproven in combat, so we had quite a selling job to do. In fact, the British wanted us to transition to Mosquitoes so we could support their night operations. But in the end we and our P-61s were assigned to Ford Airdrom, near Brighton. Soon, five teams of us were assigned to chase V-1 Buzz Bombs that were hitting targets in England at that time.

On our first combat night operation, in July 1944, I was diving on a Buzz Bomb when the tail cone in my P-61 disintegrated and left Eddie Kopsel sitting in the open. He was trying to talk to me on the intercom, but I could not understand him because of the noise of the wind coming through that big hole. I thought we'd gotten shot down on our very first time out. I throttled back and found that the airplane was still flying and that I could control it, so we went back to base.

The next night, we went out again after we replaced the missing tail cone with a piece of flat Plexiglas, and were able to shoot down a Buzz Bomb. It was the first target shot down by a P-61 in the European Theater.

The first manned German airplane I shot at was an Me-110 twin-engine fighter, but I was going too fast when I saw it, and I overshot before I could get my guns to bear. This was an important lesson. Fortunately, the P-61 was a good, stable airplane at low speeds. On several occasions, I got the speed down to only 80 miles per hour, but I still had the airplane under control. It was a very stable gunnery platform for night work, which required slow speed and precise instrument control. Also, the four fixed 20mm cannon that were mounted in the belly of the P-61s I flew were very effective, and we had very little trouble keeping them operable. I did fly one mission with an airplane that had a four-gun turret on top of the fuselage, but I only got a few rounds off in the straight-ahead position before the firing circuit failed.

The first manned airplane I shot down was an Me-110 two-place fighter that I got near Munster Eiffel, Germany, at 0240 hours on November 27, 1944. At the time, the 422d Night Fighter Squadron was operating from Advance Landing Ground A-78—the Florennes/Juzaine Airdrome near Charleroi, Belgium—as part of the IX Tactical Air Command, which was serving in support of the U.S. First Army. My next kill was a Ju-87 Stuka dive-bomber, which I shot down over friendly lines at 0523 hours on December 17. Then I shot down a Ju-188 twin-engine bomber near Monschau, Belgium, at 0025 on December 27; and I damaged a Ju-88 in the same area the very next night. On New Year's Eve, at just past midnight, my P-61's nose wheel was shot out by the gunner aboard an Me-110; it was the only time a target ever fired back at me. On top of that, he got away because my guns quit firing.

On the morning of March 2, 1945, at 0348 hours, my P-61, with 1st Lieutenant Eddie Kopsel as radar observer, took off from Advance Landing Ground A-78. We were not originally scheduled to fly on March 2, but one of the other pilots was on duty at Operations while getting over an eye problem, and he had called me in the wee hours to see if I wanted to fly a mission, because there was more activity than usual going on out over the area between the First Army bomb line and the Rhine River. At the time, Eddie and I were very close to our seventy-mission tour limit, and it looked like the war in Europe was getting close to finished. If I was going to shoot down two more German airplanes and make ace, it would have to be soon, so Eddie and I agreed to fly that night.

When we got out to the patrol area, NUTHOUSE, our ground-control radar station, had too many airplanes on the scope, so we were told to hold off for a few minutes. I started circling behind our lines, but our own antiaircraft started shooting at us. One shell caused some damage to the shutters on one of the oil coolers, but we weren't losing any oil and our radar was still working, so we elected to stay. But we went on over to the German side of the lines, where is wasn't so hot.

In another few minutes, at about 0450 hours, NUTHOUSE called with a target for us. The range to this target, which was over our lines, was only two miles, and it was at an altitude of 6,500 feet. Using his on-board AI radar set, Eddie helped me close the range to 1,400 feet and then I obtained a visual on an Me-110, which immediately began taking hard evasive action. At no time did the evasive action stop, but after great difficulty I closed the range to 400 feet and fired a deflection burst with my 20mm cannon as the enemy aircraft was undertaking a turn to starboard. We observed strikes on the fuselage, and then the enemy aircraft went into a violent peel-off to starboard. It was 0450. We observed the Me-110 as it burned and crashed, but we later learned that our antiaircraft guys also claimed it, so we accepted a credit for damaging the German fighter rather than shooting it down, because our antiaircraft boys needed to get some credit, too.

We had no sooner recovered from shooting down the Me-110 than NUTHOUSE called to vector us to another target. Eddie secured the contact at a range of two miles, an altitude of 5,500 feet, and an indicated air speed of 120 miles per hour. We closed the range to 1,000 feet and I obtained a visual sighting and positive identification on a Ju-87. When I first saw it, the Stuka was at about 12 o'clock and taking hard evasive action. I closed to 500 feet and opened fire from astern with a slight deflection. I observed 20mm strikes at the wing roots and on the fuselage. The 87 went straight down into the ground and exploded on impact. Burning debris was scattered over a large area. The action terminated at 0457. We did not see any parachutes open.

Shortly after 0500, NUTHOUSE again provided us with a target, and Eddie made radar contact at a range of two and a half miles. At that moment, the enemy airplane, which was taking evasive action, had an indicated air speed of 110 to 120 miles per hour at an altitude of 5,500 feet. With Eddie guiding us, I closed to 1,000 feet and obtained a visual sighting on another Ju-87, which was at our 12 o'clock. I continued to close. At 0506, as I came to about 300 feet astern of the enemy dive-bomber, I fired two three-second bursts at a slight deflection. Eddie and I both saw strikes on the wings and fuselage, whereupon the enemy aircraft started to fall very rapidly in what appeared to be a fairly wide flat spin. I attempted to follow the 87 down but lost sight of it when it passed beneath our P-61. A short time later, Eddie observed a large flash on the ground. There were no antiaircraft gun flashes in the area at this time and, though neither of us actually saw the 87 crash, the explosion we observed must have been caused when it struck the ground. We claimed this Ju-87 destroyed, and the victory credit was awarded. We were aces.

As soon as we reported back to NUTHOUSE, we were released from our mission.

Captain Herman Ernst rotated to the United States at the conclusion of his seventy-mission combat tour. After the war, he transferred into the Tennessee Air National Guard and served on active duty several times before retiring in 1978 as a lieutenant colonel. At this writing, Ernst still flies his privately owned airplane once or twice a week, for the pure pleasure of it.

JUMPED

1st Lieutenant IVAN HASEK, USAAF
353d Fighter Squadron, 354th Fighter Group
Near Limburg, Germany—March 16, 1945

Ivan Hasek was born in Sioux City, Iowa, on October 23, 1923, and was in his second year at the University of Nebraska when he enlisted in the Army Air Forces in order to avoid being drafted into the Army Corps of Engineers. He was inducted in February 1943 and sent to Santa Ana, California, for his Pre-flight training at the Spartan School of Aeronautics. He took Primary training at Phoenix; Basic at Merced, California; and finished with Advanced at Luke Field, Arizona, where he graduated with Class 44-B.

In due course, 2d Lieutenant Hasek was shipped to England and posted to the IX Fighter Command's elite 354th Fighter Group, then based in France, in July 1944. First Lieutenant Hasek was credited with his first victory, an FW-190 he shot down near Relange, on December 26, 1944.

On March 16, 1945, we were ordered out on an armed reconnaissance mission, but due to a slip-up I was not at the briefing and didn't know about taking off until five minutes before press time. Then one of the fellows stopped by the tent and saw me. "Aren't you on this mission?" he asked. I said "Sure." "Well you better get going as they are getting ready to take off," he announced.

I grabbed a map and helmet, and began to run for my airplane, *Little Rascal*. This was not a very auspicious start for what was to prove my toughest and most exciting day in combat.

A heavy overcast hung over most of the area we covered. Near Frankfurt, we dropped down below the clouds and skimmed along the autobahn running toward Limburg. We sighted several trucks and destroyed them by strafing. Our flight of four became separated from the rest of the squadron at this point. I was glad that 1st Lieutenant Bruce Carr was leading as I didn't have any of the courses. At this time, Bruce was the top locomotive buster of the Ninth Air Force and a three-time ace.

We passed over a large field and, looking back, I saw a herd of men working on it. I think it was a new airstrip the Germans were working on. Anyhow, I called it in to Bruce, who said, "Let's go back and check them for size."

We swung around. Down below, I could see many of the workmen hurrying toward two wooden shacks. Others jumped into foxholes. We circled the field, came back, and shot up the buildings. Those wooden slats weren't much protection against .50-caliber bullets. No one ran out. We also sprayed the foxholes before pulling up.

It was about this time that I looked down and saw two airplanes skimming along close to the deck. I thought they were other P-51s because a burst of 20mm flak broke below us. Then I saw the black crosses painted on their wings. By the time we turned around, the airplanes were gone in the overcast. We headed towards home.

I was madder than hell and started to curse myself for being a stupid so and so. That's when Carr called, "Thirty one-owe-nines above. Keep your tails clean and get busy." By that time we were right in the middle of the 109s.

Some of the German pilots were aggressive as hell. Why wouldn't they be—against four of us and having the advantage of altitude! I climbed up to four of them with my wingman, 2d Lieutenant Willie Johnson, on my tail. He stayed there like a hawk all during the battle. That's the kind of a guy to have around in a scrap. If he hadn't been there to cover me, the story might be different.

The first one I tagged onto I missed with two bursts. Then I got the range and hit him in the cockpit. He went straight on down, blazing furiously.

I picked out another—there were so many it wasn't hard to choose one. I was 100 yards away when I opened up, and I got him right off the bat. He went flaming down.

A third Messerschmitt made a banking turn to the left. I fired from an angle. My shots tore chunks off the plane, and the second burst tore his right wing off. My fire missed Johnson by a few feet. That Jerry had had it. I didn't have time to see if the pilot got out or not. Things were happening too fast. Airplanes were dropping all around.

The next one I tackled started to dive for the deck. I scored hits on him. As he went by, Johnson pumped some more bullets into it, but I don't think he got it, either.

The fifth 109 was in a steep bank and started to turn into us. He loomed up in front of me like a locomotive. I thought for sure that he was trying for a head-on collision. I pressed the gun trigger and my bullets peppered the 109. Pieces flew off and the ship went into a spinning dive. I think the pilot was killed.

After that I saw an airplane above and took off after it. It proved to be Carr, who had lost his wingman and had been hit; he was heading home. By this time, the rest of the 109s had scrammed, so Johnson and I escorted Carr back to the base.

In all, we dropped nine German planes. Carr got credit for three, and his wingman got one. The total boosted our squadron over the 300 mark. Not a bad day's work for a bum start.

In the 353d Fighter Squadron's official tally for the mission, 1st Lieutenant Ivan Hasek was credited with two Bf-109s destroyed, and two and a half probably destroyed. Lieutenant Bruce Carr was credited with three Bf-109s "unconfirmed destroyed" and a Bf-109 "unconfirmed damaged." Hasek's wingman, 2d Lieutenant Willie Johnson, was credited with half a probable, and Carr's wingman, 2d Lieutenant Ernest Widlund, was credited with a full victory. The 354th Fighter Group was one of only a few Ninth Air Force units to award credits for "unconfirmed destroyed" aircraft. As a result of this policy, a Bf-109 downed by Lieutenant Ivan Hasek near Halle on April 4, 1945, was also credited as an "unconfirmed destroyed," a bookkeeping quirk that denied Hasek ace status until an eyewitness came forward in 1985 to correct the record. Only then was Ivan Hasek awarded the full victory, and only then did he achieve a status that had been denied him four decades earlier.

On August 1, 1945, 1st Lieutenant Ivan Hasek was honorably discharged from the service.

PART III

At War in the Middle East

ENGAGEMENT OVER SINAI

RUDY AUGARTEN
101 Squadron, Israeli Air Force
El Arish, Egypt—December 22, 1948

Rudolph Augarten was born in Philadelphia on June 16, 1922, the son of Austrian immigrants who had resettled in the United States following World War I. As a boy, Rudy Augarten thought about becoming a pilot, but the dream was beyond his reach due to his family's limited financial resources. Following his graduation from high school, Augarten worked briefly and then enlisted in the U.S. Army in January 1941 and was posted to an artillery unit. He wanted to apply for flight training, but he was prevented by the two-year college requirement until it was dropped immediately following the entry of the United States into World War II. After passing the new college-equivalency exams, Private Augartern was accepted as an aviation cadet.

Rudy Augarten earned his wings and commission at Moore Field, Texas, in January 1943 and trained as an instructor at Randolph Field, Texas. He taught the Basic flying course until his constant requests for transfer to a combat unit were finally answered with orders to the P-47 school at Richmond, Virginia. From there, 2d Lieutenant Augarten sailed for England and eventual posting in May 1944 as a replacement pilot to the Ninth Air Force's 371st Fighter Group, and finally to the 406th Fighter Squadron.

In the weeks leading up to the invasion of France, the 371st Fighter Group undertook daily ground-attack missions against airfields and transportation targets, as well as missions escorting Ninth Air Force bombers. On June 8, 1944, Augarten was a member of a four-plane flight patrolling the invasion coast when his fighter was hit by ground fire over Caen. Augarten bailed out of his burning P-47 to begin a sixty-day odyssey behind German lines that involved evasion, capture by the German Army, escape, recapture, another escape, and a successful return to American lines. By then, the 371st Fighter Group was operating from an airfield in France, and though as a former prisoner of war Augarten qualified for immediate return to the United States, he elected to return to his unit. On October 3, 1944, 2d Lieutenant Rudy Augarten earned the Distinguished Flying Cross for an action over the Marne River in which he shot down a pair of Bf-109s. Captain Augarten rotated home to the United States in March 1945.

After I left the Army Air Forces at the end of 1945, I entered college on the GI Bill. First I went to McNeese College, which is a branch of Louisiana State College, and then I transferred to Harvard College in Cambridge, Massachusetts.

In early 1948, I was concerned with the fighting that was happening in Palestine. My religious training had inculcated me with a deep concern for the drive for a Jewish homeland. I felt that there was something I wanted to do, that I could do. I was put in touch with an organization that was looking for pilots, and they wanted to send me overseas in April 1948.

I told my parents about my plans, but they were very upset. They still remembered the missing-in-action telegram they had received from the War Department in 1944. I was missing for more than sixty days, and they just didn't want me to fight in another war. I listened to them and returned to Harvard, but as the fighting got worse, I decided I had to do something. So I made arrangements to go to Italy, where I would join up to fight in Israel. I did not tell my parents ahead of time; I just dropped them a letter at the airport, telling them of my plans.

I flew to Rome, made a contact with someone there, and was sent to Czechoslovakia, where I joined a group of about eight ex-World War II pilots. Most of us were Jewish from the United States and South Africa. We were sent to a Czech Air Force base in a city called Cheskie-Budivichi, which is in South Bohemia. We were given a familiarization ride in a German-built Arado Ar-96, which is similar to a North American AT-6 trainer. Next, we were given an orientation ride in a two-place Czech-built Bf-109.

The Czechs had built Bf-109 single-seat fighters for the Germans throughout World War II. After the war, they continued to build 109s, but they no longer had access to the German-made powerplants. The original powerplant for the 109 was a Daimler-Benz engine, but the Czechs had to substitute another engine, the Jumo, which was built in Czechoslovakia. The Czech version with the Jumo engine was designated the S-199 and was euphemistically called the Mule. It was identical in all respects to the Bf-109, except the Jumo power plant was not as good, because it was heavier and not as powerful, and thus the flying characteristics were much different.

I made nine flights totaling seven hours at the Czech air base. This was my first piloting in three years. I hadn't flown at all since I had left the Army Air Forces. There was no gunnery involved.

After our check flights, our group of pilots was flown into Israel on the night of July 4, 1948, during one of the truce periods between the Arabs and the Jews. At the time the Israeli forces had just one fighter squadron, the 101st, which was based at Akia, an ex-Royal Air Force base about two miles south of Tel Aviv. Akia had concrete runways, but it was very unsuited for the S-199, of which the 101st Squadron had about eight. When we arrived, however, the squadron was in the midst of being moved to a new airport that was being built near Herzlia, which is about fifteen miles north of Tel Aviv. The new base had one dirt runway, no hangars, and open parking in the surrounding banana groves.

That particular truce was to end around July 10. To conserve aircraft, no flying at all was done until the fighting started again. The fighting did start up on schedule, but I did not fly my first mission until July 18, 1948. In fact, another truce was to start that evening. That was the nature of that war in that period; the fighting started and stopped based on truces brokered by the United Nations.

We had many more pilots than airplanes. Although all of our pilots had been highly trained during World War II, most of us hadn't flown for years and had been given inadequate conversion to the type of planes that were available. The situation with regard to maintenance was worse. There were few manuals available, and the mechanics' training was very limited. As a result, the aircraft's serviceability was very low and accidents were frequent.

The squadron started with the S-199s and then acquired a few Spitfires that were put together from parts left behind when the British pulled out at the start of Israel's War of Independence. Later, we acquired more Spitfires—Mark IXs—from the Czech Air Force, which itself had been formed around several former Czech-manned Royal Air Force squadrons. We also had two P-51 Mustangs. The 101st Squadron was never able to put more than four planes in the air at one time, and most missions comprised just two planes or even single-plane sorties. But the squadron was very successful in stopping indiscriminate bombing of Israeli cities and towns by the Arab air forces, mostly the Egyptians. We even shot down five British planes—one Mosquito, three Spits, and one Tempest—when they intruded over Israeli territory. To my knowledge, we only lost one of our fighters to enemy aircraft.

Through the course of the War of Independence, I scored four aerial victories, all Egyptians. This is the highest individual total in our squadron during the war. My victories were against all types. One of them was a Spitfire I shot down while flying an S-199, two were Spitfires I shot down while flying Spitfires, and another was a C-47 I shot down while flying a P-51. I also shot up an Italian-made fighter while it was landing at El Arish in Sinai. At the time, I identified this enemy plane as a Fiat, but it was confirmed many years later as an Italian-built Macchi Mc.205Z.

The attack against the Macchi occurred on December 22, 1948. I was then the 101st Squadron operations officer, and we were flying from the former Royal Air Force base at Kastina, which is about thirty miles north of Be'ersheba in the Negev Desert. We were flying only Spitfires and P-51s at the time. We also had a few S-199s, but most of the pilots in that squadron hadn't checked out in them, and the maintenance of them was inferior to the other types.

On December 22, I was on standby with an ex-Royal Canadian Air Force pilot named Jack Doyle. When we were scrambled by headquarters, we were told to head south, because some Arab planes had been observed in the area.

I was in a Spit and Jack was in a Mustang. I don't believe either of us had oxygen. We flew down parallel to the coast at 6,000 to 8,000 feet, looking for other aircraft. We ended up just west of Gaza, but we couldn't find anything in the air, so I decided to go see what was happening at the forwardmost Egyptian air base at El Arish, which was about forty miles inside the Sinai, on the Mediterranean coast.

As we circled the air base at El Arish, I noticed that an airplane was in the downwind leg of the landing pattern. I thought, What an opportunity, catching a plane landing! But at the same time, I recalled from my World War II combat experience that strafing airfields was extremely dangerous. They tended to be very heavily fortified, the gunners had an open field of vision, and it usually did not pay to be attacking airfields, particularly if they had some advance knowledge that you were in the area. On the other hand, this was an Arab air base, so I felt the circumstances might be a little different.

I told Doyle I was going to go down and see what I could do. I cut my throttle, went down, and caught up with the Egyptian plane just as it was turning onto the final approach its the wheels and flaps down. He was about 100 to 150 feet above the ground. By this time, I had chopped my throttle and fishtailed to keep from closing too quickly. I fired several bursts and noticed strikes on the enemy airplane. I kept getting closer to the ground and then I overran him. As I did, I went to full throttle, flew as close to the ground as possible, and veered away at about 45 degrees to the runway.

I kept on course for five to eight minutes. Then I pulled up sharply, climbed to about 10,000 feet, and headed back to El Arish. As I made radio contact with Jack Doyle, I saw that the flak was coming up from the base, so I took some evasive action while keeping the base in sight. I spotted a crash site just off the runway. I didn't observe any violent burning, but I did notice that the plane I had fired on had crashed there.

Doyle's experiences were a little different. He had stayed high during the whole episode, because, as he told me when I returned, his engine was running very rough. In fact, on the way home, he switched to one magneto. He had caught a lot of attention from the flak protecting the Egyptian base.

We headed back to Kastina, where I reported the damaged Egyptian airplane as being a Fiat. This was first time we had seen an Egyptian fighter that was not a Spitfire.

This phase of the War of Independence ended on January 7, 1949. That day, a flight of four Spitfires from our squadron shot down four British-made fighters without any loss or damage to themselves. Unfortunately, I was not in that flight. This ended all the air fighting in that part of the world until the Sinai Campaign of 1956.

In February 1949, I started a training program for the four most advanced Israeli pilot trainees who had been given preliminary training in Europe. This course was conducted at Kastina while I was still a member of the 101st Squadron. When my two-month course ended, these pilots became the first Israelis to pin on pilot wings in Israel. One of them was Mordechai Hod, who later became head of the Israeli Air Force and led it during the 1967 war. When the course ended, I was transferred to Akia, the base at which I had landed when I first arrived in Israel. There, I conducted a course for the next class of about twelve Israeli advanced cadets, who received their wings later in 1949.

I then returned to the United States and resumed classes at Harvard, from which I graduated in 1950. I returned to Israel for two more years to command the base at Ramat Aviv in northern Israel. Based there was a wing of two fighter squadrons, a Spit squadron and a P-51 squadron. Many of the fighter pilots were my former students. During this time, there was no formal fighting, but a couple of actions were taken in conjunction of political events there.

The Israel Defense Force had a program which took people from various organizations and put them through a two-week parachute course. I made five jumps and got my parachute wings. I was the first person in the Israeli services to earn two sets of wings.

I learned many years after my December 22, 1948, fight over El Arish that the pilot of the Macchi was Lieutenant Shalabi al-Hinnaway, who would become commander of the Egyptian Air Force immediately following the 1967 Arab-Israeli War.

PART IV

At War Over Korea

IT GOES WITH THE TERRITORY

Lieutenant Colonel JERRY BROWN, USAF
39th Fighter-Bomber Squadron, 35th Fighter-Bomber Wing
Tokchon, North Korea—November 30, 1950

Gerald Brown was born on December 2, 1917, in Globe, Arizona, and was raised in Phoenix. He earned his wings and an Army Air Forces commission at Williams Field, Arizona, on March 10, 1943, and was assigned directly to the 55th Fighter Group, which was training in P-38s for eventual service in Europe.

While flying with the 55th Fighter Group's 38th Fighter Squadron, Brown shot down four German fighters and a medium bomber between January and April 1944. When his combat tour ended a few days after he achieved ace status, Captain Brown opted to remain in England with an Eighth Air Force P-38 replacement training unit. Right after D-Day, he volunteered for a combat assignment and was posted to the 4th Fighter Group, then flying P-51s. Brown was forced down in enemy territory by a malfunctioning engine on September 6, 1944, but he was rescued by the French Resistance and returned to his unit in England. He continued to fly combat missions until ordered to return to the United States in November 1944.

Following World War II, Major Jerry Brown opted for a career in the Army Air Forces, and he transferred into the United States Air Force when it was created in 1947.

I was the commander of the 39th Fighter-Bomber Squadron, 35th Fighter-Bomber Wing, stationed at Yokota Air Force Base, Japan, when the Korean War started on June 25, 1950. We immediately went on full alert with blackouts, digging slit trenches, and all the other panic procedures that normally follow an alert announcement.

On July 1, the wing headquarters and the 39th and 40th squadrons went to Ashiya Air Force Base on the island of Kyushu, which would allow us to support operations in Korea if called. The 41st Fighter-Bomber Squadron stayed back at Yokota for air defense, just in case. Our group had converted from F-51s to F-80s in February, and we had passed an operational readiness inspection in April.

We went operational on July 3 in support of retreating U.S. Army and Republic of Korea ground troops near Seoul. We carried six 5-inch air-to-ground rockets on the F-80s, but they weren't too effective against the T-34 tanks of the North Koreans. Because of the distance from our base to the combat area, we could not stay over the targets very long. It was decided to open up bases in South Korea in order to provide better support for the ground troops, who were being pushed back toward the Pusan Perimeter. New airfields—K-2 at Taegu and K-3 at Pohang— were opened up about the middle of July, which allowed us to provide quicker and longer ground support. Additionally, our group had to convert back to F-51s in order to take advantage of the large numbers of National Guard F-51s that were being brought to Japan from the States on Navy carriers.

When the transition back to 51s was completed, we moved our group from Ashiya to K-3. Now we could start using napalm, which was the only way to stop a tank in the mountainous areas of South Korea.

Due to the rapid approach of the North Koreans, we had to evacuate K-3 in August and go back to Kyushu where we opened up the small air base at Tsuiki. After the Inchon landing in September, we moved back to K-3 and operated from there until we moved in the first part of November to K-27 at Yonpo, on the east coast of North Korea near the twin cities of Hungnam and Hamhung. We shared the base with a Marine Corsair squadron, VMF-312. The wing continued to operate from Yonpo until the first part of December, when another evacuation was made due to the entrance of the Chinese People's Liberation Army into the Korean War.

On November 30, 1950, my squadron was assigned to several sorties in support of our ground forces in the middle part of Korea, near the small city of Tokchon, which was important because it had rail service. We were advised before the mission that the Chinese had indeed entered the Korean War and had broken through the South Korean lines near Tokchon.

At 0900 hours, I took off with my flight of four F-51s, each carrying six 5-inch air-to-ground rockets and the usual 1,800 rounds of .50-caliber machine-gun ammo. At 0930, I asked for target information from an airborne controller who was flying a T-6 over central North Korea.

The controller directed us on to Tokchon. He said that the Chinese had ambushed a mechanized convoy of South Korean vehicles, and he told us to destroy all the vehicles in order to deny their use to the Chinese.

When he arrived over the target area, we discovered that the Chinese had actually set up several ambushes around Tokchon. There were about forty vehicles north of the city, thirty or more to the east of the city, and others to the west. We also noticed a medium-size motor pool inside the city itself.

I directed my element leader to start working on the vehicles north of the city while I remained at 2,500 feet with my wingman, to provide top cover. There had been reports that North Korean MiG-15 jet fighters were making passes on our ground-support aircraft, and I didn't want to expose my flight to this possibility. Besides, an element of two aircraft can work better while strafing and using rockets.

After about twenty minutes, I told the element leader to break off and assume the top cover while I took my wingman down to continue the destruction of the remaining vehicles. I told my wingman to always keep me in sight while picking his own targets.

After we finished off the northern, eastern, and western targets, we turned our attention to the motor pool inside the city. On about my fifth pass on the motor pool, my F-51 was hit by small-arms fire in the engine and cockpit areas. Coolant immediately started streaming out and I discovered that my throttle and fuel selector had been knocked loose.

I knew that friendly lines were approximately twenty miles south of Tokchon, but the condition of my airplane would probably ensure that I did not make it that far. There were also mountains in the area around Tokchon, but I quickly decided that I could not even get high enough to bail out.

I had set my power to 2,800 RPM and 45 inches of mercury prior to starting my strafing passes, so that at the bottom of each pass I was doing about 275 miles per hour. At that speed, after being hit, I was able to zoom over a small hill in order to decide what to do next. After reviewing my situation, I advised my flight that I had been hit and directed my element leader to call Air Rescue to come get me.

I noticed a small corn field right next to the city and alongside the railroad track. I made the decision to try to make a gear-up landing there. My throttle was inoperable, but I was able to adjust my speed with the fuel-mixture control.

Pucker time had started. I had to depend on all my time in fighters, on all my training, in order to pull this landing off without splitting my wick.

I jettisoned my canopy, locked my shoulder harness, and dropped full flaps while on the downwind pass. Then I turned onto a short base leg and angled onto final. I put the bird right at the beginning edge of the corn field and slid to a stop just on the edge of a drop-off at the other end.

I left the airplane immediately because it was still smoking and burning, and I came to a stop about fifty feet from the right wing. There I was greeted by a pair of Chinese soldiers carrying submachine guns.

My captors took me to a small hut just off the edge of the field and tied my hands and arms behind my back with telephone wire. In about forty minutes, a chopper from Air Rescue arrived, but it left after ten minutes or so, which did not lift my spirits.

I was held in the hut for two days and then was joined by several U.S. Army troops and an Air Force forward air control team that had been captured about ten miles from Tokchon the day before. I also learned that I had landed right in the midst of a whole Chinese division that had bivouacked in Tokchon. This was the division that had made the first breakthrough the United Nations line on November 28.

I could not have imagined at the time that I was to spend more than one thousand days as a prisoner of war in such a godforsaken place as North Korea. I found little solace in the saying, "It goes with the territory."

What followed was a harrowing, inhumane three-year captivity in which many of his fellows POWs succumbed to malnourishment and disease. Thanks to his incessant efforts to instill pride in his fellow captives while aggressively thwarting the wishes and propaganda opportunities of his captors, Lieutenant Colonel Jerry Brown spent many long periods in isolation during his thirty-three-month captivity. He was finally repatriated to United Nations lines on September 6, 1953, and remained in the Air Force until retiring with the rank of colonel in 1967.

GLIDER TIME

Captain BROOKS LILES, USAF
336th Fighter Squadron, 4th Fighter Interceptor Wing
Korea—March 15, 1952

Brooks Jonathan Liles was born in Johnston County, North Carolina, on June 3, 1923, and enlisted in the Army Air Corps at the age of seventeen in December 1940. He eventually qualified for the Aviation Cadet program and earned his wings and a commission in May 1943. Thereafter, Lieutenant Liles served as a P-51, P-47, and P-40 instructor in a replacement training unit and was posted to the VIII Fighter Command's 55th Fighter Group in England in October 1944.

As a member of the 343d Fighter Squadron, Liles shot down an FW-190 near Salzwedel, Germany, on January 14, 1945, and was also credited with destroying three German aircraft on the ground and twenty-two locomotives, including eight on one mission. He was on his seventieth combat mission, a fighter sweep, on March 3, 1945, when he was shot down by flak as he strafed an airdrome near Prague. Although another member of the squadron, 1st Lieutenant Bernard Howes, attempted to rescue Liles, the takeoff went awry and both pilots spent the last two months of the war as prisoners.

Liles remained on active duty after World War II, in both flying and staff assignments, and he was posted to the 4th Fighter Interceptor Wing's 336th Fighter Squadron in Korea in November 1951. Captain Brooks Liles scored his first jet victory on February 21, 1952, when he downed a MiG-15 over North Korea, and he downed another MiG-15 on March 11.

The March 15 mission started like so many others. We all felt the excitement and anticipation of perhaps another tangle with a Soviet-built MiG-15 as the 4th Fighter Wing F-86 Sabres filled the take-off end of the runway at K-14—Kimpo Airdrome—on this clear, brisk morning. Some forty-eight pilots were running up their engines at 100-percent power. This created a dense black cloud of smoke, out of which each pair of Sabres emerged and thundered off into the sky. Some of them were wallowing clumsily as the pilots fought to handle the jet wash ahead of them.

Check-ins went smoothly when my squadron switched to the combat frequency and climbed steadily into North Korea. The high-speed climb to altitude—usually around 35,000 feet—allowed us to level off at near-maximum cruising speed and maintain that speed as we spread our four-plane flights out in combat formation.

As we neared our patrol area parallel to the Yalu River, there were some radio calls that went something like, "Bogeys at two o'clock high. Looks like eighty-sixes," or "Contrails at one o'clock high. Can't identify yet." Then we took a big, swinging 180-degree turn, trying to maintain speed and altitude. This brought my flight around to a southeast heading, paralleling and some fifty miles south of the Yalu. I knew we had only about twenty minutes of patrol time, because we were flying clean birds—no drop tanks.

Scanning the sky around me, doggedly looking for any bogey that might be a MiG, I spotted some flashes below me and took my two-ship element to 20,000 feet for a look-see. I didn't see anything for about five minutes and was about to call Bingo fuel and head for Kimpo. Then I spotted two Republic of Korea Air Force F-51s making a firing pass at ground targets—and crossing above them were two MiG-15s! The MiGs were apparently uninterested in the Mustangs and they continued to head north at high speed.

I called my wingman to hang on and dived to cut the MiGs off. I leveled out behind them at about 3,000 feet and realized I didn't have closing speed. Knowing I was well out of effective firing range, I opened fire anyway in the hope of a lucky hit, or to cause them to break so I could cut them off. At this low altitude, we were burning JP-4 at a very high rate, and I knew it was time to break it off and head for home. I also noted the Yalu River as it passed underneath. We had strict rules about crossing that river even though we sometimes fudged a bit.

By now, I was below Bingo fuel, so I called my wingman again to hang on and pulled straight up to about 12,000 or 13,000 feet. I rolled out and nosed down to gain speed. A couple of MiGs flashed by, going north, but at this time my only interest was on my fuel gauge. I knew I didn't have enough to get back to Kimpo. My wingman was a little better off, so I told him to break away and head straight home.

I felt I had to plan my flight to give me a shot at Chodo for a bailout over that island off the coast. I really did not want anything to do with a bailout into that cold water. Even if the ejection seat worked, I would still have to separate from the seat, open my chute, get free of all the junk, and then get into a dinghy in the always-choppy water. Then I could only hope that a Dumbo aircraft or helicopter could spot me. I thought, Hell, I'm trying for Kimpo! It all hung on how much "glider" time I could coax out of my F-86.

Climbing steadily, I reached 30,000 feet and decided to shut the engine down to save ten gallons of fuel for a restart and landing. I set up a glide at 150 miles per hour and figured I had 120 miles to go.

I never knew it could be so quiet without the familiar hum of my engine, but it was really a nice ride down to about 10,000 feet. The weather was clear and I could see that this wasn't going to work. I would have to use that ten gallons I had saved. The engine restarted just like the manual said it would, and I had climbed to 15,000 feet by the time it flamed out again. Once more, I glided at 150 miles per hour and covered the remaining 50 miles to Kimpo.

I arrived over the end of the runway for a simple 360-degree overhead approach and landing. The dead-engine landing patterns I had practiced since first checking out in jets served me well, and I even rolled to a taxiway, turned off, and cleared the runway. I never realized the F-86 would glide and glide . . . and glide some more.

Captain Liles downed his third MiG-15 on March 25, 1952, and a fourth fell to his guns on April 21. Counting the FW-190 he had downed over Germany in 1945, Brooks Liles was an ace.

THE LONGEST DOGFIGHT

1st Lieutenant CECIL FOSTER, USAF
16th Fighter Squadron, 51st Fighter Interceptor Wing
North Korea—September 7, 1952

Born in Midland County, Michigan, on August 30, 1925, Cecil Glenn Foster enlisted in the Army Air Corps Reserve upon graduation from high school and was sworn in on August 12, 1943. He completed basic training at Jefferson Barracks, Missouri, and was ordered to Knox College in Illinois. Although he had qualified as an aviation cadet, an urgent need for combat infantrymen nearly upset the plan, but Foster rode out the pressure and remained on course. He was then sent to Preflight training and on to the navigator training program at San Marcos Field, Texas.

Second Lieutenant Foster graduated from navigator school on February 10, 1945, got married, and went on to be trained as a radar navigator-bombardier in B-24 heavy bombers. He then served as a navigation flight instructor until his transfer to flight school was finally accepted in January 1947. He flew F-51s Mustangs and F-80 Shooting Star jets in flight school and later instructed Air Army Forces reservists in T-6 and T-11 training aircraft. He flew with an F-80 unit in Alaska until he left active duty with the Air Force in January 1950.

I was recalled to active duty with the U.S. Air Force in August 1951—as a radar navigator. Following a navigation refresher course at Mather Air Force Base, California, I was reassigned as a qualified pilot. I checked out again in jets at Williams Air Force Base, Arizona, and received combat training in F-80s at Nellis Air Force Base, Nevada. In April 1952, I was selected to train in the F-86. I had first flown F-80 aircraft while attending pilot training in January 1948, and I was very excited to fly the F-86.

Upon arrival at K-13 in Suwon, Korea, in early June 1952, I completed the usual area checkout, including a week-long ground school on F-86 aircraft systems in Japan. Then I was assigned to D Flight, 16th Fighter Interceptor Squadron, 51st Fighter Interceptor Wing. I flew the wing position for the first thirty missions and encountered MiG-15s on several occasions. I was then checked out as an element leader, where I would have a much greater chance to engage with my own skills.

On September 7, 1952, I was enjoying a rare day off. I dressed in a blue uniform, took my camera, and proceeded to the flight line to photograph the Sabres as they returned from a "maximum effort" mission. I planned to watch for the planes with black noses caused by the gunsmoke from their six .50-caliber machine guns. Those of us not flying were naturally very curious, and we all wanted to talk to those pilots who were able to engage the enemy, to hear all about the combat activity.

I arrived early at the flight line of the 16th Fighter Interceptor Squadron. No aircraft had returned yet, so I entered our operations building and saw 1st Lieutenant Robert Sands, the A Flight commander. He was briefing several newly assigned pilots on combat theater procedures.

Captain C. T. Weaver, our operations officer, was standing behind the counter when the field telephone from wing headquarters jangled. I overheard him confirm that we had four in-commission Sabres available. Our squadron had the strip-alert responsibility for this day, but the alert flight had already been scrambled, so Captain Weaver said, "Stand by one." He asked Lieutenant Sands if he could provide pilots for four planes to go on alert until the scrambled alert flight returned and could again assume the alert responsibility. Sands agreed but stated that he did not have a qualified element leader available. I stepped up to Captain Weaver and volunteered, but he felt that, since this was my flight's day off, he would seek someone else. He was then directed by Wing Operations to man the alert flight as quickly as possible, so he agreed that I should fill in until another element leader became available.

Lieutenant Sands, Captain Hunt, and 1st Lieutenant Les Erickson were in flying gear and already headed for their Sabres as I ran to our personal equipment building to change into flight gear. Before I could run three steps, Captain Weaver yelled, "Scramble!" Activity exploded.

I rapidly stripped off my blue uniform, donned my flying suit and boots, grabbed my helmet and parachute, and was given an airplane number as I ran toward the revetments where the aircraft were parked. One of the new pilots followed me up the side of my Sabre and straddled the nose in a backwards position. He then reached into the cockpit and started my engine as I was strapping in with an assist from the crew chief. Two other new pilots performed the exterior pre-flight check for me. As soon as they gave me the OK signal, I began taxiing.

I was the second aircraft to reach the runway. I took off behind Lieutenant Sands and was followed by Captain Hunt and Lieutenant Erickson. Sands immediately aborted because his landing gear would not retract. (The F-86's emergency gear-lowering system, which was often used by maintenance personnel, required resetting prior to departure to permit manual gear retraction.) This left me leading two newly assigned pilots whom I had never met, to accomplish an entirely unplanned mission.

As we formed up, I was informed that we were to provide air cover for the withdrawal of the main force of F-86 aircraft. They were low on fuel and a large number of MiGs was airborne and forming up. We tested and armed our six .50-caliber machine guns as we crossed the Bomb Line on our way to the Yalu River area.

As we passed Chodo Island, off the coast of North Korea, I directed Captain Hunt to orbit the island until I was certain that Lieutenant Erickson's plane was okay. Shortly thereafter, I released Hunt to return to K-13 because the policy in effect at that time forbade single ships to enter combat intentionally.

It was a bright, clear day, so I could easily see a large number of contrails above and in front of me. As we approached the Yalu area at 38,000 feet, I spotted eight MiGs. They were flying two abreast with elements in trail.

We jettisoned our drop tanks and attacked them from their 7 o'clock position. As I closed to within 2,000 feet, Les called a second flight of eight MiGs attacking us from our 6 o'clock! The first MiG flight had initiated a left climbing turn to evade us.

I was able to get off a quick burst of gunfire, and then I broke hard left. This caused the second flight to overshoot. I reversed my turn and did a barrel roll over the MiGs, then rolled out in a stern position on the second flight. As I was positioning on their number-seven man, they also began a rapid climb in a left turn. As they did, Les called out a third flight of eight MiGs lining up on our stern, and then this flight began to fire at us!

The MiG pilots appeared to be very well trained and disciplined. They maintained their formations very well and did a good job of positioning on us.

I fired a long burst into the seventh MiG-15 of the second flight. Then we broke hard left and were able to reverse and roll out again in a stern position on the third flight. By now we had twenty-four MIG-15s against our two F-86s in a high-altitude Lufbery. I felt, however, that we had the advantage because we could shoot at anybody, but they had to get position on us before they could fire. I honestly believe that Les and I each scored hits on several MiGs, but we didn't have confirmation.

The action went on for about forty-five minutes. Whenever I shot at a MiG, Les cut inside and lined up, and then I covered him while he shot at the MiGs. We took turns covering and shooting whenever we could. We alternated between being the hunter and the target.

Flying at 38,000 to 40,000 feet required a feather-light touch on the controls to prevent stalling and losing position. It required several miles of airspace to complete each orbit in the Lufbery, so the action appeared to be in slow motion.

It was incredibly exhilarating as this was the very first time that I had ever shot at anything except a towed target. To see an enemy airplane settle in my sights and then to pull the trigger is a feeling that is hard to describe. The chatter of six .50-caliber guns is such an awesome sound. The recoil of the guns noticeably slows the aircraft, so each time, after firing, we would nose down to regain airspeed and then try to reposition ourselves for another shot.

Suddenly, Les called a single MiG-15 sliding in toward us from our right side. This one was not a member of the twenty-four earlier MiGs. In fact, it appeared to be joining up with *us!* Heaven only knows what this MiG pilot was trying to accomplish, but I did not waste any time trying to figure it out. I made a quick pull-up and rolled to the right, ending up a thousand feet dead astern of the errant MiG. I fired my remaining ammunition in several bursts. Les and I both saw the sparkles on the MiG as my bullets struck. Its wings remained level, but the MiG began to turn, and it entered a slow descent toward the sea. At this point, Les called that one MiG flight was now at our 6 o'clock position, firing at me.

We were at Bingo fuel and I was out of ammo. It was time to exit. We performed a modified split-S and headed for K-13 at maximum speed. It was a huge relief to observe that no MiGs followed us.

We returned to K-13 without further incident. Les and I were the last aircraft to recover on this mission. During our intelligence debriefing, Les and I both claimed one damaged MiG, because that was all that we could visually confirm for each other. We were too busy to watch each other shoot every time. On September 26, 1952, I was informed that the claims board had certain information that upgraded my damage claim to my first official kill.

As far as I can determine, this was the longest continuous MiG-15— F-86 combat of the war. There was a lot of chatter around the debriefing area as we told how we had "cornered" twenty-five MiGs by ourselves. Neither of our aircraft sustained any damage from the MiGs that fired at us, and our confidence was greatly enhanced by this combat experience.

First Lieutenant Cecil Foster downed two MiG-15s on September 26, 1952, another on October 12, and he achieved ace status when he downed his fifth MiG on November 22. He was credited with his sixth victory on December 7, and was soon promoted to the rank of captain. He downed a seventh MiG on January 22, 1953, and, on his very last day of combat, Captain Foster downed one MiG on each of two separate combat missions—a total of nine aerial victories in his six-month combat tour.

Captain Foster remained on active duty following the Korean War. He served a combat tour in Vietnam, where he commanded a tactical fighter squadron from mid-1968 to mid-1969. He was shot down by antiaircraft fire on one occasion but was rescued by a helicopter.

Lieutenant Colonel Cecil Foster retired from the Air Force on July 1, 1975.

OUT OF CONTROL

Lieutenant Colonel ED HELLER, USAF
16th Fighter Squadron, 51st Fighter Interceptor Wing
Yalu River Area—January 27, 1953

Edwin Lewis Heller was born in Philadelphia on December 5, 1918. Though he long aspired to a career in aviation, he was a Pennsylvania state policeman on Pearl Harbor day, because he did not have the required college time to qualify for flight training. The following day, however, the eligibility requirements for Army Air Corps flight school were relaxed. As soon as Trooper Heller heard, he took a day off to go to Philadelphia to enlist as an Army Air Corps flying cadet. He was called up within a month and ordered to report to Maxwell Field, Alabama, to attend Pre-flight school as a member of Class of 43-B. He earned his wings and commission at Spence Field in Moultrie, Georgia, in March 1943. While serving as a member of the 352d Fighter Group in England, Lieutenant (later Captain) Ed Heller flew two combat tours—a total of 520 combat hours—and was credited with downing 5.5 enemy aircraft and destroying fourteen more on the ground. After the war, he decided to stay in the service.

Major Ed Heller arrived in Korea toward the end of 1952 and was assigned to command the 51st Fighter Interceptor Wing's 16th Fighter Squadron. In forty-seven missions over North Korea, Heller was credited with downing 3.5 MiG-15 jet interceptors—one MiG-15 on November 17, 1952, a shared MiG-15 on December 8, and two MiG-15s on January 22, 1953.

There was still an hour before start-engine time as I gathered the three members of my flight together in the squadron operations room. All three were old hands, so the briefing was short. I reviewed our hand signals for close formation and discussed radio discipline and how I wanted them to fly combat formation. A few minutes after that, we broke up and headed for the personnel equipment hut. It was a bitter cold day.

The personnel equipment hut was somewhat like the locker rooms of professional athletes. It was where we got dressed for our sport—

aerial combat. First I put my wallet and other personal effects in the drop of a locked box, to be recovered on my return from the mission. Next, I undressed to my underwear and pulled on my two-piece woolen immersion suit liner. I then struggled into my vulcanized, waterproof immersion suit. When I was suited up, the only parts of me showing were my hands and head. Around my wrists and neck was close-fitting elastic that would prevent icy water from entering if I had to eject over the sea. I fitted a soft scarf under my neckpiece to prevent chafing, and then I slipped my anti-G suit over my abdomen and legs. I was then ready to gather my fiberglass helmet, gloves, parachute, and escape kit—some 80 pounds of gear, all together—and go to my waiting airplane.

My crew chief—that most wonderful of men whom fighter pilots stake their lives and seldom lose—met me and took my gear. He placed the escape kit in the bucket seat for me to sit on and the backpack parachute in the recess made for it. As we made a cursory visual inspection of my beautiful F-86 Sabre, my crew chief told me of minor defects with the aircraft that were not serious but which I should know about. He told me he had put an extra "rat"—a piece of metal—in the tailpipe to enable me to get a little extra thrust from the engine. Thanks to the addition of the rat, I could now get 102 percent of normal power to use in an emergency, but I could also lose some turbine blades from prolonged use of the engine.

In peacetime training situations, where every flight was in a different airplane with a different crew chief, I paid great attention to my preflight inspection. I would study the maintenance form and question the crew chief closely about to any defect write-ups. In a combat situation, however, I didn't pay much attention to those things. This may sound incongruous, but in combat I had my own airplane and my own crew chief. I knew his name, his wife's name, and the names of his children. I knew his hometown, if there was any illness in the family, and who he had played cards with last night. And he knew just as much about me. He also knew very well how much I relied on him. It was up to me to show my trust, so he would bust his ass to get *our* plane in the best possible shape before I took off on a combat mission. And I knew my plane. There were no peculiar noises that were unidentifiable. I knew the exact RPM when the engine would vibrate a little, and I knew the gauge that would stick a little. The plane was part of me. I knew it thoroughly.

I took a last drag on my cigarette and heeled it out on the tarmac. I climbed up and wiggled comfortably into my cockpit. My crew chief helped me strap on the parachute and buckle the escape kit to its harness. I then fastened my shoulder straps to my lap belt, locked the belt, plugged in my G-suit, put on my helmet, fastened the chin strap, attached the oxygen hose, pulled on my gloves, and signaled for the external power unit. As soon as the crew chief flipped on the unit, my instruments jumped into place and began warming up. The second hand of my watch slowly came up on zero—start-engine time. I momentarily pressed the starter button, then flipped it on the battery position. The power unit labored to turn the engine over. As the tachometer read 6 percent, I cracked the throttle open. With satisfaction, I heard the dull sound of combustion as the fuel lit. The engine accelerated to idle—12 percent—and the throttle was placed around the stop to the idle position as the piercing sound of the turbine settled into steady RPM. I turned the radio on, pushed the squadron-frequency button, and while waiting for it to warm up, clipped my oxygen mask over my face and tested it for 100 percent oxygen. Then I lowered the helmet visor over my eyes.

As the radio volume came up, I pressed the mike button on the throttle and spoke into the mike within the oxygen mask: "Tiger Flight, check in." "Two", "Three", "Four" they crisply called back. "Tiger Lead. Roger. Let's roll!"

I signaled the crew chief with a thumbs-up motion, and he removed the wheel chocks. I then flipped the electric switch to close and lock the canopy, increased power to 70 percent to get moving, and quickly reduced it back to idle as soon as the airplane started moving. I left the revetment with a thumbs-up to my crew chief, and he saluted me.

Tiger-2, Tiger-3, and Tiger-4 fell in behind me as we taxied to the runway. I, as Tiger Lead, fell in behind two other flights, and another flight fell in behind me. The sixteen of us taxied onto the runway, each flight behind the other in fingertip formation. As flight leader, I was to the left of the centerline and my wingman, Tiger-2, was to my left, near the edge of the runway. My element leader, Tiger-3, was to the right of centerline, and his wingman, Tiger-4, was to the right of him, near the edge of the runway.

At a signal from the mission leader, we all ran our engines up to 100-percent power. I jammed the toe brakes on as my plane lurched and bucked from the jet blasts ahead of me. I carefully checked to see that the exhaust temperature was within limits, scanned other engine instruments, and listened as the flights ahead of me released brakes for takeoff at five-second intervals between elements. As my turn approached, I leaned my head back in preparation for the nod signal to my wingman to release brakes.

Go! In unison, my wingman and I released brakes, and our two aircraft began the take-off roll together. I reduced throttle to 98 percent to give my wingman room to maneuver. He kept perfect formation, looking up the leading edge of my wing into my cockpit. At 90 knots, I signaled with a palm-up motion and trimmed the stick back slightly. The nose wheel gently rose from the runway. At about 105 knots our planes became airborne. My wingman was still tucked in right beside me, with our wings overlapping. I gave him the thumbs-up signal for gear retraction, and with the execution signal—a nod of the head—both our landing gears gracefully folded into the wings in perfect harmony.

We zoomed over the rice paddies as I kept low to gather speed. The Korean farmers never lifted their heads, so routine had the event become for them. As my airspeed indicator approached 400 knots, I eased back on the stick and we began to climb. The two of us followed the black exhaust trails of those ahead, roared through a saddleback in a mountain range ten miles north of the field, and climbed out on course at the rate of 6,000 feet per minute.

Within minutes, we had streaked over the muddy, meandering Han River and turned slightly to port to pass safely west of the restricted Panmunjon "Holy Land." My element finally overtook us, so I increased power to 100 percent as we spread out a little. After we passed the Holy Land, I rocked my wings as the signal to test-fire guns, and each of us fired a short burst to determine if there were any jams.

As we passed Chodo Island, the GCI (ground-control intercept) station there began to warn us of MiGs. It always frustrated and angered me that, no matter how secret we tried to keep our mission timetables, the Communists always knew exactly when our time over target was.

"Attention John aircraft," the GCI radioed, "Bandit tracks One and Two forming up in Centerfield. Approximately thirty aircraft each track." A track was a radar blip, and in baseball parlance, the mouth of the Yalu

River was "Home Plate," up the Yalu was the "First Base line," and up the Yellow Sea coast was the "Third Base line."

"Attention John aircraft. Bandit track Three forming over Home Plate. Twenty-five aircraft."

I had the old feeling we were going to mix it up again today. It made no difference how many times I had been in combat before, the knowledge that I was approaching it again always got my body chemistry working. The palms of my hands began to perspire, the adrenalin began flowing to give me added energy, and I became the hunter with my eyes. It was always the same; sometimes I could control the stomach cramps, but even experienced as I was, the old body symptoms were there. The nearness of air-to-air combat, individual yet impersonal, and most likely to the death, always got that body chemistry working overtime. I began to breathe that raw oxygen a little faster.

We leveled at 45,000 feet just as our external fuel tanks ran dry. I signaled with a porpoise of the plane to jettison tanks. I trimmed the aircraft finely and punched the jettison button. Both tanks came off cleanly. If there was the slightest yaw, it was possible for a jettisoned tank to roll out to the wing's leading edge and take off the Pitot tube— the airspeed indicator inlet. Relieved of the drag burden, my plane leaped forward like a stallion.

We were in enemy territory now. The members of my flight and I all knew that sense of teamwork that bonds a flight of professional fighter pilots.

I put my flight in combat formation. My wingman was about 45 degrees to my rear, on the opposite side from my element and about four shiplengths away. My element was about 2,500 feet higher and about 1,500 feet down-sun from me. We kept our speed up to .88 mach. I concentrated my vigil in the half of the sky my element was in, to guard his rear, and he was doing the same for my element. However, I was also searching the whole sky. The sky at this altitude is a deep and brilliant blue, which made it difficult to pick out objects. I kept my head turning constantly, taking in the entire horizon. As my eyes came through the nose of the plane, I instinctively covered my important instruments with one glance and my rearview mirror with another. We were all as alert as possible. There was no room there for a weak sister, as he would have jeopardized the entire flight. The four of us were a perfect team; we complemented each other. After all, this was not a training exercise; every move we made was a matter of life or death.

The visibility was perfect. Ahead I could see the remnants of contrails. They were right above the mouth of the Yalu, which confirmed the GCI report. I knew from the weather forecast that the condensation level was between 25,000 and 30,000 feet. Within that altitude spread, tailpipe exhaust would condense to form a cloud. This was what I saw from afar over the Yalu River. I became even more alert and watchful. I searched the sky through the sun and away, using the airman's trick in the process—I did not stare at any one piece of sky but simply let my eyes move, allowing my peripheral vision to pick up any object out there.

There! A glint!

"Tiger Lead here. Bogeys ten o'clock high." I kept scanning the sky. In a moment, I picked them up again. MiGs! They were high, coming on in the opposite direction. The combined closing speed was in excess of 1,200 miles per hour. I knew they would be out of sight before I could turn to give chase. I gave the GCI people the MiGs' position and vector, and we continued on patrol.

We approached the Suiho Dam (First Base) and began a gentle 180-degree turn back to Home Plate. While in the turn, I picked something up. "Tiger Lead here. Bogeys coming in at nine o'clock. Let's turn into them."

As I spoke, I tightened my turn to port in case they were MiGs. This would make us head-on to them and give us little time to fire.

"Tiger Lead. Three here. Break left . . . *now!*"

Before the last word was out, I was already in a hard diving turn, bending my head around to see what was endangering us. I saw four MiGs bouncing us from above. That meant at least eight of them were around. And I soon picked up the other four.

The next thing I knew, there were MiGs all over the sky. I knew we were really in for it.

"Tiger Lead to John aircraft. Mixing it with twelve-plus at First Base. Angels forty-five [45,000 feet]."

There was no more time to talk, so radio silence prevailed among the other flights heading our way. For Tiger Flight, it was just a matter of getting down to business and turning to the offensive.

I made a defensive maneuver and succeeded in losing my immediate pursuer. I was then ready to attack. I quickly cleared my tail—my wingman was in perfect position—and then caught a glimpse of a MiG below me, in a good position for me to attack.

As I rolled over for my bounce, I cleared my tail once again. I saw a MiG coming up in a zooming climb to attack me. I was not concerned, because my attacking wingover was a perfect defensive maneuver against this MiG's attack. Also, he was only going to get a split-second shot at me, with even less time to track me. We often purposely put ourselves in this position to give MiGs a 50-degree angle-off shot in order to draw them into a fight.

I loosened up my turn to keep from approaching a stall, and increased the lead required by the MiG. I could actually see the 37mm rounds—they looked like burning golf balls—zooming over my canopy. I instinctively ducked behind the armor plate and waited for him to complete his pass on me.

Suddenly there was a terrific explosion. It felt like a 500-pound bomb going off right beside me. It momentarily stunned me. I thought my plane had exploded, but when I came to my senses I realized I had been hit. I felt the ripping pain of steel through my right arm, which was limp. I lifted the useless hand off the stick grip rest and placed it on my lap. Then I surveyed the damage to my plane.

The MiG had passed me by, but I was approaching a vertical dive. I grabbed the stick with my left hand to pull out of the dive, but to my horror, the entire stick came away. I couldn't fly the airplane at all without the stick. I held it up in front of my face and pulled the trigger. When that didn't fire the guns, I threw the stick down with a curse.

The cockpit was a mess. The right console, where the radio controls were, was smashed, and either blood or hydraulic fluid was oozing over it. The instrument panel was completely shot away, and so were the wind screens. I had been hit somewhere over my right shoulder with a 37mm explosive shell. The armor plate took most of the shrapnel, which saved my life, but shrapnel had broken my right arm, taken out the instrument panel, windscreen, and stick while miraculously missing my legs.

I knew I was through, that I had to get out. There was no way to fly the plane, and I was now in an uncontrolled vertical power dive, approaching the speed of sound. In preparation to eject, I locked my shoulder harness with the lever under the left arm rest and brought my feet up under my knees. I then strained to reach the ejection lever to eject the canopy. I pulled, but nothing happened. I desperately pulled harder, bringing the lever against its stop. Still nothing. To my utter horror, I realized that I was trapped inside the cockpit. The electrical motor wouldn't run it back at this speed. I realized the ejection system had also been shot away. I could not eject the canopy or myself.

It was futile to grab the pull handle of the canopy, but I did anyway. It would not budge. I was in a vertical dive and the ground was directly in front of me. I was fascinated by how rapidly the ground was approaching.

Somewhere between 20,000 and 16,000 feet, the plane began a pull-out from the dive. This was natural because the heavier lower air reacted differently on the control surfaces than the thin upper air. The centrifugal forces became immense. My head sank between my knees, the oxygen mask came loose from my face, saliva poured from my mouth, and mucus from my nose and eyes felt like it was popping from my head. In spite of my anti-G suit, which helped to keep the blood in the upper part of my body, I blacked out and lost consciousness. I must have pulled 10 to 12 Gs—ten or twelve times my body weight.

As the plane came through the horizon and started back in its dive, the G forces let up and I recovered. I threw my head back in relief. At once, I saw the hole from the shell. As I was again speeding toward the ground, only seconds away from a crash, I did not hesitate. I flipped open my lap belt and stood up. The next thing I knew, my helmet was ripped off my head and I was sucked through the canopy, enlarging the shellhole as I went. I felt a tick in my left leg, and then I was torn by the air rushing at my face.

I knew I must wait a few seconds to slow down before I pulled the chute open. My eyes were blasted shut, but after a few seconds, I placed my left thumb under the ring and jabbed a punch outward. A tremendous shock hit me and I blacked out again. A moment later, I recovered and found myself floating quietly to earth. It was just a moment, though, before the ground came up and I collapsed on into it. I heaved a great big sigh and took stock of myself. My left foot was underneath my knee—that was the tick I had felt going through the canopy. I was helpless.

In a couple of minutes, I heard a noise and looked around to see that several men were coming toward me. They carried me down to a truck and drove me off to their village.

Though the Korean War came to an end only seven months after he was shot down, Lieutenant Colonel Ed Heller spent nearly two and a half years as a prisoner of the People's Republic of China, for that is where he landed. For two years, he lay on his back in isolation, until Chinese surgeons finally repaired his shattered leg in the last of four operations. When Heller could walk again, he joined three other American prisoners for a trial in Peking. There, the three were found guilty of spying, and their punishment was deportation from China.

Ed Heller resumed his flying career and participated in the Cuban Missile Crisis of 1962. He retired from the Air Force as a lieutenant colonel in 1967.

CROSSING THE RIVER

Major JACK BOLT, USMC
39th Fighter Squadron, 51st Fighter Interceptor Wing
Yalu River Area—July 11, 1953

John Franklin Bolt was born in Laurens, South Carolina, on May 19, 1921, and raised in Sanford, Florida. He attended the University of Florida for two years, ran out of tuition money, and enlisted in the Naval Aviation Cadet program in order to claim the $500-per-year bounty offered to four-year Navy Reserve aviators. He earned his wings at Jacksonville Naval Air Station and was commissioned a Marine second lieutenant on July 18, 1942, following his advanced course at Opa-Locka.

Lieutenant Jack Bolt arrived in the South Pacific in July 1943, was assigned to the pool of reserve pilots, and shortly made his way into VMF-214, a veteran combat squadron retraining for its second combat tour in the Solomon Islands.

While flying F4U Corsairs with VMF-214, Lieutenant Bolt downed six Imperial Navy Zero fighters between September 23, 1943, and January 4, 1944—from the northern Solomons to Rabaul. In May 1945, while training for carrier operations with VMF-472 in Hawaii, he set an endurance record by staying aloft in a Corsair for just over fourteen hours. He spent the closing months of the Pacific War with VMF-472, bombing bypassed islands and preparing for the invasion of Japan.

Following World War II, Bolt stayed on active duty in the Marine Corps and advanced through a number of routine flight and staff assignments. The start of the Korean War found him on duty with the 2d Marine Aircraft Wing, and from there he served as an exchange pilot with the U.S. Air Force, flying F-86 jet fighter-interceptors in the United States. Though the F-86 was not rated for night operations, Bolt took part in many night missions while serving with an Air Force Reserve squadron charged with defending the Oregon coast against an anticipated Soviet air attack.

Major Jack Bolt arrived in Korea in May 1952 and was assigned to Marine Air Group 13. While serving with VMF-115 and flying the Grumman F9F Panther jet, he completed ninety-four combat missions, mostly in support of United Nations ground forces.

While on my first R&R in Korea, I made contact with an Air Force squadron commander named George Ruddell, whom I had met at March Field in 1947 or 1948, when I'd gone there to try to promote jets with the Marine Corps. All my buddies were in Japan, whooping it up, but I was at K-13, where the 51st Fighter Interceptor Wing was based. Ruddell, a lieutenant colonel at the time, was commanding the 39th Fighter Interceptor Squadron. I showed him that I had a hundred hours, not only in the F-86, but in the F-86F. His was the only squadron of F-86Fs on the field, so I had experience he could use. Ruddell was friendly toward me and let me fly his birds. I just took some familiarization flights with a few guys.

I did my second R&R trip that Christmas—1952. At this time, the Air Force's soon-to-be-great ace, 1st Lieutenant Joe McConnell, had been grounded. He'd had some flight infraction, and Ruddell was punishing him by grounding him. But Ruddell sent him up to teach me some tactics. I flew two or three flights with McConnell, and he was good. They were just familiarization hops. McConnell really taught me lots of things. He became the leading ace of the Korean War and entirely deserved the fame he achieved. He was killed soon after the war on a test flight at Edwards Air Force Base.

We got three R&Rs during a regular combat tour—one about every six weeks. This was my second one, so my tour was winding down. I put in for an Air Force exchange tour, but our group personnel officer said, "Bolt, I know you've been trying to worm your way into this, but you've had a year with the Air Force, and you ain't going up there. You think you are, but I'm telling you now that it ain't gonna happen." They felt that I'd had more than my share of gravy assignments. So I got in touch with Ruddell, and he got the Air Force general up there to send a wire down to our Marine Corps general. They only had two F-86 wings in Korea, the 4th and 51st, and they had two Marines in each. One of them was leaving, and this was the opening I wanted. The time was ripe for me. Another guy from our squadron, Major Tom Sellers, went to the 4th Group, but he was killed by a MiG. So the Air Force general sent a wire to the Marine general, saying, "We're willing to have your pilots, but they come up here having never flown the plane, and they present a training burden on our people. But now we have a rare instance of a pilot who's shown enough initiative to come up here and get checked out, and he's ready to go. Would you mind appointing John Bolt?" Well, there was nothing my group could do; it came down from the 1st Marine Aircraft Wing. So they put me in Ruddell's 39th Fighter Interceptor Squadron.

McConnell became the top ace through the first half of 1953—he shot down sixteen MiG-15s between January and May—and I was flying on his wing when I first got up there, for my first half dozen or dozen flights. I was in his flight—Dog Flight. Ruddell was really nice to me, too. Although he was a very tough guy, he was as nice to me as he could be. When McConnell left in May, I took over the command of Dog Flight, a quarter of the squadron, about twelve pilots.

The "kill rules" were that if you got seven hits on a MiG, they would give you a kill. The MiGs didn't torch off at high altitude. They simply would not burn because of the air density. So our intelligence people would count the incendiary hits on them. They figured that if you got seven hits in the fuselage, the odds were the MiG was dead, and they'd give you a kill. We had very good gun cameras, and they could count the incendiary hits. They knew that every third round was an incendiary, so if you got three incendiary hits on the gun-camera film, they would say that it was a dead MiG.

The salvation of the F-86 was that it had good transonic controls, and the MiG's controls were subsonic. We could cruise at about .84 Mach in the F-86. The MiG had to go into its uncontrollable range to attack you, and its stick forces were unmanageable. The kill ratio between the MiG and the F-86 was about eight to one. This was due almost exclusively to the F-86's flying tail, although there were other superior features, such as the gun package. The MiG-15's gun package was designed to shoot down B-50 bombers—a 37mm and two 23mm cannons. It was overkill, and not very good against fighters. Although the F-86 package used essentially the same .50-caliber machine guns as we had used in World War II, the rate of fire had been doubled, and it was a good gun for shooting down fighters.

Down low, where you were out of that transonic superiority range, we had a G-suit, and they didn't. You can fight defensively when you're blacked out, but you can't fight offensively. If you had enough speed to pull into a good 6G turn, you'd go black in 20 to 30 degrees of turn, but they couldn't follow you while blacked out themselves. You're still conscious, but you have three to five seconds of vision loss. When you thought you'd gone about as far as you could carry that, you could pop the stick forward and you'd immediately regain your vision. You'd already started your roll, and they were right there in front of you, every time, because they'd eased off in their turn since they didn't have G-suits and your G tolerance was about twice theirs. They were usually right there in front of you, probably because they had overshot you.

The F-86 also had a better rate of roll than the MiG-15, which in a scissor is a good maneuver. And we could simply outrun them if we could get enough distance to bring the speed advantage into effect.

My first jet kill came on May 16, 1953, at about 43,000 to 44,000 feet. I had missed a couple of kills before that. I missed them by not being determined or aggressive enough, and at this point I was almost desperate for a MiG kill. I was the leader of Dog Flight, but I'd screwed up a couple of bounces. My self-esteem and my esteem among the other pilots in the flight were low. I just determined that the next MiG I saw was a dead man, and I didn't care where he was. The next MiG was in a gaggle; there were MiGs as far as I could see. I had a good run on one of them and pulled into a firing position, but other MiGs were shooting at me and my wingman. They were sufficiently close. I got some hits on the one I was aiming at, but he went into a scissor. The MiG-15 was lighter than the F-86, so he could gain altitude in a scissor. But the F-86 had a better rate of roll. As he was scissoring—a good tactic—I was trying to shoot as he passed through my firing angle. Well, each time I shot, I delayed my turn, so he gained on me and was drifting back. He almost got behind me and was so close that his plane just blanked out the camera. But I think he realized that I would have crashed into him rather than let him get behind me, so he rolled out of it and dived away. Then I got a bunch more hits on him, and he pulled up. The pilot was probably dead by this point. I'll bet I put 500 rounds into that guy. The whole time, other MiGs were shooting at my wingman and me, and so we pulled out.

My self-esteem and my esteem in the flight went up with that. From then on, I didn't botch up many opportunities. This first guy sure knew what he was doing. The scissor was the right thing to do; he just shouldn't have broken it off. He was really getting back to a position where he could've taken the initiative.

By this time, Ruddell had five MiG kills, but the MiGs quit coming south of the Yalu River, and we weren't supposed to go north, into China. If you went north of the river, it was at the risk of your professional career if you got caught. The Chinese were yelling and screaming about the "pirates" that were coming over there, but that's where the action was. Ruddell wasn't getting any MiGs because they weren't coming south of the river. He'd been threatening everybody that he'd kill 'em—cut their heads off, decapitate 'em—if they went north of the river. But he weakened one night. He'd had a few drinks, and he called me into this little cubbyhole where he had his quarters. During the discussion, tears came to his eyes; they were running down his cheeks as he was saying how he wanted to be a good Air Force officer, and how he loved the Air Force, and if they told him to do something he'd do it, and if they told him to not do something he'd not do it. But getting those MiGs meant more to him than his career and life itself. And since he had been beating up on his own flight about not going across the river, he'd be embarrassed to ask any of them to go across the river with him. He didn't know whether they would want to anyway. They would have been in big trouble if they'd been identified as going up there. I don't know if the pilots who were shot down north of the river were ever disciplined when the war was over, or what. But at this time we took the threat seriously, and it hung very heavily over us.

Ruddell said, "Would you give me some of your flight? I want to go across the river. I've gotta have some action." They'd gone day after day after day with no action. I said sure, I'd be delighted. So we planned one for the next day. I was going to fly his second section. I was going across every flight, anyway, and I had learned that it was useful to have guys in your flight who didn't go across.

On a river-crossing flight, we took off and went full bore all the way. We'd put those planes at a 100-percent power setting until we got out of combat; they drew 100 percent all the time. The F-86's engine life was planned for 800 hours, but we were only getting about 550 or so. Turbine blade cracks were developing. Also, we were running them at max temperature. You could put these little constrictors in the tailpipe—we called them "rats"—and you could "rat 'em up" until they ran at max temperature, so they were really hot rods. We would run our drop tanks dry just about the time we got up there. If we didn't have a contact, we weren't supposed to drop the tanks, but we skinned them every time. By the end of the flight, on at least four occasions, I had been to over 50,000 feet in that bird. When you were lighter and still hadn't pulled power back—still at 100 percent—you could really get up there. The MiG-15 could get up there, too—to 50,000.

So, for me, this flight with Ruddell was a typical flight. We got up there and skinned the drops—at least the pilots going across the river did. We had a code. We would say, "Twin," and the call-back was "City." Then we would switch from the combat frequency to the training frequency. We were so far away from our bases that we didn't have all the usual training chatter going on. We'd come up on the training frequency, where the next call might be, "Sioux," and the call-back would be, "Falls." That's all; there was no other radio contact, but we knew we were all up on the same frequency. With that channel switch, the leader strangled his IFF—his squawk—and another guy picked up the squawk and turned down short of the Yalu while we sailed across. We were splitting our flight; just two of us went over, and two stayed back, so the controllers thought they had a radar image on all four. We were beyond range of voice control. We'd "choked our parrot," but they thought they had four planes because one IFF squawk was all they were expecting to read. That was typical of the way Dog Flight did it before Ruddell joined us, and we briefed him on all of this.

The first flight with Ruddell was on June 30, 1953. We got up there and he and I went over the river. There were big clouds up. It was early in the morning—0800 or 0900—and we heard on the radio that there was a fight going on, that there were some MiGs flying this day. We came from the sunny side of the clouds to the back side of this big cumulus cloud. There was some antiaircraft down there that had been shooting at something—there were black flak puffs—and there were some planes down there. We were half blind from the diminished illumination on the back side of the cloud, and it was a confusing situation, but we dived down there and, by God, there was a MiG. Ruddell spotted a MiG, and we tore down from probably about 43,000 feet to about 15,000. We just dropped straight down. Ruddell got into shooting position behind the MiG, but then he didn't shoot, didn't shoot, didn't shoot. I tore past him and blew up the MiG.

I had experience at jumping planes, and one of the things you did when you came down from extreme altitude to the deck, which is frequently where you found them when north of the river, was put your armored-glass defroster on full bore. It would be so hot, it would almost be painful, but it kept the front windscreen clear. Another thing you did was test your guns to be sure they were firing. You tested your G-suit, too, because you were going down low where the G-suit could be very important to you.

Ruddell's windscreen had fogged over. He was sitting there in a kill position, but he couldn't shoot. So I went by him and got the MiG. I was a "MiG killer" by this time; I'd gotten three others—one each on May 16, June 22, and June 25.

We got back, and all the guys—everybody in the 39th Squadron—knew what was going on. The squadron was just abuzz that the colonel had started crossing the river and he'd gotten aced out of his first kill over there; Ruddell had gone across the river, he'd had a chance to kill one, he didn't do it, and I took it. The pilots were going bananas. When we got back they had all these signs pasted up all over the Dog Flight

Quonset hut. One of the signs said, "Marine wetback steals colonel's MiG!"

Another day, we got bounced. We went across the river and jumped these planes that had just taken off from an airfield called Fenchen, which was twenty or thirty miles north of the river. They were alerted to our presence, probably by the tower, and they'd dropped their tanks and were sucking their gear up by the time we arrived. All I got was a "damaged" that day. He was going about 150 knots, and I was doing about 600. I just got a skim shot through him.

They had a combat air patrol up, and it came down on us. From then on, they were taking all the pictures! We had a hell of a fight trying to shake them. My wingman and I were immediately separated, and it took about five minutes of twisting and turning at high Gs. We were doing all sorts of things to keep from getting shot. Finally, coming out, I was just totally exhausted. I was calling my wingman, 1st Lieutenant Fritz Kuhlman—first on this frequency we'd gone to, the private frequency—but there was no answer. Then I called him on all the other frequencies. No answer. I just knew I'd lost him. I'd never lost a wingman in World War II, but I figured I'd lost Fritz. But I hadn't. He was all shot up and his radio was shot out. I beat him back to K-13; he came in about five minutes after I did. He was killed in a dumb stunt over in Japan a few weeks later, probably after the war ended; he flew up a box canyon in a Mustang and couldn't Immelmann or turn out of it.

On my last two MiGs—July 11, 1953—my wingman was 1st Lieutenant Jerry Carlile. This was the only time I ever felt any sympathy or compassion for an enemy in a dogfight. We were north of but still close to the Yalu River, and these two MiGs were tearing along, right down at ground level, skimming the treetops. We were down at about 20,000 feet for some reason. By this time, I'd killed four, and I knew right away that those guys were dead men. It was just the ideal situation. We dove right onto their tails, and I started shooting at one. Jerry, who was to my left, also started shooting. He almost shot me because I'd drifted over really close to him and both of us were shooting. Jerry shouldn't have been shooting, and he quit just in time to avoid shooting me. I got a good burst into the trailing wingman. When the leader made a hard turn to the right, I followed around and tried to hit him. The first burst missed him, but I managed to get him as soon as he rolled out and leveled off.

I got good gun-camera footage on the second one. With the first one, we were kind of transonic wobbling, and he was down so low there were trees in the background. It was not good film, but if you looked closely, you could see the first kill. The second one had good film coverage on it.

It was fairly early in the flight, so I turned the lead over to Jerry and said, "That's enough for me, Jerry, you get some." And I started flying his wing. Jerry had one kill, and he was some guy, a tenacious wingman.

Major Jack Bolt was the only Marine fighter pilot to achieve ace status both in World War II and Korea, one of only seven American aces to do so. He served in a variety of assignments following the end of the Korean War, earned his bachelor's degree in 1956, and retired from the Marine Corps as a lieutenant colonel in 1962. After spending several years in private industry, Jack Bolt completed a law degree and practiced in Florida until 1991.

NAVY NIGHT ACE

Lieutenant GUY BORDELON, USN
VC-3
South Korea—June 29–July 16, 1953

Guy Pierre Bordelon, Jr., was born in Ruston, Louisiana on February 1, 1922. He graduated from high school in Alexandria, Louisiana, in the spring of 1939 and went on to college at Louisiana Polytechnic Institute and Louisiana State University. Bordelon quit LSU and enlisted in the Navy flight program in July 1942, and he was designated a Naval Aviator and commissioned as an ensign on May 23, 1943, at Corpus Christi, Texas. He served as a flight instructor for fourteen months at Kingville, Texas, and was training as a combat team leader with a new FM-2 Wildcat unit in Sanford, Florida, when the war with Japan ended.

Lieutenant Bordelon received a Regular Navy commission and served in a variety of peacetime billets in the United States and overseas.

During the early part of the Korean War, I served on the staff of the commander of Cruiser Division 3, based aboard the heavy cruiser USS

Helena. This was a good "black-shoe Navy" indoctrination but was very frustrating for a thoroughly trained and motivated Navy fighter pilot. What I really wanted was to be back in the air, carrying the war to the "Reds", and I felt the cockpit of a Navy fighter was the best place to realize that ambition. I was therefore greatly pleased when, in 1951, I was ordered to one of the U.S. Navy's top-line all-weather fighter squadrons, Composite Squadron 3 (VC-3), then headquartered at Moffet Field, California.

This large squadron of 175 pilots was charged with creating, training, equipping, and supporting night-fighter teams for each *Essex*-class carrier of the Navy's Seventh Fleet engaged in combat with the Communists in the Korean War. Normal complements for such teams were five F4U-5N propeller-driven night-combat-equipped aircraft, five specially trained pilots, nearly forty maintenance, ordnance, and electronics specialists, and necessary supplies and spare parts. For administrative support, we were attached to the onboard air group and, if possible, to a squadron of similar aircraft. My night-fighter section was attached to Fighting Squadron 152, which has equipped with F4U-4 Corsair day fighters. We were well supported by VF-152 and the personnel of the USS *Princeton* (CV-37).

At the time, the *Princeton* was making her second nine-month deployment of the Korean War. She was what we Navy types call a "happy ship." That means that she had a reputation for outstanding concern for the comfort and efficient support of her embarked air group on each deployment. And she didn't let us down!

As night fighters, we were a special unit, like nothing else aboard the *Princeton,* and thus we had special support problems that drove us and the ship's supply officer to the brink at times. For example, our -5Ns were considerably heavier and more complex than the -4s flown by VF-152. As usual, the Bureau of Aeronautics planners who worked up the parts allowances for each deployed detachment had erred drastically on the side of fragility and so-called cost savings. At least half of our aircraft down time was due to such errors. Even the tailhook, that essential part that snares the arresting wire for a safe landing aboard the carrier, was different and required unique parts. The hook was beefed up by specially hardened H-11 steel at the attaching point. This part, designed to last indefinitely, usually failed every third or fourth landing! It was easy to replace if you had the required part, but we soon ran through the ship's support allowance of two! During early deployment, my unit had three "down" aircraft out of the five until the *Princeton's* outstanding supply officer personally manufactured reliable replacements out of common ship's boilerplate! We were never short of this part again, and the boiler plate lasted five times longer than H-11 steel and cost one hundred times less! We wanted to award the commander a medal, but he modestly declined.

Beginning our night combat missions under the late-October moon of 1952, we launched on pre-briefed roving strikes by individual aircraft against color-coded and numbered truck and rail routes that were being heavily used by the Communists. Our targets were along a line roughly parallel to but north of the 38th Parallel, extending all the way across the Korean peninsula.

Our mission was interdiction of enemy road and rail links used to resupply their ground forces. "Search and Destroy" was the name for the missions we flew at low altitudes in a nightly effort to eliminate anything that moved. As our day aircraft had long since made any type of movement by day extremely costly, if not impossible, the Reds turned more and more to night travel in a desperate effort that we countered with bomb- and ammo-laden F4U-5N Corsair fighter-bombers and Douglas AD-5N Skyraider attack aircraft. It was a dangerous mission because we were forced to fly up steep mountain passes at ground-scraping altitude in order to reach our targets as they ascended on twisting and turning mountain roads and rail lines.

The enemy did everything possible to stop our attacks by positioning thousands of antiaircraft guns along every route and equipping each truck convoy with machine guns and cannon. Our tactic to prevent detection was to start our attacks at around 7,000 feet and make power-off dives for silent approach. When in range, we would open fire with our four 20mm cannon, targeting the lead trucks to stop the convoy's forward movement and then making a second attack against the rear trucks to prevent escape. This was very effective.

To prevent our use of flares for target illumination, the enemy forces set many smoke fires on clear nights. The resultant haze combined with the flares to create a milkbowl effect that gave the attacking pilots instant vertigo. After this happened to me on an otherwise clear night, I seldom used flares again. The smoke was a common defense tactic used to protect rail-tunnel entrances and coastal rail lines. Training in proper use of the eyes at night became very important to our missions. "Pull away from bright explosions!" was our watchword. Night blindness is difficult to get rid of in a hurry, and it can be deadly.

Among other measures adopted by the Communists to protect their rolling stock was setting fires inside railroad tunnels. This was to make us think that trains were hiding in the tunnels. The idea was that we would use up our bombs attempting to create earth slides to seal the tunnels. The answer to that game was not to bomb tunnel entrances unless we had actually seen trains entering them. It took a while to learn that lesson, however.

To protect their trucks, the Reds converted entire villages into drive-through "garages". When we were in the area, the enemy ran their trucks into such villages, walls were raised, and the trucks parked inside, out of sight, until we left the area. Daylight photography revealed rutted tracks leading into the concealing hooches, and we ended their little trick.

With the onset of winter weather, our job became more hazardous. We were forced to wear the infamous "poopysuits" that supposedly gave us a few more minutes of life in the icy waters of the Sea of Japan. Five minutes of exposure after ditching was supposed to be the limit, then unconsciousness and death soon followed. The exposure suits were extremely uncomfortable as they choked the wearer. I frequently returned from a four-and-a-half-hour flight with a horrendous headache and feeling more than a bit dizzy, all because of the poopysuit's tight fit.

Finally, in June 1953, our ardent dreams came true! The Fifth Air Force requested our services in the Seoul area to destroy the slow, low-flying World War II-vintage propeller-driven aircraft that the Reds were using to harass our installations, bomb supplies, drop agents, and generally raise hell. When the call came, a group of these "Bedcheck Charlie" aircraft had just destroyed millions of gallons of aviation fuel, large quantities of munitions intended for our front-line forces, and large quantities of other essential combat supplies. Air Force all-weather jet interceptors had been unable to deal with these aircraft because the prop-driven airplanes flew so low and so slow. Several jet interceptors had been lost flying into the "hard centers" of the mountains around Seoul. Our Navy boss, Admiral Joseph "Jocko" Clark, the Seventh Fleet commander, volunteered our services because we flew the hazardous "low and slow" missions every night. His offer was snapped up and four of us flew from Seventh Fleet carriers to Seoul.

After our briefing at the Joint Operations Center, Korea, we were assigned to K-16, a U.S. Marine Corps air base at Pyongtaek, thirty-five miles south of Seoul. This was ideal. The Marines operated F4U-4s and -5s, and virtually identical AU-1s, so they had plenty of spare parts and trained maintenance personnel. We flew several area-familiarization hops and then settled in to begin our mission. Our quarters were screened huts that had somehow managed to attract hundreds of the infamous "biting" black flies. The only way we could sleep was to pull heavy wool blankets over our heads and literally sweat it out. I slept like a baby.

We had action almost immediately after we got started. On the night of June 29, 1953, I was on alert when enemy aircraft intruded into our area. I was launched and controlled by a Marine ground-control sergeant who soon vectored me on to the tail of an unknown aircraft. Closing to point-blank range, I identified the bogey as a Yak-18. As I made my report, the rear-seat gunner began to spray the area to my left and below me with machine-gun fire. I immediately opened fire with my four 20mm cannon, which were loaded with high explosive incendiary shells. These rounds literally blew the Yak out of the sky. The explosion blinded me momentarily, but I managed to maintain control until I could see again.

I reported the kill to my ground controller and was told that another bogey had just "popped up." This one was to the north and west of me. Once again, I was vectored into contact with a second Yak-18. Upon reporting "Enemy," I was cleared to fire. As I pulled in tight, I saw that I was being fired on by the rear-seat gunner, but his tracers were going beneath my Corsair. I opened up with my 20mm cannon and saw the incendiary shells begin to burn him. Then I saw a big explosion. The Yak seemed to break into several large pieces, each burning furiously.

My controller reported that the sky was clear and directed me to return to base. I did so gladly. I was feeling very fatigued, yet elated. My reception on the ground was tumultuous, but all I wanted was to sleep.

The following night, June 30, I was scheduled to fly a combat air patrol from the port of Inchon north to the Imjin River and then east up the river to two distinctive bends we called "Marilyn's Left" and "Right One." As I arrived on station, I reported in to the Joint Operations Center, Korea, and was immediately vectored toward unknown targets to the north of my position. The bogeys appeared to be headed southeast toward Inchon. I maneuvered in behind the two aircraft, which I was soon able to identify as Lavochkin La-11 fighters.

The La-11s were in a loose trail formation, so I pulled in right behind the rear aircraft and gave a "Tallyho!" on enemy bogeys. I was cleared to fire and at once opened on my targeted La-11. Two short bursts of cannon fire was all it took. This La-11 began to burn, and it dove straight down into the ground.

The lead fighter started to follow the burning aircraft down, but I closed to point-blank range and immediately opened fire on it. This target turned left, then right, and started to climb as I gave him another burst. With that, he exploded in flames and fell apart. I followed the largest burning mass down to 500 feet and saw it crash near my first kill. "Over so fast?" I thought.

The next two weeks were not as fruitful because the North Koreans suddenly stopped sending Bedcheck Charlies down to us. However, we were kept busy intercepting and identifying unidentified and uncleared friendly aircraft. On three occasions, I was forced to repeat my identification report of "friendly aircraft" to the joint operations center, where controllers were insisting that I fire because they had no flight clearance requests on the aircraft I had intercepted. Once I came in on a large rescue helicopter, which the center controllers insisted I shoot down despite my request that they check with the in-port Navy hospital ship for information about choppers in our area. Finally, I received the order, "Do not fire!" What a relief!

One mission was a real disappointment. I intercepted two Tupolev Tu-2 aircraft headed east toward Inchon. I was cleared to fire, but I could not because a wire had been left unconnected after my new automatic direction finder gear had been installed. I drove the Tu-2s off by flying ahead of them and then turning in with my landing light on. One dove down to the right and the other pulled hard left and almost straight up.

About one week later, on July 16, 1953, I was launched to take over an intercept for my wingman, Lieutenant Ralph "Hoppy" Hopson, when his aircraft radar suddenly went out just as he was closing on a bogey. As I arrived in the area, I checked in with the joint operations center and was vectored against a fast-moving target. After several minutes of full-power chase, I finally acquired the target on my radar. Then I got a visual on him and made a positive identification; the flame pattern of his engine exhausts was that of an La-11. I reported "Tallyho!" on an enemy target and was immediately cleared to fire.

Our frequency was being monitored, for as soon as I was cleared to fire, the La-11 began evasive turns and reversals. However, I had closed to firing range and was able to stay right with him as he led me over Kaesong, where a battery of large antiaircraft guns fired continuously just behind us. As we cleared the AAA fire, the La-11 suddenly rolled level, and I was able to fire a long burst from my four cannon directly into him. He exploded like a bomb. I saw one wing flying just above me. Blinded once again, I was able to flick on my autopilot, and my bird, *Annie-Mo*—named for my wife—straightened up to level flight like the champion she was. I could have kissed her!

I was soon presented with the Navy Cross by the Fifth Air Force commanding general in Korea. I was the only Navy ace, the only night-fighter ace, and the only propeller fighter ace of the Korean War. However, my top award was my swift return to my family's arms.

After the Korean War, Guy Bordelon remained in the Navy and undertook a wide variety of flying and shore-based assignments in the United States and overseas—a typical naval career of the day. Among other notable assignments, he was involved in recovering Apollo astronauts. When he retired from the Navy in 1969, Commander Guy Bordelon had amassed more than 15,000 flight hours over his twenty-seven-year career.

PART V

At War Over Vietnam

THE HANOI POL STRIKE*

Major JIM KASLER, USAF
354th Tactical Fighter Squadron, 355th Tactical Fighter Group
Hanoi, North Vietnam—June 29, 1966

James Helms Kasler was born in South Bend, Indiana, on May 26, 1926, and raised in Indianapolis. After graduating from high school in 1944, Kasler enlisted in the Army Air Forces and served as a B-29 gunner in combat over Japan near the end of the war. He left the service in May 1946 and attended Butler University for three years before entering the Air Force's pilot training program in January 1950. Second Lieutenant Kasler earned his commission and pinned on his silver wings at Williams Air Force Base, Arizona, in March 1951, and following gunnery training in F-84s ended up in Korea in November 1951.

During his combat tour in Korea, in the course of flying one hundred combat missions with the 4th Fighter Wing's 335th Fighter Squadron, 1st Lieutenant Jim Kasler downed six MiG-15 fighter-interceptors

---

* This story is a slightly edited version of an article appearing in the October 1994, issue of the *Air University Review*. It is used here with the author's permission.

between April 1 and May 25, 1952. He remained in the service after the Korean War, served in a rotation of staff and flying assignments, and completed his bachelor's degree in 1963. In February 1966, Major Jim Kasler was assigned to the 355th Tactical Fighter Wing's 354th Tactical Fighter Squadron, then based at Takhli Royal Thai Air Base.

Until mid-1966, the U.S. Air Force's aerial bombardment of North Vietnam was restricted to targets of comparatively little importance. These restrictions were a direct result of the notion expressed by Secretary of Defense Robert McNamara, when he declared that "the targets that are influencing the operations in the South, I submit, are not the power, the oil, the harbor, or the dams. The targets are the roads and the war material being moved over the roads." There were also no-strike areas surrounding Hanoi and Haiphong, which made a virtual sanctuary of these areas. The North Vietnamese were well aware of this sanctuary and took the utmost advantage of it, especially when positioning strategic war materials.

As it became increasingly obvious that the destruction of targets such as vehicles, roads, small bridges, and river traffic was hardly affecting the Communists' ability to carry the war to the South, in June 1966 Washington decided not only to increase the tempo of air strikes against the North but also to include targets of greater strategic significance. The first of these targets was the great petroleum, oil, and lubricant (POL) facility located just outside Hanoi. The following account is my recollection of the day I led Thailand-based aircraft of the 355th Tactical Fighter Wing on one of the most spectacular and successful missions of the air war. At the time, I was operations officer of the 354th Tactical Fighter Squadron.

On the afternoon of June 28, I had just returned from a mission and, after my intelligence debriefing, stopped in at the wing command post. The deputy for operations motioned me into his office and told me that my squadron had drawn the lead for the strike against the Hanoi POL storage complex. He also informed me that the wing commander, Colonel William Holt, would lead the mission and that Colonel Holt had asked that I finalize the navigation and attack plan and prepare the combat mission folders for the strike. On June 21, when we had first been informed of the upcoming strike, we had been directed to identify to Wing Operations those pilots who were to participate. They were to be selected according to their skill and experience. It was one of the most difficult decisions I ever had to make, because there was no pilot in the squadron whom I considered to be unqualified, and I knew how disappointing it would be for those not selected. Two of my most experienced flight commanders, Captain Lewis Shattuck and Captain Norman Wells, assisted me in planning the mission.

Air-to-ground combat is the most exacting type of flying in the Air Force and certainly the most dangerous, as the combat casualty records of World War II, Korea, and Vietnam bear out. Moreover, low-level navigation at speeds in excess of 500 knots requires the utmost skill since a one- or two-degree heading error can throw a plane miles wide of the route in a just few minutes. In addition, timing is essential because each element of the attack must mesh exactly or the mission's effectiveness will suffer. I feel that there are three elements necessary to increase the air-to-ground combat pilots' chances of survival: planning, execution of the mission, and luck. Of course, experience and skill in the planning and execution phases decrease one's dependence on luck.

We spent six hours planning, checking, and double-checking every facet of the mission. This was our first detailed study of the defenses in the Hanoi area, and we found little in the aerial photographs to give us comfort. The enemy's air defenses, formidable from the start, were becoming more formidable each day. By every estimate, Hanoi had the greatest concentration of antiaircraft weapons ever known in the history of aerial warfare. In Vietnam itself, there were from 7,000 to 10,000 rapid-firing antiaircraft weapons of 37mm or larger caliber. In addition, the Russians had provided the Vietnamese with a sophisticated radar and communication network for detecting attacks and coordinatimg their surface-to-air missiles (SAMs) and MiG fighters.

Surprise was pretty well ruled out as a possibility in our attack plans. For one thing, Navy attack fighters were to strike the Haiphong POL complex fifteen minutes before our time over target (TOT). For another, the defenses would certainly be alerted in the Hanoi area because our twenty-four aircraft would be preceded in the attack by eight aircraft from the 388th Tactical Fighter Wing.

To an outsider, the intelligence planning room would resemble a madhouse located in a paper factory. Once the mission leader has laid out the route and attack plan, every pilot must prepare his own charts. The charts are cut, glued, and then folded in accordion fashion. Routes are drawn down the center of the page and ticked off in time and distance. Each turn requires another chart, because the route line must remain centered for ease of navigation.

By midnight, we were satisfied with our work and headed for our quarters. Usually, the briefing for the first mission of the day was scheduled between 0100 and 0900 hours, but this one was special. Except for a few selected strikes, involving only a few aircraft, the Hanoi raid was the only one scheduled for our wing on the 29th. Our briefing time was scheduled for 0830, with time over the target at 1210.

On the morning of the strike, I walked into the wing intelligence building at about 0810. Major General George Simler, the deputy for operations of the Seventh Air Force, was standing by the door with Colonel Holt. General Simler looked at me and said, "Major Kasler, how would you like to lead this mission?" I said, "Yes, Sir, I certainly would!" General Simler handed me the combat mission folder that I had prepared for Colonel Holt the preceding day. I looked at Colonel Holt, who did not appear too happy, and said, "I'm sorry about that, Colonel." Holt muttered something and stalked into the briefing room. I had not meant for it to come out the way it sounded, because I knew how anxious he was to lead the mission, and I was sincerely sorry. Every fighter pilot dreams of leading a mission of this importance, but few ever have the opportunity.

As it turned out, all the wing commanders whose units were participating in the Hanoi raid, whether as the strike force, top cover, or support role, had scheduled themselves to lead their wings. But they were all removed from the mission by order of General Joseph Moore, commander of the Seventh Air Force.

When we entered the briefing room, I took the mission commander's seat. The briefing officer almost had a heart attack, and he kept motioning that I was in the wrong chair until Colonel Holt finally gave him the word.

The general briefing preceding a mission is little more than a refresher of those items that the pilots have already learned and memorized about the route, tactics, and target defenses. The things the pilots are most interested in are the weather and bombing winds in the target area. The weather for the Hanoi area that day was perfect for fighter-bomber operations. It was forecast as clear with light and variable winds to 10,000 feet.

General Simler concluded the briefing with a short talk, in which he emphasized the importance of the Hanoi POL complex to the Vietnamese supply lines. He pointed out that the Hanoi facility contained twenty percent of all North Vietnam's petroleum supplies. He also made it clear that under no circumstances, even if hit, was any pilot to jettison his bombs into the city of Hanoi.

The role of our sister wing, the 388th, which was based at Korat, Thailand, was to initiate the attack on the POL complex with eight aircraft. Their plan was to approach the Communist capital from the south, low behind the screen of high mountains southwest of the city. At the mountains, they would pop up and then dive in low over Hanoi and strike the target.

The 355th was to strike from the north. The plan was to cross the Red River 100 miles northwest of Hanoi, turn east, and descend to low altitude to avoid SAM missiles. Our route took us parallel to and north of Thud Ridge, the 5,000-foot-high razorback mountain running west to east through the heart of North Vietnam. The eastern tip of the mountain ends about twenty-five miles due north of Hanoi. We would screen ourselves behind the mountain until we reached the eastern tip, then make a 90-degree turn south toward Hanoi. The operations order had also directed that all attacks would be executed on a south-to-north heading, to preclude tossing a hung bomb into the city of Hanoi. Approaching from the north, we would have to make a 180-degree pop-up maneuver to strike the target as ordered.

What the attack order meant was that every aircraft would be rolling into the bomb run at approximately the same spot, heading in the same direction. Not too smart from the pilot's viewpoint, but in the interest of protecting civilian populations, such orders were commonplace in Vietnam. Ideally, attacks should be on divergent headings to confuse the gunners and thus prevent them from zeroing in on one spot.

General Simler's remarks were followed by a short briefing with the other three flight commanders. Each aircraft was carrying eight 750-pound bombs armed with a split-second delayed fuse. When I gave my briefing, I directed that the fusing of the two bombs carried on the outboard wing stations be changed to an instantaneous setting, to ensure that there would be some flying shrapnel among the fuel storage tanks in the event of a near miss. A final briefing was held in the squadron before the pilots headed for their aircraft.

The crew chief greeted me as I stepped from my pickup. He walked around the aircraft with me as I made the pre-flight inspection. I told him that if I gave him the abort signal after I had started the engine he was to get the ladder back up immediately because I was heading for the ground spare. He said, "Major Kasler, my assistant and I have spent the last nine hours checking every system on this airplane, and you aren't going to abort." He was right! I have never found more dedicated or experienced airmen than those who worked on our aircraft in the Vietnam War. In the ninety-one missions I flew there, I never had a single abort or armament malfunction—a fantastic achievement.

We started engines and taxied to the marshalling area at the end of the runway, where the maintenance crews made a final inspection of the aircraft. We then lined up on the runway and were cleared for takeoff. Our takeoff weight was around 51,000 pounds, the maximum gross weight for the Republic Aviation F-105 Thunderchief. In the hot Thailand summer, this meant a long ground roll and a lift-off speed of 235 knots.

I breathed a sigh of relief when my gear was in the well, not because I was concerned about the takeoff, but because 95 percent of our aborts occurred on the ground. I was airborne with a perfectly functioning aircraft, leading the biggest mission of the Vietnam war to date.

As the rest of the flight slid into position, I completed a slow turn back to the north and contacted our radar site. They gave me a bearing to our tankers, 250 nautical miles to the north.

Approaching the tankers, I could see a row of ominous thunderstorms stretched across the horizon to the north. It was obvious that the tankers were not going to be able to maintain their briefed refueling route. Fighters can refuel and even effect join-ups in thin cirrus clouds, but the turbulence and lack of visibility associated with heavy cumulus clouds create an impossible situation.

We began taking on fuel, but the tankers were unable to maintain their track because of the thunderstorms. Ten minutes before our drop-off time, the tanker lead advised that he had to turn back because he was unable to circumnavigate the storms ahead. We had all refueled, but we were not able to recycle through again to top off as planned.

I rejoined my flight in close formation, flicked on my radar, and picked my way between the thunderstorm cells. We were sixty miles southeast of our desired point of departure when we left the tankers. It was imperative that our timing be exact, so I had selected a prominent river junction in Laos as my starting checkpoint. As luck would have it, we broke out in a small hole directly over the point of departure. I was three minutes ahead of schedule, so I made a 360-degree turn to use up time and set course to the north.

We immediately re-entered the clouds, and when we next broke out after twenty minutes, we were directly over the Red River northwest of Yen Bai. My Doppler was functioning perfectly, and we were directly on course and time. I turned right and began a descent through several layers of clouds. Vietnam north of Thud Ridge was covered with ground fog. I continued the descent to 300 feet, which was just above the fog bank. At higher altitudes, SAM missiles had a nasty way of popping up through clouds at an unsuspecting pilot, but 300 feet was a fairly safe altitude to prevent this from happening.

We were skimming along the base of Thud Ridge, which towered above us to the right. As we approached its eastern tip, our external fuel tanks showed empty, and I ordered them dropped. I could hear Lieutenant Colonel James Hopkins, leader of the 388th, departing the Hanoi target area, and I asked him what the weather was. He said, "It's clear in the target area, but there are MiGs airborne."

Looking far to the east, I could see smoke rising from the POL tanks at Haiphong, which the Navy fighters had already struck. When we passed our Initial Point at the end of Thud Ridge, I called the flight to push it up and started a turn south toward Hanoi. As we turned, the fog bank faded away beneath us and we broke into the clear. At that same instant, flak began bursting around us. I glanced to the right, toward Phuc Yen Airfield, and could see the flak guns blinking at us. Despite the fact that we were only 300 feet above the ground, the Vietnamese had leveled their heavy 85mm and 100mm guns and were firing almost horizontally at us.

I called the flight to start jinking, a series of irregular evasive maneuvers designed to confuse ground gunners.

We were running parallel to the northeast railroad that leads into the city of Hanoi. This was North Vietnam's most important supply link with the People's Republic of China, and it was protected by flak guns of every caliber and description. Ahead, I could see two gray smoke columns rising, one on each side of the Hanoi POL field just struck by the 388th. The sky was dotted with hundreds of white, gray, and black puffs—the remaining traces of shells that had been fired at the departing Korat aircraft. Thus we had a good idea of what was awaiting us over the target.

We approached slightly left of target. I called for afterburner and began my pull-up. I climbed through 8,000 feet and began a slow turn to the right until I reached my roll-in point at about 11,000 feet. I cut my afterburner, dropped dive brakes, and rolled into the bomb run. As I was turning in, I could see three ten-gun 85mm batteries on Gia Lam Airfield frantically firing. Ignoring these as best I could, I began my bomb run. I saw that one large tank on the extreme left side of the complex and one on the right side were smoking. As I rolled in, I could hardly believe my eyes—my entire view was filled with big, fat fuel tanks! I pushed my pickle button and made a rolling pullout to the right. When I cleared the smoke, I made a gentle left turn around the target complex. The huge fuel tanks were erupting, one after another, sending up immense billowing fireballs.

By the time I had circled to the southwest corner of the target, each of my flight members had also made his bomb run and had rejoined me. The smoke now merged into one huge boiling red-and-black pillar, an unbelievable sight. As I climbed back to about 5,000 feet, I could see flames leaping out of the smoke thousands of feet above me.

After my number-four man had rejoined the formation, I swung around to the north toward Phuc Yen Airfield. I had seen a MiG on the end of the runway when we began our dash toward Hanoi and thought we might get a shot at it if it got airborne. I changed my mind when I saw the fantastic intensity of the flak bursting around us. I then banked my Thunderchief to the south, and as I did so, I looked at the ground; there were so many guns firing that the valley reminded me of a desert city viewed from the air at night.

After we crossed south of the Red River, the flak diminished as the gunners apparently switched their attention to the fighter-bombers behind my flight. We headed west, searching the roads for targets of opportunity. As we approached Hoa Binh on the Black River, I noticed that a new road had been cut up the side of a high plateau that extended east back toward Hanoi. I popped over the rim of the plateau and dropped my nose to investigate. There, directly under my gunsight pipper, was a truck. I squeezed the trigger, and the 20mm cannon shells tore into the truck, setting it on fire. All told, we found twenty-five trucks on the plateau. We set twelve afire and damaged at least six others. It appeared that the Vietnamese were floating supplies from China down the Black River on rafts to Hoa Binh, transferring them to trucks, and moving them across the plateau to Hanoi.

As I pulled out of one of my strafing passes, I looked back at Hanoi, thirty-five miles to the east. It was a windless day, and the black smoke formed a perfect pillar reaching above 35,000 feet.

By now our fuel was running low; we were forced to head for home. We did not have enough fuel to reach Takhli, so I planned a recovery at Ubon if we could not get fuel from the airborne tankers. Looking back toward Hanoi, I could still see the smoke column more than 150 miles away. The GCI controller found us a KC-135 tanker, so we refueled over the Mekong, and headed for home.

The Hanoi POL strike was one of the most successful missions of the Vietnam War. The complex was over 90-percent destroyed and was one of the few targets in North Vietnam that never required a restrike, as the Vietnamese abandoned the facility altogether.

Amazingly, only one of the strike aircraft was lost to flak in the raid. The pilot, Captain Neil Jones, was interned in North Vietnam until February 1973. Three aircraft suffered battle damage, with one pilot receiving minor wounds.

On the other hand, the MiGs were conspicuously absent; they engaged only one flight of SAM-suppression aircraft. They inflicted minor damage on one F-105, but the pilot was credited with a probable MiG kill in the brief aerial battle. By comparison with the first World War II Ploesti oil raid, when German Bf-109 pilots flew through their own flak to get at the B-24s, the North Vietnamese MiG pilots' efforts were far less courageous.

One of the puzzles of the raid was why the Vietnamese had not fired any of the dozens of SAM missiles that rimmed Hanoi. On the day following the raid, they began firing SAMs in volleys at our aircraft, which was a complete change in the tactics they had used previously. The answer to this question was learned two months later, when I was shot down and captured by the North Vietnamese.

Shortly after my capture on August 8, 1966, I was questioned by a Vietnamese interrogator while lying in a hospital room in Hanoi. The interrogator tried to get information from me concerning the Hanoi POL strike. He asked: "What did you think about our defenses during the Hanoi raid?" I said, "I figure you got a new air defense boss." Just a guess on my part, but apparently a correct one, as he became quite agitated and left. A short time later, my room was invaded by four very stern-looking Vietnamese, who spent the next two days trying to figure out how I knew they had had a shake-up in their air defense command.

The Hanoi POL strike was a supreme feat of courage, fortitude, and airmanship. The pilots who participated in the raid felt at the time that it was a major step toward shortening the war. Ironically, despite an almost perfectly conceived and executed mission, there was no perceptible slow-down in the North Vietnamese POL supply system, as Soviet tankers continued to discharge fuel supplies at Haiphong harbor until 1972. Had the port been closed and the fighter-bombers and B-52s used in conjunction with the strategic targets struck in 1966, as they later were, America might very well have avoided the agonizing years of war that followed.

Following his repatriation in 1973, at the conclusion of the Vietnam armistice negotiations, Lieutenant Colonel Jim Kasler attended the Air University and served as a deputy fighter wing commander until he retired from the Air Force with the rank of colonel in May 1975.

Bibliography

Belote, James H., and William M. Belote. *Titans of the Seas: The Development and Operations of Japanese and American Carrier Task Forces During World War II.* New York: Harper & Row, 1975.

Blackburn, Tom, with Eric Hammel. *The Jolly Rogers: The Story of Tom Blackburn and Navy Fighting Squadron VF-17.* Pacifica, California: Pacifica Press: 1997.

Bond, Charles R., Jr. and Terry H. Anderson. *A Flying Tiger's Diary.* College Station, Texas: Texas A&M University Press, 1984.

Carter, Kit C., and Robert Mueller. *The Army Air Forces in World War II: Combat Chronology, 1941-1945.* Washington, D.C.: Office of Air Force History, 1973.

Copp, DeWitt S. *A Few Great Captains: The Men and Events that Shaped the Development of U.S. Air Power.* Garden City, NY: Doubleday, 1980.

_____. *Forged in Fire: Strategy and Decisions in the Airwar Over Europe, 1940-1945.* Garden City, NY: Doubleday, 1982.

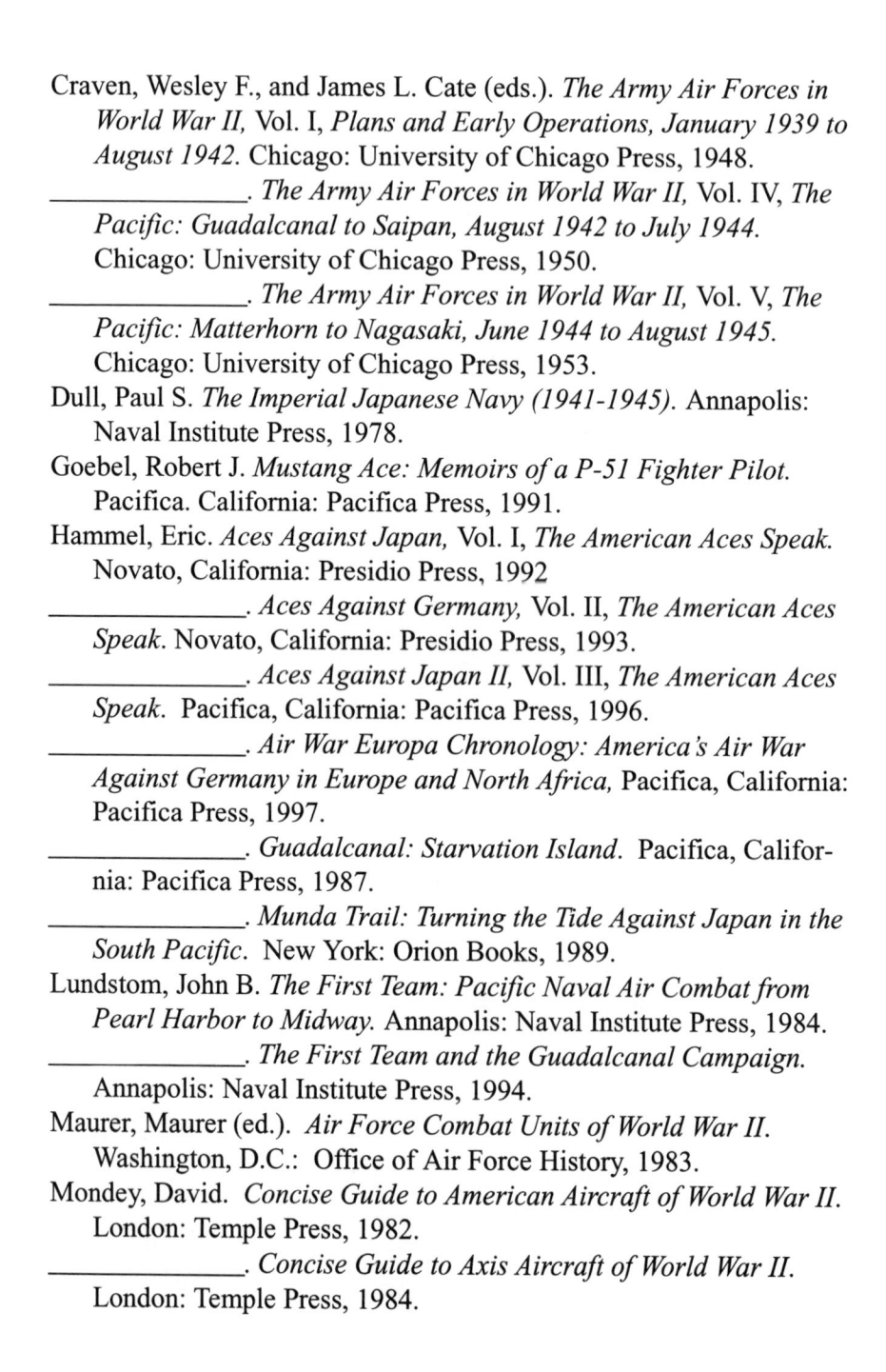

Craven, Wesley F., and James L. Cate (eds.). *The Army Air Forces in World War II,* Vol. I, *Plans and Early Operations, January 1939 to August 1942.* Chicago: University of Chicago Press, 1948.

_____. *The Army Air Forces in World War II,* Vol. IV, *The Pacific: Guadalcanal to Saipan, August 1942 to July 1944.* Chicago: University of Chicago Press, 1950.

_____. *The Army Air Forces in World War II,* Vol. V, *The Pacific: Matterhorn to Nagasaki, June 1944 to August 1945.* Chicago: University of Chicago Press, 1953.

Dull, Paul S. *The Imperial Japanese Navy (1941-1945).* Annapolis: Naval Institute Press, 1978.

Goebel, Robert J. *Mustang Ace: Memoirs of a P-51 Fighter Pilot.* Pacifica. California: Pacifica Press, 1991.

Hammel, Eric. *Aces Against Japan,* Vol. I, *The American Aces Speak.* Novato, California: Presidio Press, 1992

_____. *Aces Against Germany,* Vol. II, *The American Aces Speak.* Novato, California: Presidio Press, 1993.

_____. *Aces Against Japan II,* Vol. III, *The American Aces Speak.* Pacifica, California: Pacifica Press, 1996.

_____. *Air War Europa Chronology: America's Air War Against Germany in Europe and North Africa,* Pacifica, California: Pacifica Press, 1997.

_____. *Guadalcanal: Starvation Island.* Pacifica, California: Pacifica Press, 1987.

_____. *Munda Trail: Turning the Tide Against Japan in the South Pacific.* New York: Orion Books, 1989.

Lundstom, John B. *The First Team: Pacific Naval Air Combat from Pearl Harbor to Midway.* Annapolis: Naval Institute Press, 1984.

_____. *The First Team and the Guadalcanal Campaign.* Annapolis: Naval Institute Press, 1994.

Maurer, Maurer (ed.). *Air Force Combat Units of World War II.* Washington, D.C.: Office of Air Force History, 1983.

Mondey, David. *Concise Guide to American Aircraft of World War II.* London: Temple Press, 1982.

_____. *Concise Guide to Axis Aircraft of World War II.* London: Temple Press, 1984.

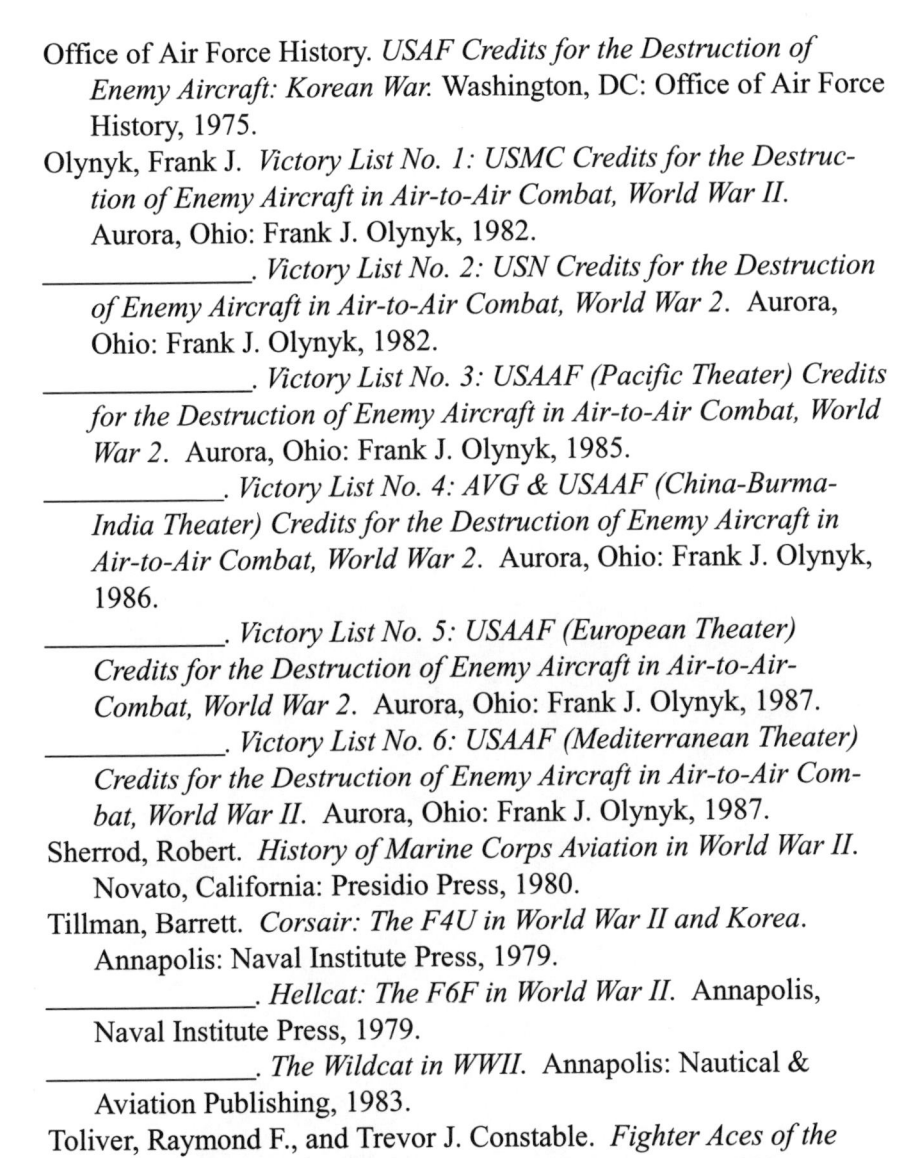

Office of Air Force History. *USAF Credits for the Destruction of Enemy Aircraft: Korean War.* Washington, DC: Office of Air Force History, 1975.

Olynyk, Frank J. *Victory List No. 1: USMC Credits for the Destruction of Enemy Aircraft in Air-to-Air Combat, World War II.* Aurora, Ohio: Frank J. Olynyk, 1982.

——————. *Victory List No. 2: USN Credits for the Destruction of Enemy Aircraft in Air-to-Air Combat, World War 2.* Aurora, Ohio: Frank J. Olynyk, 1982.

——————. *Victory List No. 3: USAAF (Pacific Theater) Credits for the Destruction of Enemy Aircraft in Air-to-Air Combat, World War 2.* Aurora, Ohio: Frank J. Olynyk, 1985.

——————. *Victory List No. 4: AVG & USAAF (China-Burma-India Theater) Credits for the Destruction of Enemy Aircraft in Air-to-Air Combat, World War 2.* Aurora, Ohio: Frank J. Olynyk, 1986.

——————. *Victory List No. 5: USAAF (European Theater) Credits for the Destruction of Enemy Aircraft in Air-to-Air-Combat, World War 2.* Aurora, Ohio: Frank J. Olynyk, 1987.

——————. *Victory List No. 6: USAAF (Mediterranean Theater) Credits for the Destruction of Enemy Aircraft in Air-to-Air Combat, World War II.* Aurora, Ohio: Frank J. Olynyk, 1987.

Sherrod, Robert. *History of Marine Corps Aviation in World War II.* Novato, California: Presidio Press, 1980.

Tillman, Barrett. *Corsair: The F4U in World War II and Korea.* Annapolis: Naval Institute Press, 1979.

——————. *Hellcat: The F6F in World War II.* Annapolis, Naval Institute Press, 1979.

——————. *The Wildcat in WWII.* Annapolis: Nautical & Aviation Publishing, 1983.

Toliver, Raymond F., and Trevor J. Constable. *Fighter Aces of the U.S.A.* Fallbrook, California: Aero Publishers, Inc., 1979.

Williams, Mary H. *U.S. Army in World War II: Special Studies, Chronology: 1941-1945.* Washington, D.C.: Center of Military History, 1984.

Index

Abbeville, France, 90
Advance Air Base K-2 (Taegu), South Korea, 202
Advance Air Base K-3 (Pohang), South Korea, 202, 203
Advance Air Base K-13 (Suwon), South Korea, 209–210, 212, 222, 228
Advance Air Base K-14 (Kimpo), South Korea, 206–208
Advance Air Base K-27 (Yonpo), North Korea, 203
Advance Landing Ground 78, Belgium, 184
Aitken, Maj John, Jr., USAAF, 159–162
Akia Airdrome, Israel, 195
Alameda Naval Air Station, California, 65
Amberley Field, Australia, 70
American Volunteer Group (AVG, Flying Tigers), 7

1st AVG Fighter Squadron, 7
Amoy, China, 50, 52
Andress, 1stLt Crystal, USAAF, 54–56
Apollo space-flight program, 86
Arab-Israeli War of 1967, 198
Armistead, Maj Kirk, USMC, 16
Arnold, Cdr Jackson D., USN, 40
Ashiya Air Force Base, Japan, 202
Atkinson, Col Gwen G., USAAF, 54–56
Atlantic City Naval Air Station, New Jersey, 34
Augarten, Rudolph, Israeli Air Force, 2dLt USAAF, 193–194, Personal narrative, 194–198
Ayres, Capt Frank L., USAAF, 85

Banks, Capt William M., 28
Bannock, Squadron Leader Russell, RCAF, 127
Barber's Point (Oahu) Naval Air Station, Hawaii, 34, 58–59

Barksdale Field, Louisiana, 97–98
Bauer, LtCol Harold W. (Joe), USMC, 17, 22
Berlin Airlift, 125, 142
Berlin Crisis of 1962, 162
Beyl, 2dLt Herman, USAAF, 78
Biskra Airdrome, Algeria, 100–101
Blackburn, LCdr John Thomas (Tom), USN, 29, 33, Personal narrative, 30–33
Bluie West-1 Field, Greenland, 98
Bocca di Falco Airdrome, Sicily, 112
Bolt, Maj John F., USMC, 221–222, 229, Personal narrative, 222–229
Bolyard, 1stLt John W., USAAF, 49, 52, Personal narrative, 50–52
Bond, Vice Squadron Commander Charles R., Jr., AVG, 7–8, 14, Maj USAAF, 14, Personal narrative, 8–14
Bordelon, Lt Guy P., USN, 229, 235, Personal narrative, 229–235
Borgo Airdrome, Corsica, 112
Bourke-White, Margaret, 100
Bowman, Capt R. L., USN, 60
Boxted Airdrome, England, 166
Brisbane, Australia, 24, 25
Brischetto, Col Roy, USAAF, 54
Brown, LtCol Gerald, USAF, 201–202, 205, Personal narrative, 202–205
Brown, 2dLt Harley L., USAAF, 155–156, 157, Personal narrative, 156–157
Budapest, Hungary, 129, 130
Burma Road, 9–10

Cactus Air Force, 17, 18
Cal-Aero flying academy, 96
Cap Bon, Tunisia, 103
Cape Nojima, Honshu, 84
Carlile, 1stLt Jerry, USAF, 228
Carr, 1stLt Bruce W., USAAF, 187–189
Carr, 1stLt Robert, USAAF, 78, 82
Carter, Capt James R., USAAF, 163, 166, Personal narrative, 164–166
Chambers, 1stLt John, USAAF, 78
Chanute Field, Illinois, 23
Chateaudun-du-Rumel Airdrome, Algeria, 101, 105
Chichi Jima, Bonin Islands, 35, 78
Chinese People's Liberation Army, 203, 204
Chodo Island, North Korea, 210, 216
Civil Aeronautics Administration, 23, 74
Civilian Pilot Training (CPT) Program, 1–3, 33, 74, 133
Clark Field, Luzon, 54–56, 70
Clark, RAdm Joseph J. (Jocko), USN, 35, 40–41, Adm., 233
Clarke, Flight Lieutenant "Freddie," RCAF, 90–92
Cole, Capt Charles H., Jr. (Tink), USAAF, 171, 182, Personal narrative, 172–182
Colerne Airdrome, England, 99
Collins, Capt Harold D., USAAF, 78
Coltishall Airdrome, England, 127
Comstock, Maj Harold E., USAAF, 164
Cordray, Lt(jg) Paul, USN, 31–32
Corpus Christi Naval Air Station, Texas, 15, 34, 42, 57, 65, 229
Craig Field, Alabama, 111, 158
Cranfill, Maj Niven K., USAAF, 166, 171, Personal narrative, 167–171
Crawford, Lt(jg) Jack H., USN, 68
Cristadoro, Maj Maurice A., Jr., USAAF, 174–175
Croydon Airdrome, England, 90
Cuban Missile Crises of 1962, 111, 221

Aces At War

Curtis, 1stLt Robert C., 111, 117, Personal narrative, 111–117
Czech Air Force, 195, 196

Dale Mabry Field (Tallahassee), Florida, 75
Daniels, 2dLt Richard H., USAAF, 168–169
Daytona Beach Naval Air Station, Florida, 57
Dean, Cdr William A., Jr., USN, 34, 37, 41
Dieppe raid, 90–91
Dieppe, France, 90–93
Divenny, Ens Percy E., USN, 30–31, 32
Dobbin, Maj John F., USMC, 16, 19–22
Dougherty, 2dLt Wayne W., USAAF, 110
Doyle, Jack, Israeli Air Force, 197
Duffy, Capt James E., Jr., USAAF, 134
Dulag Luft (Frankfurt, Germany), 179, 181
Duxford Airdrome, England, 107

Eagle Farms Airdrome, Australia, 25
East Wretham Airdrome, England, 167
Egyptian Air Force, 198
Ehmen Airdrome, Germany, 168
El Arish Airdrome, Egypt, 197
Eniwetok Atoll, Marshall Islands, 35
Erickson, 1stLt "Les," USAF, 209–212
Ernst, 1stLt Herman E., USAAF, 182, 186, Personal narrative, 182–186
Evans, 1stLt Leo, USAAF, 78
Ewa (Oahu) Marine Corps Air Station, Hawaii, 15–16

Fairfax Airport (Kansas City) Kansas, 15

Fast Carrier Task Force, *see* USN, Task Force 58
Fighter-1 Airstrip, Guadalcanal, 18, 21
Ford Island (Oahu) Naval Air Station, Hawaii, 16
Ford, 1stLt Joseph S. USAAF, 156
Fortier, Capt Norman J. (Bud), USAAF, 133, 142, Personal narrative, 1–4, 133–142
Foshee, Ben D., AVG, 13, 14
Foster Field, Texas, 155
Foster, 1stLt Cecil G., USAF, 208, 212, Personal narrative, 208–212
Fowler, Cdr William, USN, 45–46
Fowlmere Airdrome, England, 159, 161
Franklin, 2dLt Dwaine R., USAAF, 122, 125, Personal narrative, 122–125
French Indochina, 70
French Resistance, 202
Fruechtenicht, Capt Richard W., USAAF, 172

Gabreski, Maj Francis S., USAAF, 163
Galer, Maj Robert E., USMC, 15, 16, 17, 19, 20, 22
Gardner Field, California, 182
Gatwick Airdrome, England, 90, 91
Gautsche, 2dLt "Don," USAAF, 78, 85
Gerard, 1stLt Francis R. (Frank), USAAF, 158, 162, Personal narrative, 159–162
German Air Force *(Luftwaffe)* 53d Fighter Wing, 117
GI Bill, 194
Gia Lam Airfield, North Vietnam, 246
Gilbert Islands invasion, 34
Gilbert, Henry, AVG, 11
Gizo Island, Solomon Islands, 22
Glenview Naval Air Station, Illinois, 34, 57

Goebel, 1stLt Robert J., USAAF, 128, 133, Personal narrative, 129–133
Goldsmith, Pete, 3–4
Gosselin, "Goose", 2
Goxhill Airdrome, England, 106
Gross Ostheim Airdrome, Germany, 164
Guadalcanal Island, Solomon Islands, 17
Guam Island, Mariana Islands, 35, 36

Haha Jima, Bonin Islands, 35, 78
Haiphong, North Vietnam, 240, 245
Hamilton Field, California, 106, 167
Hanoi, North Vietnam, 240–242, 245–246, 248
Hargreaves, Lt(jg) Everett C. (Connie), USN, 33, 42, Personal narrative, 34–42
Harmon, George, 2
Hart, LtCol John N., USMC, 17
Hasek, 1stLt Ivan, USAAF, 187, 189, Personal narrative, 187–189
Hayden, 2dLt, USAAF, 120–121
Heller, LtCol Edwin L., USAF, 213, 221, Personal narrative, 213–221
Henderson Field, Guadalcanal, 17, 18
Herbst, Maj John C. (Pappy), USAAF, 50, 52
High Ercall Airdrome, England, 99
"High Flight" (poem), 1
Hills, Flying Officer Hollis H. (Holly), RCAF, 89–90, Lt (USN), 94, Personal narrative 90–94,
al-Hinnaway, Lt Shalabi, Egyptian Air Force, 198
Hirsch, Al, 3
Hoa Binh, North Vietnam, 247
Hod, Mordechai, Israeli Air Force, 198
Hollandia, New Guinea, 35
Holloman, 2dLt Joseph W. (Peewee), USAAF, 123–125
Hollowell, 2dLt George L., USMC, 14–15, 22, Personal narrative, 15–22
Holmsley South Airdrome, England, 128
Holt, Col William, USAF, 240, 242
Hopi, New Guinea, 26
Hopkins, Harry, 99
Hopkins, LtCol James, USAF, 245
Hopson, Lt Ralph (Hoppy), USN, 235
Hostetler, Capt "Ernie," USAAF, 78
Hovde, Capt William J., USAAF, 136
Howard, Capt Ronald M., USAAF, 172
Howes, 1stLt Bernard, USAAF, 206
Hulett, 2dLt Wesley J., USAAF, 72, 73
Hutchinson Naval Air Station, Kansas, 42
Huxtable, LCdr Edward, USN, 44

Israel Defense Force, 198
Israel War of Independence, 194
Israeli Air Force, 198
  101st Squadron, 196
Iwo Jima, Volcano Islands, 35, 41, 76, 77, 85

Jackson, Capt Michael J., USAAF, 164
Jackson, Lt(jg) Robert H. (Hal), USN, 31
Jacksonville Naval Air Station, Florida, 15, 221
Jasper, Flight Lieutenant Clarence M., RCAF, 126, 128, Personal narrative, 126–128
Johnson, Lt(jg) George C., Jr., USN, 66, 68
Johnson, 2dLt Willie K., USAAF, 188–189
Joint Operations Center, Korea, 233
Jones, Capt Neil, USAF, 247

Kanchow, China, 49
Karachi, India, 49
Kasler, Maj James H., USAF, 239, 248, Personal narrative, 240–248
Kasserine Pass, Tunisia, 100
Kastina Airdrome, Israel, 196, 198
Kearby, Col Neel E., 24, 25, 26
Kelly Field, Texas, 23, 74, 97, 118, 163
Kelly, 2dLt George W., USAAF, 120–121
Kennedy, 2dLt Mathew H., USMC, 16
Kenney, MajGen George C., USAAF, 25
Kindred, 2dLt Ray, USAAF, 54–56
Kingsville Naval Air Station, Texas, 34, 229
Kita Iwo Jima, Volcano Islands, 79
Klippgen, Oberleutnant Rolf, 117
Kopsel, 1stLt Edward H., USAAF, 183, 184–186
Korat Royal Thai Air Base, 243
Korean War, 22, 49, 73, 162, 171, 202, 222, 229, 239
Kozu Island, Japan, 78
Kuhlman, 1stLt "Fritz," USAF, 228
Kunming, China, 8
Kwajalein Atoll, Marshall Islands, 34–35
Kweilin, China, 49

La Sebala Airdrome, Tunisia, 112
La Senia Airdrome, Algeria, 100
Langensbold, Germany, 164
Langley Field, Virginia, 7
Lechfeld Airdrome, Germany, 136, 140–141
Leyte Island, Philippine Islands, 42, 53
Liles, Capt Brooks J., USAF, 205, 208, Personal narrative, 206–208
Lindbergh, Charles, 1, 25, 70, 71, 171
Lingayan Gulf, Luzon, 54

Little, Flight Leader Robert L., AVG, 8, 13–14
Loisel, Maj John S., USAAF, 69, 73, Personal narrative, 70–73
Londeree, 2dLt Jimmy, USAAF, 183
London, Capt Charles P., USAAF, 108
Luke Field, Arizona, 166, 172, 181, 187

MacArthur, Gen Douglas A., USA, 25, 42
MacLean, 2dLt Edward F., USAAF, 120
Madna Airdrome, Italy, 122
Magdeburg, Germany, 172
Magoffin, Col Morton D., USAAF, 118, 122, Personal narrative 118–122
Maher, 1stLt Philip J., USAAF, 78, 83–84
Majuro Atoll, Marshall Islands, 35
Malone, Lt(jg) Donald, USN, 31–33
March Field, California, 106
Marianas Turkey Shoot, *see* Philippine Sea battle
Marianna Field, Florida, 122
Marilinan, New Guinea, 26, 28
Marine Corps Air Station K-16 (Pyongtaek), South Korea, 233
Marshall Islands, 22
Marshall, Capt Bert W., Jr., USAAF, 145–147, 149–153
Marshall, Gen George C., USA, 99
Martin, Flight Lieutenant O. A., 127
Mather Air Force Base, California, 208
Mather Field, California, 69, 106, 182
Maxwell Field, Alabama, 23, 213
May, Lt(jg) Earl, USN, 30–32
Mayer, 2dLt Raymond D., USAAF, 160
McConnell, 1stLt Joseph, USAD, 222

McGraw, Ens Joseph D. (Jojo), USN, 42, 49, Personal narrative, 42–49
McNamara, Secretary of Defense Robert, 240
McPherson, Ens Donald M., USN, 57, 64, Personal narrative, 57–64
McQuoid, Flying Officer Ray, RCAF, 93
Mekong River, 247
Mickelson, Wingman Einar I. (Mickey), AVG, 8
Midway Atoll, 76
Midway battle, 75, 76
Mindoro Island, Philippine Islands, 53
Mines Field, California, 97
Minter Field, California, 172
Mitchell, Lt(jg) Henry E., Jr., (Hal), USN, 66–68
Mitscher, VAdm Marc A. (Pete), USN, 36, 39
Montgomery, Col Robert P., USAAF, 172
Moore Field, Texas, 193
Moore, 1stLt DB, USAAF, 78
Moore, BriGen Ernest (Mickey), USAAF, 86
Moore, Gen Joseph, USAF, 242
Moore, Capt Robert W. (Todd), USAAF, 78
Morrissey, Lt Jack L., USN, 46–48
Muroc Dry Lake, California, 97

Nadzab Airdrome, New Guinea, 26-28
Nagasaki, Japan, 56
Nagle, 2dLt John, USAAF, 27
Nashua (New Hampshire) Municipal Airport, 2–3
National Aeronautic and Space Administration (NASA)
  Manned Space Program, 133
Nationalist Chinese Air Force, 172

Neale, Squadron Commander Robert H., AVG, 8, 13–14
Nellis Air Force Base, Nevada, 209
New Jersey Air National Guard, 162
Nittigahara Airdrome, Japan, 62–63
Noemfoor Island, Schouten Islands, 53
North Africa campaign, 112
North Africa invasion, 29
North Island (San Diego) Naval Air Station, California, 15
Northwest Africa Air Force
  Air Support Command, 112
  Coastal Command, 112
Nouvion Airdrome, Algeria, 100

O'Hare, Cdr Edward H. (Butch), USN, 34
O'Neill, 1stLt Lawrence F., USAAF, 23, 28, Personal narrative, 23–28
Opa-Locka Naval Air Station, Florida, 29, 34, 221

Palau Islands, Caroline Islands, 35
Panama Canal Zone, 128
Panmunjon, Korea, 216
Paoshan, China, 8–9, 13
Paris, France, 108
Patterson Field, Iceland, 98
Patuxent River Naval Aviation Test Center, Maryland, 69
Pearce, Lt James L., USN, 64, 69, Personal narrative, 65–69
Pearl Harbor (Oahu), Hawaii, 16
Pearl Harbor attack, 4, 77, 166
People's Republic of China, 246
Pete Goldsmith's Flying School, 2
Philippine Sea battle, 36
Phuc Yen Airfield, North Vietnam, 245, 246
Ponape Island, Caroline Islands, 35
Popp, Ens Wilbert P. (Beads), USN, 30–31

Port Moresby, New Guinea, 25
Price, Maj Jack C., USAAF, 106, 111,
  Personal narrative, 106–111
Priest, 2dLt Royce W. (Deacon),
  USAAF, 142, 155, Personal
  narrative, 142–155
Pusan Perimeter, South Korea, 202
Pyle, Ernie, 100

Quonset Point Naval Air Station,
  Rhode Island, 34

Rabaul, New Britain Island, 19
Ramat Aviv Air Base, Israel, 198
Randolph Field, Texas, 95, 97, 193
Randolph, Col John P., USAAF, 168
Rangoon, Burma, 11
Red River, North Vietnam, 243, 247
Republic of Korea Air Force, 202, 207
Republic of Vietnam Air Force, 182
Rice Field, California, 158
Richards, Dr., AVG, 12–14
Rickenbacker, Edward, 105
Riemensnider, Capt Robert, USAAF,
  177
Roberts, LtCol Eugene P., USAAF,
  108, 109
Robinson, Capt James G., USAAF,
  160
Roddy, Maj Edward F., USAAF, 52,
  56, Personal narrative, 53–56
Roosevelt, President Franklin D., 1
Roseberry, 2dLt Bob, USAAF, 78
Ross, 1stLt George L, USAAF, 105
Rostock, Germany, 127
Royal Air Force, 90, 93
  Eagle squadrons, 107
Royal Canadian Air Force (RCAF), 90
  414 Squadron, 89–90, 94
  418 Squadron, 126-128
  Empire Training Program, 90

Ruddell, LtCol George I., USAF, 222–
  223, 225–227
Runyon, Capt Theodore H., USAAF,
  100

Saipan Island, Mariana Islands, 35
Salween River, 10
Samar Island, Phillipine Islands, 43
San Bernadino Strait, 43
San Diego Naval Air Station, Califor-
  nia, 58
San Marcos Field, Texas, 208
Sands, 1stLt Robert, USAF, 209–210
Sauer, 1stLt Robert R., USAAF, 105
Sears, 1stLt Meldrum L. (Sammy),
  USAAF, 101–103, 105
Selfridge Field, Michigan, 97
Seller, Maj Tom, USMC, 223
Shaffer, 2dLt Joseph D. R., USAAF,
  99
Shahan, 2dLt Elza E., USAAF, 99
Shattuck, Capt Lewis, USAF, 241
Sherman, RAdm Frederick C., USN,
  60
Sherren, 1stLt "Al," USAAF, 78
Simler, MajGen George, USAF, 242-
  244
Sinai Campaign of 1956, 198
Smith, Maj John L., USMC, 15, 22
Smith, Wing Commander Doug,
  RCAF, 90
Soffe, Lt Carlos R., USN, 61-63
Sorenson, Sgt Raymond, USMC, 18–
  19, 20
South China Sea, 70
South Field, Iwo Jima, 78
Southerland, Cdr James J., II (Jack),
  USN, 60
Southwest Pacific Area, 25
Spartan School of Aeronautics, 187
Spence Field, Georgia, 49, 133, 213

Steeple Morden Airdrome, England, 143, 153
Stone, Lt(jg) Carl V., USN, 68
Suiho Dam, North Korea, 218

Tacloban Airdrome, Leyte, 44–45
Tafaraoui Airdrome, Algeria, 100
Takhli Royal Thai Air Base, 240, 247
Tanimizu, WO Takeo, IJN, 52
Tapp, Maj James B., USAAF, 73, 86,
    Personal narrative 74–86
Tennessee Air National Guard, 186
Teschner, Maj Charles G., USAAF, 119
Texas National Guard, 7
Thud Ridge, North Vietnam, 243, 245
Thunderbird Field, Arizona, 171–172
Tobera Field (Rabaul), New Britain Island, 30
Tokchon, North Korea, 203–205
Tokyo, Japan, 81
Tre Island, French Indochina, 73
Truax, Ens Myron M. (Melton), USN, 61–62
Truk Atoll, Caroline Islands, 35
Tsuiki Air Force Base, Japan, 202–203
Tyler, Capt James O. (Tim), USAAF, 122–123

Ubon Royal Thai Air Base, 247
Ulithi Atoll, Caroline Islands, 60
United Nations, 205
United States Air Force (USAF)
    4th Fighter Interceptor Wing, 206, 223
    Fifth Air Force, 232, 235
    Seventh Air Force, 242
    16th Fighter Squadron, 209, 213
    39th Fighter Squadron, 222, 223, 227
    39th Fighter-Bomber Squadron, 201–202
    41st Fighter-Bomber Squadron, 202
    336th Fighter Squadron, 205–206
    354th Tactical Fighter Squadron, 240
    355th Fighter Squadron, 239
    355th Tactical Fighter Wing, 240
    388th Tactical Fighter Wing, 241, 243, 245
    51st Fighter Interceptor Wing, 222, 223
United States Army Air Corps (USAAC)
    Flying Cadet training program, 52, 69, 74, 95, 106, 133, 163, 166, 171
    Hawaiian Air Force, 118
United States Army Air Forces (USAAF)
    1st Fighter Group, 99–100, 102, 105
    1st Pursuit Group, 97–98
    2d Bombardment Division, 119
    2d Fighter Squadron, 112, 117
    3d Heavy Bombardment Wing, 108
    Fourth Air Force, 105
    4th Fighter Group, 107, 108, 201
    4th Fighter Squadron, 122
    Fifth Air Force, 25, 75-76
    V Fighter Command, 25, 53–54
    5th Fighter Squadron, 122, 125
    VII Fighter Command, 75, 77, 86, 118
    VIII Bomber Command, 108
    VIII Fighter Command, 107, 108, 110, 119, 133, 163, 164, 167
    IX Tactical Air Command, 184
    Ninth Air Force, 121, 187, 194
    9th Fighter Squadron, 105
    Twelfth Air Force, 128
    Thirteenth Air Force, 76
    14th Pursuit Group, 106
    Fifteenth Air Force, 122
    15th Fighter Group, 76–78, 80, 85
    15th Pursuit Group, 118

20th Fighter Group, 111, 156, 172, 174
20th Pursuit Group, 166-167
21st Fighter Group, 77, 85
27th Fighter Squadron, 94, 99, 100–102
27th Pursuit Squadron, 97
31st Fighter Group, 111, 128
33d Fighter Squadron, 99
36th Fighter Squadron, 70
38th Fighter Squadron, 201
45th Fighter Squadron, 76
52d Fighter Group, 111–112, 117, 122, 123
55th Fighter Group, 201, 205
55th Fighter Squadron, 171
55th Heavy Bombardment Wing, 129
56th Fighter Group, 53, 107, 108, 163–164, 166
58th Fighter Group, 52–53, 56
61st Fighter Squadron, 164, 166
62d Fighter Squadron, 164–166
63d Fighter Squadron, 164
66th Fighter Wing, 158
67th Fighter Squadron, 18
67th Fighter Wing, 110
71st Fighter Squadron, 101, 102, 104
73d Fighter Squadron, 75
73d Very Heavy Bombardment Wing, 77, 78
74th Fighter Squadron, 49-50
77th Fighter Squadron, 172
78th Fighter Group, 106–108, 110
78th Fighter Squadron, 73, 75, 77, 84
82d Fighter Group, 101, 104
83d Fighter Squadron, 108
84th Fighter Squadron, 106, 108
98th Heavy Bombardment Group, 98
308th Fighter Squadron, 128
310th Fighter Squadron, 54
311th Fighter Squadron, 54, 75
339th Fighter-Bomber Group, 158
340th Fighter Squadron, 26
341st Fighter Squadron, 26
342d Fighter Squadron, 23–24, 26–27, 53
343d Fighter Squadron, 205
348th Fighter Group, 24
352d Fighter Group, 213
353d Fighter Squadron, 187, 189
354th Fighter Group, 187, 189
354th Fighter Squadron, 136, 137, 141–143
355th Fighter Group, 133–134
357th Fighter Squadron, 136–137
358th Fighter Squadron, 136
359th Fighter Group, 167–168
362d Fighter Group, 118
368th Fighter Squadron, 167
369th Fighter Squadron, 167
370th Fighter Squadron, 168, 170
371st Fighter Group, 194
378th Fighter Squadron, 119
422d Night Fighter Squadron, 182-183
432d Fighter Squadron, 70
433d Fighter Squadron, 70
475th Fighter Group, 70, 73
503d Fighter Squadron, 162
531st Fighter Squadron, 77
Aviation Cadet training program, 23, 205
Aviation Mechanics School, 23
Central Instructor School, 172
Far East Air Forces, 70
School of Applied Tactics, 14
United States Marine Corps
  2d Marine Aircraft Wing, 15, 222
  Marine Air Group 13, 222
  Marine Air Group 22, 75
  Marine Fighter Squadron (VMF) 111, 22

Marine Fighter Squadron (VMF) 115, 222
Marine Fighter Squadron (VMF) 212, 17, 18
Marine Fighter Squadron (VMF) 214, 221
Marine Fighter Squadron (VMF) 221, 75
Marine Fighter Squadron (VMF) 223, 15, 17-19
Marine Fighter Squadron (VMF) 224, 14, 15, 17–19, 22
Marine Fighter Squadron (VMF) 312, 203
Marine Observation Squadron (VMO) 251, 17, 18
Marine Scout-Bomber Squadron (VMSB) 231, 16–17
Marine Scout-Bomber Squadron (VMSB) 232, 17
United States Military Academy (West Point), 118
United States Navy (USN)
  Aviation Cadet training program, 15, 34, 42, 57, 65
  Composite Squadron (VC) 3, 230
  Composite Squadron (VC) 10, 42, 49
  Composite Squadron (VC) 80, 45-46, 49
  Cruiser Division 3, 229
  Escort Carrier Fighter Squadron (VGF) 29, 29
  Fighter-Bomber Squadron (VBF) 17, 66-68
  Fighting Squadron (VF) 2, 33–40, 42
  Fighting Squadron (VF) 5, 18, 19
  Fighting Squadron (VF) 6, 34
  Fighting Squadron (VF) 17, 29–30, 64–66
  Fighting Squadron (VF) 18, 35, 65
  Fighting Squadron (VF) 27, 42
  Fighting Squadron (VF) 32, 94
  Fighting Squadron 83, 61
  Fighting Squadron (VF) 100, 58-59
  Fleet Carrier Air Group 2, 36, 40
  Fleet Carrier Air Group 6, 34
  Fleet Carrier Air Group 83, 59, 64
  Naval Aviation training program, 221
  Scouting Squadron (VS) 52, 65
  Seabees, 18
  Seventh Fleet, 43, 233
  Taffy 1, 43
  Taffy 2, 43, 45
  Taffy 3, 43
  Task Force 58, 35, 36, 60–62
  Task Group 58.1, 40–41, 66
  Task Group 58.3, 60
  Task Group 77.4, 43
  Task Unit 77.4.3, 43
  USS *Arizona*, 58
  USS *Belleau Wood*, 68
  USS *Bunker Hill*, 29, 35, 65
  USS *Enterprise*, 34
  USS *Essex*, 60, 63-64
  USS *Gambier Bay*, 42–43, 49
  USS *Haddo*, 94
  USS *Hancock*, 60
  USS *Helena*, 229–230
  USS *Hornet* (CV-8), 16, 17
  USS *Hornet* (CV-12), 35–36, 38–40, 65-66, 69
  USS *Independence*, 42
  USS *Kalinin Bay*, 35
  USS *Kitty Hawk*, 16
  USS *Langley*, 94
  USS *Lexington*, 34
  USS *Long Island*, 16
  USS *Manila Bay*, 45–46, 48–49
  USS *Princeton* (CV-37), 230
  USS *Sable*, 58
  USS *Saratoga*, 19
  USS *Sitkoh Bay*, 76

USS *Wolverine*, 57, 58
USS *Yorktown*, 40
Utter, Cdr H. T., USN, 60

Vande Hey, Maj James M., USAAF, 77-78
Vietnam War, 22, 171, 212
Vieweg, Capt Walter, USN, 44
Vila Harbor (Efate), New Hebrides Islands, 16

Wakde Islands, New Guinea, 35
Ward, Lt(jg) Lyttleton T., USN, 61
Weaver, Capt C. T., USAF, 209–210
Weil, 1stLt Burton L., USAAF, 100
Welch, Capt Darrell, USAAF, 94, 106, Personal narrative, 95–106
Wells, Capt Norman, USAF, 241
Weltman, Maj John W. (Bill), USAAF, 99
Westover Field, Massachusetts, 24, 118, 167
Wetmore, Capt Ray S., USAAF, 168, 170
Wewak, New Guinea, 26

Wheeler Field (Oahu), Hawaii, 75, 77, 118
Widlund, 2dLt Ernest J. A., USAAF, 189
Williams Air Force Base, Arizona, 181, 209, 239
Williams Field, Arizona, 182–183, 201
Winfield, Lt(jg) Murray, USN, 68
Woleai Atoll, Caroline Islands, 35
Wolford, 1stLt John L., USAAF, 101
Wood, 2dLt Thomas L., USAAF, 154
Woolard, Flight Officer Marion L., USAAF, 154

Yalu River, 210, 216–218, 225-226, 228
Yap Atoll, Caroline Islands, 76
Yellin, 1stLt Jerome. USAAF, 78
Yen Bai, North Vietnam, 245
Yokota Air Force Base, Japan, 202
York, 1stLt Robert M., USAAF, 170
Your Navy Wings of Gold (movie), 15

Zeola, Ens Leo, USN, 43